1001 *MAD* PAGES
YOU MUST READ BEFORE YOU DIE
(Crammed into 864 Actual Pages!)

1001 *MAD* PAGES
YOU MUST READ BEFORE YOU DIE
(Crammed into 864 Actual Pages!)

METRO BOOKS
NEW YORK

Jacket design by Sam Viviano

ISBN 978-1-4351-2268-0

Printed and bound in the United States of America

First edition
1 3 5 7 9 10 8 6 4 2

Visit *MAD* online at www.madmag.com

FOREWORD

If you knew you had only a short time left to live, how would you spend it? Reuniting with loved ones? Twittering wisdom gleaned from your life experience for the benefit of others? Traveling to all the places you always wanted to see?

Not a chance.

Your impending hook-up with the Grim Reaper wouldn't change you one bit. You're a *MAD* reader. By definition you're lazy, not too bright, and prone to throwing your money away on questionable products — which brings us to this book!

We've put together *1,001 MAD Pages You Must Read Before You Die* to guarantee you'll die laughing. (We've crammed it into 864 pages because, quite frankly, given the deteriorating quality of health care in this country, we want to be sure you're able to finish the book before settling down for that long dirt nap.)

As many critics have recently noted, the material presented in this book, gathered from over 500 issues of *MAD*, is the *last* thing you'll want to read. So, at least we got the title right.

I implore you to read this book now, while you're still alive. There are currently no Barnes & Noble locations in the afterlife.

Goodbye and remember to go towards the light (by the cash register).

John Ficarra
Editor, *MAD*

MAD ISSUES 1-100
"MURMURS AND MUMBLINGS"

WRITERS AND ARTISTS: SERGIO ARAGONES · DAVE BERG · BOB CLARKE · JACK DAVIS · MORT DRUCKER
DON MARTIN · NICK MEGLIN · NORMAN MINGO · JOE ORLANDO · ANTONIO PROHIAS · DON REILLY

SST! THE DOOR, SWEETHEART! OPEN IT NICE AND EASY LIKE... THEN GET OUT OF THE WAY! I MIGHT HAVE TO PLAY A SYMPHONY WITH A HOT LEAD TEMPO! THEY'VE BEEN LOOKING FOR ME!... JUST *CAN'T* GET RID OF THEM *BILL COLLECTORS!*

KANE KEEN PRIVATE

THE DOOR SWUNG OPEN... AND *SHE* WALKED IN... A SYMPHONY IN CHANNEL #5, TABU AND BURMA-SHAVE! AND BY THE SLIGHT BULGE IN HER HAND-BAG, I WOULDN'T SAY SHE WAS FLORENCE NIGHTINGALE!

GAD! *ANOTHER* BEAUTIFUL GIRL CLIENT! *WHY CAN'T AN UGLY OLD MAN COME UP SOMETIMES? WHY ONLY BEAUTIFUL GIRLS?*

LISTEN, KANE! MY NAME IS LASSIE ROVER! MY UNCLE IS ROLLOVER ROVER! YOU'VE GOT TO HANDLE MY CASE! MONEY IS NO OBJECT!

YOU MEAN YOUR UNCLE IS ROLLOVER ROVER, THE RETIRED VAUDEVILLE ACTOR WHO HAD THE FAMOUS DOG ACT?

YES! EVER SINCE HE CAME OVER FROM DOVER ON THE GOOD SHIP PLOVER WHERE HE WAS PLANTING CLOVER, HIS LIFE HAS BEEN IN GREAT DANGER!

RING-A-LING

HELLO! KANE KEEN DETEC-TIVE AGENCY! ALSO NOTARY PUBLIC AND INCOME TAX RETURNS FILLED OUT!

HELLO KEEN?

LISTEN! MY NAME IS ROLLOVER ROVER! I'M GOING TO BE KILLED! MY MURDERER IS...IS...

GET AWAY FROM THAT PHONE...

DROP THAT PHONE!

...IS...IS... IS...IS... IS...

KTOW BLAM BLAM BLAM

SEE? IT HAPPENS *EVERY TIME!* JUST AS THEY'RE ABOUT TO TELL YOU WHO THE MURDERER IS... THEY GET KILLT!

2

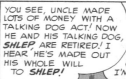

QUICK! TO YOUR UNCLE'S HOUSE! SOMEHOW I HAVE A HUNCH SOMETHING'S WRONG! YOU KNOW HOW SOMETIMES YOU CAN JUST SENSE HUNCHES! IT MAY JUST BE A WILD GUESS...

FILL ME IN ON THE WAY ON THE REST OF WHICH I SHALL CALL... THE CANINE CAPER!

YOU SEE, UNCLE MADE LOTS OF MONEY WITH A TALKING DOG ACT! NOW HE AND HIS TALKING DOG, SHLEP ARE RETIRED! I HEAR HE'S MADE OUT HIS WHOLE WILL TO SHLEP!

AHA! I CAUGHT YOU OPENING THE DOOR! TRYING TO TAKE IT ON THE LAM, EH?

I'M SUPPOSED TO OPEN THE DOOR! I'M THE BUTLER!

WELL... JUST DON'T GO AWAY!

EEK! IT'S MY UNCLE ROLL-OVER! KANE! IS HE... IS HE... DEAD?

...WE'LL HAVE TO WAIT FOR THE CORONER'S REPORT!... HA! HERE'S A SUSPICIOUS-LOOKING CHARACTER!

IT IS MY DUTY TO WARN YOU, SIR, ANYTHING YOU SAY WILL BE HELD AGAINST YOU! ...JUST DON'T GO AWAY!

AND I'M HOLDING YOU AS CIRCUMSTANTIAL EVIDENCE, SO... JUST DON'T GO 'WAY!

KANE! KANE KEEN!

KEEN KANE KEEN!

LOOK! SHLEP'S DOG HOUSE! IT HASN'T BEEN SHLEPT IN! SHLEP HAS BEEN KIDNAPPED!

AHA! AND SHLEP WAS THE ONE THE MONEY WAS WILLED TO! LIKE A JIGSAW PUZZLE, THE FINE STRANDS ARE COMING TOGETHER!... LIKE A WEB... THE PIECES ARE FITTING INTO PLACE!

HERE SHLEP BOY!

WHERE ARE YA, SHLEP?

OOPS!

HELLO, SHAMUS! I JUST WANT TO GIVE YOU A WORD OF WARNING!

SHLEP! SHLEP, OL' BWAH!

COME-A HYAR, SHLEP!

I'M WARNING YOU TO KEEP OFF OF THIS CASE!

CLONG

HOOP

3

A SYMPHONY OF A THOUSAND RIVETING MACHINES RIVETED ON A RIVET THAT WAS MY HEAD! WHEN I OPENED MY EYES... *SHE* STOOD THERE SPRINKLING WATER ON MY BROW...

OH KANE! I AM ROLLOVER'S WIFE! WHEN I HEARD WHAT HAPPENED, I RAN RIGHT OVER!... YOU SEE... I'M JUST *DYING* TO *MEET* YOU!

ROLLOVER'S WIFE, EH!... SOMEHOW I HAVE A HUNCH THAT YOU DIDN'T LOVE YOUR HUSBAND! IT MAY BE A WILD GUESS...

OOH... HAHAHA! DON'T BE RIDICULOUS, KANE! *WHATEVER* GAVE YOU THE SILLY NOTION THAT I DIDN'T LOVE MY HUSBAND?

(PUFF, PUFF) JUST A HUNCH! (PUFF) SOMETIMES YOU FOLLOW A HUNCH (PUFF, PUFF) AND IT BLOWS UP IN YOUR FACE!

HA HA HO

HEE HOO, THAT'S RICH

NOW TO USE SOME COLD AND CALCULATING REASONING TO DEDUCT WHAT DIRECTION I SHALL TAKE NEXT!

PTOO!

HA! I GO *THAT* WAY!

ALL RIGHT, EVERYONE! STAY WHERE YOU ARE! OPEN UP IN THE NAME OF THE LAW!

CRUNCH

I HEARD THERE WAS A MURDER HERE AND I RUSHED RIGHT OVER!

I RUSHED BECAUSE I WANTED TO BEAT THAT PRIVATE EYE NAMED KANE KEEN! HE ALWAYS GETS TO THE MURDER BEFORE I DO, BUT THIS TIME... THIS TIME...

KANE KEEN, PRIVATE EYE! YOU DID IT AGAIN! YOU BEAT ME TO THE MURDER!

STUPID FOOL! SHVIENHUNT POLICEMAN! GET OUT OF MY WAY!

WAAH! EVERY TIME THERE'S A MURDER... HE COMES FIRST! ...EVERY TIME!

DUMKOPF! AND KEEP OUTTA MY WAY OR I'LL CALL A COP!

4

I STROLLED THROUGH THE ROVER MANSION LOOKING FOR THE MURDER WEAPON! SUDDENLY ALL CONCENTRATION WAS BLASTED BY A SYMPHONY OF LIPSTICK, HIGH HEELS AND A PAIL OF SLOP!

IT WAS THE UPSTAIRS MAID DOWNSTAIRS CLEANING... CLEANING A COLT 45! I BACKED AWAY...THEN RAN... NOT FROM THIS BEAUTY! I RAN BECAUSE I HAD UNWITTINGLY BACKED INTO THE *MURDER WEAPON!*

DANG DANG DANG DANG DANG

OOPS! YOU AGAIN!

HEY, SHLEP!

HEY, BWAH!

SHLEPPY!

SHAMUS! ARE YOU STILL ON THIS CASE!

I'M TELLING YOU FOR THE SECOND TIME... *KEEP OFF OF THIS CASE!*

WHO CASE? WHAT CASE? WHERE...

HOOD

A THOUSAND HAMMERS PLAYED A SYMPHONY BY SPIKE JONES IN MY BRAIN! I BREATHED A PRAYER THAT NONE OF THE CRACKS IN MY HEAD, FROM PREVIOUS CAPERS, HAD OPENED!

CRASH

HAH! KANE KEEN! I JUST WANT TO TELL YOU YOU'RE NOT SO SMART! I JUST WANT TO TELL YOU I FOUND OUT WHAT THE MURDER WEAPON WAS BEFORE YOU FOUND OUT! BY TEDIOUS DEDUCTION I KNOW IT WAS CAUSED BY A LONG THIN SWORD...

YOU MEAN AN ÉPÉE... A DUELING SWORD LIKE... *THIS?*

5

WAAAH! EVERY TIME! **EVERY TIME** HE FINDS OUT BEFORE I FIND OUT!... I'LL KILL MYSELF! I'LL **RUN AWAY!**

GAD... HOW THESE POLICEMEN **DO** GET IN THE WAY OF THE LAW!

BUT I'M SICK AND TIRED OF THIS NONSENSE! I'M SICK AND TIRED OF BEING HIT ON THE HEAD BY THIS CHARACTER! I'M SICK AND TIRED OF BEING KICKED AROUND BY TWO-BIT GUNZELS! HE'S A SLIPPERY ONE, NO DOUBT!

HE'S PROBABLY HIDING OUT RIGHT NOW... WAITING TILL THE HEAT'S OVER! BUT **I'LL** GET 'IM! **I'LL** TRACK 'IM DOWN! US CANADIAN MOUNTIES **ALWAYS** GET OUR MAN! **ALWAYS!** AND **WHEN I DO**, BOY...

...WHEN I DO...

SHLEP!

SHLEP, BOY! WHERE DAT OL' SHLEP?

HA! **SNAP ON THE HANDCUFFS BOYS! WE GOT 'IM WHERE WE WANT 'IM! TYPE UP A CONFESSION! HE'LL SIGN IT! HE'S THE MURDERER! HE WANTED ME TO GET OFF THE ROVER CASE!**

CONFESSION? MURDER? I'M ROLLOVER ROVER'S LAWYER! I DON'T WANT YOU TO GET OFF OF THE **ROVER** CASE! I WANT YOU TO GET OFF MY **BRIEFCASE! YOU KEEP STEPPING ON IT!**

ONCE AND FOR ALL... GET OFF OF THE CASE!

CLONK

6

HA! SUDDENLY MY MIND IS CLEAR AS A BELL!

THE SOLUTION HAS SUDDENLY STRUCK ME!

I WANT EVERYBODY IN THIS ROOM! THE SOLUTION TO THE MURDER IS SIMPLE... FASCINATING! I WAS A FOOL NOT TO SEE IT RIGHT OFF! WHO HAD TO PROFIT BY ROLLOVER'S DEATH? HIS NIECE? YES! THAT GIVE HER AN EXCUSE TO MEET *ME*, (LUCKY GIRL)!... THE BUTLER? YES THE BUTLER IS *ALWAYS* THE MURDERER! HIS WIFE? YES! EVERYONE HAD A MOTIVE FOR MURDER! I WAS BACK WHERE I STARTED!

SO I TOSSED A COIN AND IT SHOWED THE MURDERER *WAS* THE BUTLER... WHO IS IN REALITY...

...*SHLEP*... THE TALKING DOG... IN *DISGUISE*!... SHLEP BEING A RUSSIAN WOLF-HOUND, I RECOGNIZED HIS ACCENT!

HEY, KANE! THERE YOU ARE! I BET *I* FIGGERED OUT SUMP'N *YOU* DIDN'T!

I FIGURE THE *BUTLER* DID IT!

CRASH

AWRIGHT, EVERYONE! DON'T MAKE A MOVE OR I'LL BITE THIS COP! I'M GETTIN' OUTTA HERE AND NO ONE'S GONNA STOP ME! AND FURTHERMORE... *RROWF...ARF...*AND BARK!

KANE! DO SOMETHING!

HE'S GETTING AWAY!

STOP HIM!

DON'T BE SILLY, GIRLS! THE 'CANINE CAPER' ENDS RIGHT HERE! THIS ISN'T A CASE FOR DETECTIVES! IT'S A CASE FOR THE DOG-CATCHERS!

7

HEY, MELVIN OF APES! HERE ME COME! HERE COME BOY!

KRASH!

HOO HA!

KLOMP!

THUMP!

HOOOOP!

THUD!

OOPS! ME GET SUDDEN CRAMP IN LEG, BUT *HERE* ME COME, MELV!

HOO HA!

CLEARUM DECK, MELV! ME GONNA SWING OUT ON VINE AN...

EEEEE EEEE

BOY MISS!

BOY! HOW MANY TIMES ME TELL YOU TO USE HANDS WHEN SWING FROM VINE! *SHOW-OFF!* ...FOR THAT YOU *WALK* HOME!

KRASH!

HO! AT LAST AFTER MUCH SWINGING SWIFTLY O'ER AERIAL SKYWAY IN TREE-TOPS, ME COME IN SIGHT OF JUNGLE HOUSE WHERE JANE WAITS!

2

3

THE OOKABALLAKONGA

STAN' BACK, JANE! ME GONNA FIGHT! ME GIVE WAR CRY OF N'GOWA...BIG BULL APE!

HOOO HAA!

HA... OOKABALLAKONGA! *PUT 'EM UP!* ME HEAR HOW YOU SHRINK HEADS!

HAH! ME KNOW HOW YOU GOT STRANGE MYSTERIOUS FORMULA TO SHRINK 'EM!

PLOP! PLOP! PLOP! PLOPLOPLOP!

HEY! BUT YOU NO SHRINKUM MY HEAD! COME ON! PUT 'EM UP... *PUT 'EM UP!*

HAH! ME KNOCK OUT ALL OOKABALLAKONGA EXCEPT DIS ONE PUNK! ME KNOCK HIM OUT, DEN GIVE VICTORY CRY OF N'GANDI, BIG BULL APE!

HOPPY FAN CLUB

OW!

POK!

PTOO!

4

MELVIN! DE OOKABALLAKONGA'S ARE TAKING US AWAY TO SHRINK HEADS!

JANE! WHERE DAT OL' 50 CALIBER FIRE STICK? YOU SURE I BUST IT?

MELVIN! WE GONNA FIX YOUR WAGON! WE GONNA TIE YOU TO FOUR ELEPHANTS AN' TEAR YOU IN FOUR EQUAL PARTS!

ANY LAST REQUESTS, OL' MAN?

YES! JUST LET MELVIN GIVE ONE L'IL OL' CRY OF BULL-APE, N'GOKKA, IN TROUBLE!

HOOO HA!

HOOO HAAAAA

MELVIN IS IN TROUBLE!

MELVIN IS IN TROUBLE!

MELVIN IS IN TROUBLE!

MELVIN IS IN TROUBLE?

HOOO HA!

HOOOO HAAA

MELVIN IS IN TROUBLE!

MELVIN IS IN TROUBLE!

MELVIN IS IN TROUBLE!

MELVIN IS IN TROUBLE!

MELVIN IS IN TROUBLE!

HOO HA!

HOOO HAAAAA

MELVIN IS IN TROUBLE!

MELVIN IS IN TROUBLE!

MELVIN IS IN TROUBLE!

MELVIN IS IN TROUBLE!

HOOOO
HAAAA

HOOOOO
HAAAA

HOOOO
HAAAAA

HOOOO
HAAAA

SURRENDER!

WE SURRENDER!

FINS, I GOT!

KAMERAD!

WHITE FLAG!

FINGERS!

MELVIN! US OOKA-BALLAKONGAS GIVE UP! YOU BIG BOSS AROUND HERE FROM NOW ON! FORGIVE US! WE GIVE YOU GIFTS AND ALL KINDS BRIBES!

FIRST WE HAVE BIG FEAST! FRIED WART-HOG WARTS AND LITTLE LEFT-OVER HAUNCH OF EXPLORER WE HAD IN ICE BOX!

DEN WE GIVE YOU GIFTS! VOODOO DOLL YOU CAN STICK PINS IN! KEEP YOU MATE IN LINE!

OWCH!

DEN WE GIVE YOU COUPLA EXTRA WIVES! DIS ONE HERE... SHE KISS YOU... *HOBOY!* YOU *STAY* KISSED!

NOW FOR MAIN GIFT OF EVENING! VERY FINE GIFT MADE BY SECRET OL' OOKABALLAKONGA FORMULA! MAKE GOOD TELEVISION SET DECORATION!

BRING SPECIAL GIFT!

CLAP! CLAP!

NO!

IT CAN'T BE!

CHIEF CHOW CHEF

IS SHRUNKEN HEAD!

...IS BOY!

UGH! GO WAY, BOY! YOU *REPULSIVE!*

AH COM'ON MELV! *ME* GOOD! ME SWING ON VINE WIT' *TWO HANDS* NOW! TAKE BOY BACK TO TREE HOUSE, WILLYA? HUH? WILLYA? HUH? HUH? WILLYA?

7

...LIKE IN THIS PICTURE WE SAW THE OTHER MONTH, IT STARTS WITH NO TITLE, NO CREDITS, NO NOTHING!...JUST A SCENE OF A HIGHWAY STRETCHING WAY OUT...

...NOTHING ELSE!...JUST A HIGHWAY!...THAT'S HOW THE PICTURE STARTS!...FOR A HALF AN HOUR, JUST A HIGHWAY!...BUT YOU KNOW, BY THE WAY THAT HIGHWAY GOES, SOMETHING'S COMING!

...YOU KNOW, BY THE WAY THAT HIGHWAY STRETCHES TO THE HORIZON, SOMETHING'S GOING TO COME DOWN THAT HIGHWAY! ... AND SURE ENOUGH...SOON YOU HEAR A NOISE!

...A FAINT ROAR COMING DOWN THE HIGHWAY! *YOU LOOK TO SEE WHAT'S COMING DOWN THE HIGHWAY! LOUDER AND LOUDER...COMING DOWN THE HIGHWAY!.. STILL...NOTHING ON THE HIGHWAY... HEY!*

...*WAIT A MINUTE!...* YOU GUYS GOT THE WRONG *HIGHWAY!... TAKE THEM MOTORCYCLES AND GO BACK AND COME UP THE RIGHT HIGHWAY!*

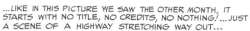

O.K.!...SO HERE WE GO AGAIN! TRYING TO EXPLAIN HOW THIS MOVIE STARTS!...SO HERE'S THIS HIGHWAY AGAIN... NOTHING ON IT!...NOUGHT... ZERO...NONE... NOTHING!

...ALL OF A SUDDEN, YOU HEAR A NOISE... AH, HERE THEY COME... A GROUP OF MOTORCYCLE RIDERS *SPEEDING* ALONG IN THE DISTANCE...*CLOSER*...*LOUDER*... *FASTER*...

...*THE SPEED BUILDS UP!... SOUND BUILDS UP!... THESE MOTORCYCLES ROAR RIGHT DOWN ON TOP OF YOU... SCARE YOU TO DEATH!... WHAT A SCENE!*

...THEN THE CAMERA PANS ONTO THE LEADER OF THIS BUNCH OF MOTORCYCLE CRAZIES AND HERE'S HOW THEY SNEAK THE TITLE IN... SOMETHING LIKE THIS...

CORRECTION!
WILD ½

VRRUM BDUM POW RRAK

ARE YOU RUN DOWN? GET AN AUTOMOBILE TIME FOR

GO BACK

STOP

?

SLOW

PAK POW

YOU ARE ENTERING **COSMOPOLIS** WELCOME WE HOPE YOU BROUGHT MONEY

AT EASE, YOU KATS!... WE'RE GOIN' TO TAKE OVER THIS TOWN AND REALLY HAVE A BALL!... I MEAN, WE'RE GOIN' TO **GO**, MAN! ...I MEAN, WE'RE GOIN' TO MAKE THE JOINT JUMP, I MEAN!

WHADZ HE MEAN?

...SAY, NOW LOOKA HERE, YOUNG FELLER! ...YOU'RE WELCOME TO STAY IN THIS TOWN, YOUNG FELLER, AS LONG AS YOU DON'T CAUSE NO TROUBLE!

...I HATE COPS!

B.B.O.P.

PUSH!

DON'T LET HIM GET AWAY WITH THAT!

GET TOUGH!

...YOU'RE THE POLICE OFFICER IN THIS TOWN!

...IF YOU SHOW THEM KIND YOU'RE SCARED, THEY'LL RUN ALL OVER YOU!

RIGHT! NOW LOOKY HERE, BWAH! I'VE STOOD ENOUGH GUFF FROM YOU!...YOU JUST STEP OUT OF LINE ONCE! I'LL SEND YOU OUT TO A PLACE, YOU CAN'T HEAR THE DOGS BARK! HEAR ME, BWAH? **NOW**, WHATAYA SAY! **NOW**, WHATAYA SAY!

GRR GRR GRR

...I HATE COPS!

B.B.O.P.

PUSH!

3

...I'D BETTER STAY INSIDE HERE BECAUSE I DIDN'T LIKE THE WAY THAT 'JOHNNY' LOOKED AT ME AND BECAUSE HE'S NOTHING BUT A HOODLUM AND BECAUSE MOSTLY I LEFT MY MAKE-UP IN HERE!

HEY, DOLL! YOU SELL BEER?

WHAT'LL YOU HAVE? SHLITZ? BLATZ? BLITZ? ZETZ?

...WHAT'S THAT?

...MY MOTORCYCLE SPEED-RECORD TROPHY!... SAY... WHAT ARE YOU DOING TONIGHT? HOW'S ABOUT A DATE?

...LISTEN!...I KNOW YOUR KIND!...YOU GO RIDING, LOOKING FOR TROUBLE AND YOU'RE NOT SATISFIED TILL YOU FIND TROUBLE AND YOU'RE ALWAYS LOOKING FOR TROUBLE!... OH, I KNOW YOUR KIND... I KNOW YOUR KIND!

NOT ONLY AM I KIND... I'M GOOD TOO!

...YOU GOT ME WRONG, DOLL! I'M JUST LOOKING FOR A BALL... I MEAN A WING-DING... I MEAN...

WHADZ HE MEAN?

...I WOULDN'T GO OUT ON A DATE WITH YOU EVEN IF YOU BEGGED ON HANDS AND KNEES... EVEN IF YOU WERE THE LAST MAN ON EARTH... EVEN IF YOU WERE THE BEST.!

...ONLY IF YOU HAD MONEY, I'D GO OUT.!

I MEAN... I JUST GOTTA FLIP... I MEAN...

WHAD'Z HE MEAN?

SHUCKS, FELLAS... LOOKS LIKE WE'VE SACKED AND LOOTED EVERYTHING IN TOWN!

...EVERY-THING?

VA VA VOOM!

POK POK POK SPA DOW!

TIP TAP TIP TAP

VRUM! VRUM! VRUM! VROOOOW

TIPPITY TAPPITY TIPPITY TAPPITY

WRAM

TIPPITY TAP TIPPITY TAP

6

WEEEOOOAWW
SLAM! SLAM! SLAM! SLAM! SLAM

COPS

PDQ

ALL RIGHT!... ALL RIGHT! WE HEARD SOME TROUBLE WAS GOING ON HERE! WE HEARD SOME MOTORCYCLE CRAZIES HAVE TAKEN OVER COSMOPOLIS! WE HEARD THEIR LEADER HATES COPS! WHERE IS HE?

...SHERIFF! WAIT A MINUTE! WAIT! WAIT!... THE MOTORCYCLE CRAZIES HAVE CHANGED!

...THEY BROKE INTO THE LAUNDRY... STOLE CLEAN CLOTHES AND THEY'VE CHANGED!

WANTED

BUT THEN, JOHNNY, THE LEADER FELL IN LOVE WITH MY DAUGHTER! SHE CHANGED HIM!... HE DOESN'T LOOK FOR TROUBLE ANYMORE! THE TROUBLE'S RIGHT THERE WITH HIM AND HE DOESN'T HAVE TO LOOK!... HERE COMES JOHNNY NOW!

Schmekonheimer's SHOES

COP

JOHNNY!... TELL THE SHERIFF HERE HOW YOU DON'T LOOK FOR TROUBLE ANY MORE!... TELL THE SHERIFF HOW YOU MET MY DAUGHTER AND FELL IN LOVE AND HOW THINGS ARE DIFFERENT NOW! ...WHATAYA SAY, JOHNNY, BWAH! ...WHATAYA SAY!

I HATE COPS!

B.B.O.P.

...SOME POLICE-CHIEF YOU ARE! NOW THEY'RE RIDING AWAY!... IF YOU SHOW THEM KIND YOU'RE SCARED... THEY RUN ALL OVER YOU!... YOU MUSTN'T SHOW THEM YOU'RE SCARED.!... YOU MUSTN'T LET 'EM SEE YOU'RE SCARED.!... JUST LET ME GET UP...

...WAIT, SHERIFF! WAIT WAIT! THINGS ARE DIFFERENT!... DON'T GET UP TO ARREST THEM 'CAUSE YOU'LL SEE IN A MINUTE THINGS ARE DIFFERENT AND THEY'VE CHANGED!

WOOD

...WHO'S GETTING UP TO ARREST THEM? I'M GETTING UP TO GET OUT OF HERE SINCE I DON'T WANT TO LET 'EM SEE I'M SCARED!

...YES.!... THE MOTORCYCLE CRAZIES ARE NOW BICYCLE CRAZIES!

..YOUTH HOSTEL... FORWARD!

...HEY! WAIT A MINUTE!... THEY REALLY HAVE CHANGED!

8

THREE MEN STRIDE DOWN THE DUSTY STREET WHICH IS QUIET BUT FOR THE QUICK SCUTTLING OF CITIZENS DISAPPEARING INTO DOORWAYS AND RAIN BARRELS!

... AND THERE'S SOMETHING ABOUT THESE MEN... NUTHIN' YOU COULD PUT YOUR *FINGER* ON... BUT SOME STRANGE SIXTH SENSE *SOME*HOW TELLS YOU THEY'RE *ORNERY!*

DYEW NOT FOR SAKE ME OH MAH DARLINK!

MARSHALL! MARSHALL! MARSHALL! LISTEN!...THEM OWL-HOOTS WHO JUST CUM INTER TOWN!...THEY'RE GOIN' DOWN TO THE TRAIN STATION!...THEY'RE GOIN' TO WAIT FOR THE HIGH-NOON TRAIN! THEY'RE GOIN' TO WAIT FOR KILLER DILLER MILLER AND THEY'RE GOIN' TO COME AND **KILL YOU!**

OH NO! WE'VE JUST BEEN MARRIED! THEY **CAN'T** KILL HIM!...NOT AT HIGH-NOON! KANE WAS GONNA TAKE ME TO THE **MOVING PITCHERS** TONIGHT!

DO NOT FOO SAKE ME

HMPH! KILLER DILLER MILLER'S BEEN OUT TO GET ME EVER SINCE I SENT HIM UP!...THERE WE WERE AT THE CONEY ISLAND PARACHUTE JUMP AND I SENT HIM UP!...I RECKON THERE'S ONLY ONE THING TO DO! I GOTTA GO MEET THAT TRAIN!

NO!

UH-OH! HE'S A-PUTTIN' ON HIS GUNS... A-PUTTIN' ON HIS HAT...AN' A-PUTTIN' ON HIS 'OLD SPICE' COLOGNE WITH THE HE-MAN AROMA!

ON THIS OUR WEDDIN' DAY!

NO, NO! DON'T GO, KANE, HONEY!...DON'T GO, KANE, SUGAR!...SUGAR KANE...DON'T MEET THAT TRAIN, BWAH!

GITCHA COTTON PICKIN' HANDS OFFEN ME, GAL! KILLER DILLER MILLER'S A-COMIN' GUNNING FER ME AND I'VE GOT TO MEET THAT TRAIN!

DEW NOT FOSAKE ME OH MAH DARLEEEEN!

KANE! IF YOU MEET THAT 12:00 O'CLOCK TRAIN, KILLER DILLER MILLER WILLER KILLER YOU... AND I'LL **NEVER** GET TO GO TO THAT MOVING PITCHER!

12:00 O'CLOCK TRAIN? WHO SAID ANYTHING ABOUT A **TWELVE** O'CLOCK TRAIN! I GOTTA MEET THE **11:45** O'CLOCK TRAIN AN' **GIT THE HECK OUTTA HYAR!**

WAN'TED DEAD!

DYEW NOT FOR SAKE ME

2

BONG BONG
BING
BONG
BONG BANG
BONG
BING FLANG DANG

DE DIVEY NOT FOR SAKE ME OH MAH etc.

MARSHALL! YO **CAIN'T** LEAVE US!

I'M A-LEAVIN'!

...YOU'LL LEAVE US TO **DIE**!

I'M A-LEAVIN'!

...YOU'LL LOSE YOUR **WIFE**!

I'M A-LEAVIN'!

...YOU'LL FORFEIT YOUR **PAY**!

...

...**I'M A**-STAYIN'!

...IT DOES MY HEART GOOD TO SEE YOU GOOD PEOPLE... AROUSED BY INJUSTICE...RALLYING ...BANDING TOGETHER TO FIGHT OPPRESSION! I SAY...TAXATION WITHOUT REPRESENTATION IS TYRANNY! THE SICK AND THE AGED GO BACK TO THEIR HOMES FOR WE DO NOT NEED SO MANY AND I KNOW YOU WILL ALL STEP FORWARD AS A MAN WHEN I ASK FOR **VOLUN**...

...**TEERS**!

...

(HOO, BOY! I COULD'VE SWARED THAR WUZ A CROWD HYAR!)

I VOLUNTEER!

HEY, MISTER!

HEY!...I RAISE MY HAND!

YAY! A VOLUNTEER!

...**PARDNER**!... YOU STAND... A BOULDER OF STRENGTH IN A SEA OF FEAR! LET THE OTHERS LOOK TO YOU AND SAY...'THERE WALKS MANLINESS AND COURAGE!'

...I HEREBY DEPUTIZE YOU TO ARREST KILLER DILLER MILLER! HERE IS YOUR STAR...YOUR PISTOL... WEB BELT... CANTEEN... CANTEEN CUP... FOOT-POWDER, M-1!

CHEE T'ANKS, MARSHALL!

HEY... WHERE **YOU** GOING?

...**WHERE DO YOU THINK, BOY?** ... **I GOTTA CATCH THAT 11:45 O'CLOCK TRAIN AND GET THE HECK OUTTA HYAR!**

3

5

HIGH NOON

BONG 12 TIMES

TWOOOOOOIE

OH TO BE TORN TWIX LUV AND DUTY

HOWDY, 'KILLER'!

THAT'S A GOOD DISGUISE, 'KILLER'!

BUT... BUT... BUT...

BUT, BUT BUT...

HYAR'S YOUR GUNS, 'KILLER'!

...LOADED WITH DUM-DUM BULLETS, KILLER! *HAW!* WHEN WE GET FINISHED WITH *KANE* HE WON'T EVEN BE GOOD FOR A *WALKING-STICK!*... AND DON'T WORRY 'BOUT NO TROUBLE FROM HIM, KILLER! HE IS UPSTANDING AND HONEST AND HE WILL NEVER EVER SHOOT US AS LONG AS OUR BACKS ARE TURNED LIKE THI... *AWK!*

BUT BUT BUT BUT...

RATATATATATATATTA

LISTEN, BOYS! LET'S GET REALISTIC ABOUT THIS THING! I AM MARSHALL AND YOU ARE OUT TO GUN ME AND I MISSED MY 11:45 O'CLOCK TRAIN OUTTA HERE AND I CAN'T GET A POSSE! AND I'M NOT SUPPOSED TO SHOOT IN THE BACK!... LOOK!... FUN'S FUN, AND I KNOW IT'S NOT IN THE ROMANTIC WESTERN SPIRIT BUT I GOTTA QUIT KIDDING AROUND! IF THE LOCAL POLICE CAN'T HANDLE THIS... I JUST CALL OUT THE NATIONAL GUARD!

SPOSE'N I LOSE MY FAIR HAIRED BEAUTY...

...WAAL...THET WUZ QUITE AN ADVENTURE, BUT I RECKON THE EXPERIENCE TEACHES ME ONE THING! THE ONLY THING TO FEAR IS FEAR ITSELF...OR FEAR OF *FEAR-ING* FEAR, FOR FEARING FEAR OF FEAR OR FEARING IS FEARING FEAR OF FEE...OF FOO FI... FEE ...

...TO SUM IT ALL UP... IT'S *HERE* THAT I BELONG! IT IS *HERE*... WHERE I SHALL STAY!... *IN OTHER WORDS* ...

MARSHALL! HORRIBLE NEWS! THAT WASN'T KILLER DILLER MILLER ON THE HIGH-NOON TRAIN! IT WAS SOMEONE ELSE!

KILLER DILLER MILLER MISSED THE HIGH-NOON TRAIN AN' HE'S A-COMIN' IN ON THE *LOW*-NOON TRAIN!

...IN OTHER WORDS...

...I'M A-LEAVIN'!

WAIT A LONG WAIT A LONG

DEAD OR ALIVE

6

C'MON, SPARRIE! LET'S GO INTO OUR MINSTREL ROUTINE! MAYBE WE CAN GET SOME FLOP-HOUSE MONEY!

TAKE ME HOME IN A TAXI HONEY WON'T BE READY TILL HALF PAST EIGHT!

PLUNKA PLUNKA PLUNKA

LOOK! A COUPLE THRUPENCE TUPPENCE HA'PENNY!

MINE!

MINE! HALFIES! HALFIES!

MINE!

TWO CENTS! ALL WHO VOLUNTEER TO DIVIDE THESE CENTS FAIR AND SQUARE... STAND UP!

ONLY TWO CENTS! NOT A THRUPENCE OR A FUPPENCE? NYAAH! STICKY FINGERS!

SAY! I'VE GOT AN IDEA! DID YOU EVER HEAR OF ROBIN HOOD?

...DIVIDE TWO CENTS! LEMME SEE... TWO INTO TWO... CARRY THE ONE...

HE TAKES FROM THE RICH AND GIVES TO THE POOR! THAT POSSE IS RICH AND WE ARE POOR! WOW! WHAT A DEAL!

MULTIPLY BY FOUR... TAKE THE SUM... PLUS THE SQUARE ROOT!

IT'S NO USE! TWO CENTS CAN'T BE DIVIDED!

LET'S GO FIND ROBIN HOOD! LET'S RAT ON THAT POSSE! C'MON, BIG JOHN! LET'S CROSS THIS LOG OVER THE STREAM!

HO, YON VARLETS!

HALT WHILE I CROSS YON LOG FIRST!

2

HOO! HOOO HAH!

...EY!

HA! ROBIN HOOD'S MERRY MEN HAVE GONE TO ROB FROM THE RICH AND GIVE TO THE POOR! LET US POOR SIT HERE AND WATCH THE BATTLE!

I'M GONNA WATCH MAID MARION!

TWANG!

TWANG!

TWANG!

METHINKS THE BATTLE WAGES HOT AND HEAVY! WHAT DO YOU THINKS, SPARKIE?

ME AIN'T GOT TIME TO THINKS!

PAM! POW ZOOOOOOO BAM!

TAC TAC TAC TAC! ZING

POW

METHINKS IT IS ALMOST TIME FOR US TO JOIN THE BATTLE SINCE METHINKS IT'S ALMOST OVER!

METHINKS I'M GETTING TIRED!

POW KRUMP! POW

ZZ ZZ

SKREEEE

ZOOO

HEY BOY! THE FIGHT IS OVER! LET'S GO GET OUR SHARE OF THE LOOT!

NOT NOW, BIG JOHN! I'M A-CLOSIN' IN!

WOW! LOOK AT WHAT ROBIN HOOD TOOK FROM THE RICH!

MONEY!

A TELE-VISION SET!

DEFENSE BONDS!

A CADILLAC CONVERT-IBLE!

5

GO YE AWAY FROM THE DAYS OF YORE! GO YE AWAY FROM MERRY ENGLAND! GO YE AWAY FROM YE DAYS WHEN YE MINSTRELS SANG IN YE FORESTS!

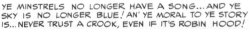

YE MINSTRELS NO LONGER HAVE A SONG... AND YE SKY IS NO LONGER BLUE! AN' YE MORAL TO YE STORY IS... NEVER TRUST A CROOK, EVEN IF IT'S ROBIN HOOD!

6

TREASURE ISLAND!

LONG JOHN SEVERIN

MY NAME IS MELVIN HAWKINS! MY MOTHER AND I RUN A MOTEL ON THE SEA-COAST OF ENGLAND! ONE STORMY DAY, I CLIMBED THE HILL BEHIND THE HOUSE...

...I HAD A MESSAGE TO DELIVER TO ONE OF OUR BOARDERS...CAPTAIN ROLLEM BONES!...ALL DAY LONG CAPT. BONES WOULD STAND ON THE HILL LOOKING OUT OVER THE COVE!

ADMIRAL BENBOW

1

ALL DAY LONG, LOOKING OUT OVER THE COVE! FULL WELL DID I KNOW THAT THE LADY'S DRESSING ROOM OF YE OLDE REPERTORY THEATRE LAY OUT OVER THE COVE!

...THERE HE STOOD, HIS SPYGLASS GLUED TO HIS EYE! IT MUST'VE BEEN GLUED RATHER TIGHTLY, FOR HE NEVER REMOVED IT AS I APPROACHED WITH THE TINY FOLDED PAPER!

I UNFOLDED THE PAPER AND WATCHED CAPT. BONES'S WAVING SPYGLASS AS IT DARTED BACK AND FORTH ACROSS THE SHEET WHICH MUST HAVE CONTAINED A LENGTHY MESSAGE!

IMAGINE MY SURPRISE WHEN I SAW THE PAPER CONTAINED ONLY A SMALL BLACK SPOT!...*THE BLACK SPOT!!* WARNING OF IMPENDING DEATH! THE MAFIA WAS AT WORK!

I COULD TELL CAPT. BONES WAS EXCITED BY THE WAY HE LEAPED OVER THE CLIFF LEAVING A FOLDED MAP BEHIND!

I UNFOLDED THE MAP! IT LOOKED LIKE A *TREASURE* MAP! IN ANY CASE...ONE THING, I KNEW, WAS CERTAIN!

I COULD NEVER FOLD THAT MAP PROPERLY AGAIN!... I STOLE AWAY, DETERMINED TO SEEK THE TREASURE!

2

THE NEXT DAY, WITH THE AID OF SQUIRE TRELAWNEY, DR. LIVESY, AND A G.I. VETERAN'S LOAN, WE PURCHASED AND OUTFITTED A SMALL TRAMP STEAMER!

FIRST WE SET THE CREW TO WORK FEVERISHLY BATTENING THE HATCHES, STOWING THE GAFF FOR THE VOYAGE! THEN WE GAVE OUT PENNICILIN FOR THE FEVERISH CREW!

I DIDN'T LIKE THE CREW! THE PURPOSE OF OUR VOYAGE HAD BEEN SUPPOSEDLY KEPT A SECRET FROM ANY PIRATES!

I DIDN'T LIKE THEIR LOOKS! SOMEHOW, SOMEWHERE, THERE WAS SOMETHING VERY SUSPICIOUS ABOUT THEM!

I DIDN'T LIKE THEIR CHIEF, LONG-JOHN ALUMINUM!...I COULD SEE BY HIS LONG-JOHNS, WHY HE WAS CALLED LONG-JOHN!

BUT DESPITE THE STRANGE NATURE OF THE CREW, WE DECIDED TO SET SAIL...AND SO, AT SUN UP, WE KEELHAULED ANCHOR, AND POINTED OUR BARNACLE FOR *TREASURE ISLAND!*

OUR SHIP SWEPT OUT OF THE HARBOR, PASSING THE STATUE OF LIBERTY! AS HE LOOKED UP AT HER TORCH, I HEARD LONG-JOHN SAY IN A FERVENT WHISPER.. *DIG* THAT *CRAZY RONSON!*

AND SO, WE HEADED FOR A TINY SPECK OF LAND IN THE VAST OCEAN! I STOOD ON THE POOP DECK... POOPED... DRINKING IN THE SALT AIR THAT SMELLT OF THE SEA ITSELF!

GOSH! THAT SALT AIR I WAS DRINKING IN SURE SMELLT LIKE THE SEA ITSELF!... AND I WONDERED TO MYSELF... WOULD WE FIND THIS TINY SPECK OF LAND IN THE VAST OCEAN?

SUDDENLY... THE SOUND OF A TWIG CRACKING UNDERFOOT CAUSED ME TO *WHIRL IN TIME TO SEE THE CREW...*

...SNEAKING UP TO STEAL MY MAP! FORTUNATELY I AM A MASTER WITH THE BLADE! MY PEN-KNIFE FLASHED IN THE SUN!

...BUT THEY OUTNUMBERED ME! I BACKED AWAY ALONG THE POOP...BACK ALONG THE STARBOARD HELM...BACK ALONG THE JIB...

...BACK, BACK ALONG THE MIZZEN SHROUDS...BACK ALONG THE MIZZEN MAINSAIL... BACK ALONG THE MAIN MIZZEN-MAINSAIL! THEN SUDDENLY I KNEW *SOMETHING WAS MIZZEN!*

...THERE WAS MIZZEN ZOME MORE MIZZEN! I WAS TRAPPED! JUST AS I THOUGHT I WAS DONE FOR... THE LOOKOUT SPOTTED THAT TINY SPECK OF LAND IN THE VAST OCEAN ...

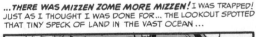

...TREASURE ISLAND! IN OUR EXCITEMENT, WE FORGOT OUR ANIMOSITY! WE ALL GRABBED OARS AND PULLED FOR THE ISLAND IN THE LONG BOAT! **WOW! WAS IT LONG!**

IN A TRICE, THE KEEL GROUND INTO THE SOFT SAND AS WE HIT THE BEACH! WE JUMPED ONTO THE BEACH AND WITHOUT DELAY STARTED INLAND!

THE DIRECTIONS ON THE MAP WERE EXPLICIT! 'NOR'- NO'REAST TO SPYGLASS HILL ...SOU'-SOU'WEST 1 MILE! THEN EA...'.

...'AFTER TRAVELLING 3 MI, EA...'. TURN RIGHT AT THE FILLING STATION... GO DOWN THREE RED-LIGHTS AND TURN UPTOWN...'.

...' THEN, 50 PACES RIGHT, 6 FEET LEFT, 9 INCHES BACK, 1/3 OF AN INCH TO THE RIGHT, AND 16 MILLIMETERS LEFT!'

OOPS! WRONG ISSUE!

...FINALLY, AFTER MUCH PAINFUL AND CAREFUL CONSULTATION WITH SLIDE RULE, LOGARITHM TABLE AND HOROSCOPE, LONG-JOHN POINTED HIS FINGER DOWN AND BID US DIG!

...POINTED HIS FINGER DOWN UNERRINGLY AT THE VERY CENTER PIN-POINT SPOT WHERE THE TREASURE WAS PRE-SUMABLY BURIED! NOW ALL THAT WAS LEFT WAS TO DIG IT UP!

5

WITH A SINGLE CRY OF JUBILATION, THE WHOLE CREW RUSHED FORWARD, AND BEFORE THEY COULD CHECK THEMSELVES, FELL TO THEIR DEATHS ON THE ROCKS BELOW! LONG-JOHN HAD FOOLED THEM!

...I SUDDENLY REALIZED HE HAD WANTED THE TREASURE FOR HIMSELF! AS HE PICKED UP OUR HEAVY EQUIPMENT IN HIS SINEWY ARMS, I THOUGHT, 'AHA...HE LET ME LIVE! *HE LIKES ME!*'

MY HEART LEAPED WITH JOY KNOWING THIS MURDEROUS MAN FAVORED ME!...A MOMENT LATER I QUESTIONED MY CONCLUSION AS I HELD OUR HEAVY EQUIPMENT IN MY SCRAWNY ARMS!

... NOW, LONG-JOHN ALUMINUM DIRECTLY LOCATED THE PLACE WHERE THE TREASURE WAS BURIED, AND WE SET UP OUR EQUIPMENT AND PREPARED TO DIG THAT CRAZY GROUND!

I PICKED UP MY SPADE, BUT LONG-JOHN WANTED ME TO DIG... NOT PLAY CARDS! THEN, MY SHOVEL KNOCKED ON SOMETHING!

...A... A HOLLOW KNOCKING SOUND... THE SOUND OF A SHOVEL KNOCKING ON A...A CHEST! *THEN*...SOMEONE KNOCKED *BACK!*

IT *WAS* A CHEST! *MELVIN MOLE'S* CHEST... OUT OF *'MAD' #2!* WHAT A RIDICULOUS STORY THIS WAS TURNING INTO!

NOW WE GOT TO WORK IN EARNEST! I ROLLED UP MY SLEEVES...SPIT ON MY PALMS...

...SPIT ON MY PALMS? OOOGH...HOW DISGUSTING! I RAN TO WASH OFF MY PALMS!

...THEN I TOOK A HITCH ON MY BELT...FLEXED MY MUSCLES...SQUARED MY SHOULDERS...

..."DID I DIG," YOU SAY?...DON'T BE FANTASTIC! WHO WANTS TO DIG?...**THEN WE FOUND IT!**

THE TREASURE CHEST.!... WE TORE OPEN THE COVER...TORE THROUGH THE WAX PAPER AND FOUND DOUBLOONS... TRIPLOONS... FOURPLOONS... AND A COUPON TO SEND AWAY FOR SILVERWARE!

...I WATCHED LONG-JOHN BITE INTO A GOLD PIECE TO TEST IT! I WATCHED HIS LOWER JAW FLAP OPEN! I WATCHED HIS EYE BALLS FLAP OUT! I WATCHED HIS TONGUE FLAP DOWN!

I DON'T KNOW WHICH CAUSED THE FOLLOWING CONVULSIONS... THE HORRIBLE DISCOVERY HE HAD MADE ABOUT THE COINS, OR THE HOT FOOT I GAVE HIM ON HIS WOODEN LEG!

...IN ANY CASE, HE WAS GONE ...AND THE TREASURE WAS MINE! ALL MINE! A WHOLE CHEST OF THOSE MARVELOUS ROUND LITTLE MILK CHOCOLATE CANDIES...

...YOU KNOW...THE ONES THAT ARE WRAPPED IN YELLOW FOIL TO LOOK LIKE GOLD COIN?!

7

ALICE IN WONDERLAND!

Alice was beginning to get very tired of sitting by her sister and having nothing to do. She had peeped into the book her sister was reading but it had no pictures...

...Suddenly a White Rabbit ran by. There was nothing so remarkable in that, but, when the Rabbit actually took a watch out of its waistcoat pocket, Alice started to her feet...

Burning with curiosity, she ran across the field just in time to see it pop down a rabbit-hole. Alice went after it...

The rabbit-hole went straight on like a tunnel and then dipped suddenly down and Alice found herself falling...

...down what seemed to be a very deep well. First she tried to look down but it was too dark to see!

Then she noticed the sides were filled with cupboards and book-shelves.

Down, down, down..."I wonder how many miles I've fallen?" she said...when suddenly...

...thump! thump! Down she came upon a heap of sticks and the fall was over.

what a mess!

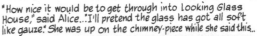

"How nice it would be to get through into Looking Glass House," said Alice..."I'll pretend the glass has got all soft like gauze." She was up on the chimney-piece while she said this...

...Though she hardly knew how she had got there, the glass was beginning to melt away like a bright silvery mist! In another moment Alice was through the glass...

By George! That "pretending" business sure can get a body into trouble!... The whole gol-durned mirror... smashed to smithereens! Alice began looking about...

...and there was the Rabbit hurrying along. Alice fancied she heard him say something like "Updok!"

At the end of the hall appeared a doorway through which the Rabbit flew with Alice right after.

However, the door being fifteen inches high, and the wall being harder than her head, Alice was unable to follow!

Suddenly, Alice came upon a table of solid glass with a tiny golden key on it and beside the key, a tiny bottle inscribed with the words "DRINK ME."

Since it would do her no good to open the tiny door, she turned to the bottle and finished it off. "How curious! I must be shutting up like a telescope!" said Alice.

And now her size was OK... the door was OK... She went to get the key... but **Alice** was too small!

So she grew big again from a cake that said "EAT ME"... got key OK... went to door...but **Alice** was too big!

...Drank more "DRINK ME" bottle...size OK... door OK...went to get key... but **Alice** was too small!

...ate cake... key OK...table OK... size OK... but the door was too big!

...more bottle...key OK...size OK... door OK... but the **room** was too small!

...more cake... door OK... size OK... table OK... but the **key** was too big.

...bottle... key OK... door OK ...size OK... table OK... but the **picture** was too small!

This whole business was getting ridiculous so Alice called the 'super' who let her out with the pass key! Outside were a March-Hare, a Mad Hatter and a Doormouse.

"No room!" they cried at Alice who said, "Gracious, a talking March-Hare!" However, the March Hare wasn't really talking. It was the Doormouse (who was a ventriloquist.)*

*And don't tell us you haven't heard **that** one before!

"Very well," said the Hatter springing from his seat. "You may join our tea-party! Come, let's put on our war-paint!"

"But what has war-paint to do with a Mad Tea Party?" said Alice. "**Mad** Tea Party? Who said **Mad** Tea Party..."

"...This is going to be a **Boston** Tea Party!" said the Hatter. But Alice had been distracted by the White Rabbit...

This time she was determined to catch him...to learn what that strange sound, "Updok" meant!..."Updok... What's Updok... **What's up-doc?**"... Now she knew!

An instant later, bravery was fear... hunter turned hunted...for Alice suddenly realized from movies she'd seen...**this Rabbit was very dangerous to chase!**

5

In any case, a cry of "The trial's beginning!" was heard in the distance. "Come on!" cried the Rabbit. Ahead of them, the King and Queen were holding court.

It seems that the Knave of Hearts stole some tarts. And so...don't ask us why, but we now come to part where White Rabbit reads most classic poem of book called "Jabberwocky!"

JABBERWOCKY.

'Twas brillig, and the slithy toves
  Did gyre and gimble in the wabe:
All mimsy were the borogoves,
  And the mome raths outgrabe.

" Beware the Jabberwock, my son!
  The jaws that bite, the claws that catch!
Beware the Jubjub bird, and shun
  The frumious Bandersnatch!"

He took his vorpal sword in hand:
  Long time the manxome foe he sought —

So rested he by the Tumtum tree,
  And stood awhile in thought.

And, as in uffish thought he stood,
  The Jabberwock, with eyes of flame,
Came whiffling through the tulgey wood,
  And burbled as it came!

One, two! One, two! And through and through
  The vorpal blade went snicker-snack!
He left it dead, and with its head
  He went galumphing back.

"!"That's a poem?" said Alice!

"That by you is a Classic poem supposed to live through ages?...

...Is it educational? Does it teach a moral? Will it sell?" said Alice!

6

"The Knave is guilty!" says the Queen. "Off with his head!" Alice flips! But the Knave says, "It's O.K.! Since I'm a playing card, I've got a head to spare!"

And that's why Alice flips...the card deck, that is, 'cause all the while she's playing solitaire...and cheating. "Off with her head!" the Queen shouts.

"Who cares for you?" says Alice, "You're nothing but a pack of cards!" At this, the whole pack rose up into the air and came flying down on her!

She tried to beat them off and found herself lying on the bank with her sister, who was gently brushing away some dead leaves from her face.

"Wake up, Alice dear!" said her sister. "You've been dreaming!" "What?" said Alice, "The old 'dream' plot?"

"Whew! That old routine where an adventure turns out to be a dream, is the corniest plot in history!"

And so she told her sister of her curious dream as well as she could remember...

...And when she had finished, her sister said, "It certainly was a curious dream" and so took Alice off to see a psycho-analyst.

WAR COMICS DEPT.: THE TRUCE HAS BEEN SIGNED IN KOREA! FOR SOME TIME, WE HAVE BEEN ITCHING TO SINK OUR TEETH INTO ONE TYPE OF LITERATURE BORN OF THE WAR!...WE THINK THE TIME HAS COME! ANY SIMILARITY BETWEEN THIS STORY AND REAL WAR IS TOTALLY ACCIDENTAL!... IT IS WITH THE SINCEREST RESPECT THAT WE DEDICATE THIS LAMPOON TO YOU *REAL* SOLDIERS WHO HAVE HAD TO PUT UP WITH THE *GLAMORIZED* WAR COMICS LIKE...

G.I. SHMOE!

OH HO HA! IT'S THAT G.I. SHMOE AND SGT. SQUIRT HAVING ONE OF THEIR FRIENDLY FIGHTS OVER A WOMAN AGAIN!

GRRR

ROWF

SNAP!

OW

SNARL

SNAP!

OW

GRR

AMMO DAISY M-1 BB GUN

WOOD.

...WHAT A RIOT THEY ARE! THEY'RE THE FASTEST OF FRIENDS... INSEPARABLE COMPANIONS... AND YET THEY STILL ALWAYS HAVE THESE SILLY LITTLE GRUDGE FIGHTS! OH MY!

BRAP

BADAP

O.K., BABY!... YOU'RE ALL MINE!

OH G.I. SHMOE... GALUSHA IGGY SHMOE! YOU HAVE FOUGHT FOR ME AND WON! MY LOVE FOR YOU CAN ONLY BE EXPRESSED IN THESE FEW WORDS WHICH ARE...

...HEY, JOE! ...YOU GOT CHEWING GUM?

1

Panel 1: G.I. SHMOE! G.I. SHMOE! LISTEN! CANNON-FIRE UP FRONT!... SOUNDS OF BATTLE!... AND YOU KNOW THAT WHENEVER WE HEAR SOUNDS OF BATTLE, WE DROP EVERYTHING AND RUN TO THE SOUNDS OF THE BATTLE!

GIMME!

CAN'T HAVE IT!

BLAM BOOM PAF! POP! K-R-RUMF FRRZT.

Panel 2: SOUNDS OF BATTLE! OH JOY! THERE'S NOTHING LIKE A GOOD BATTLE (SNIF)...TO DIE AND LEAVE EVERYTHING (SNIF) FOR A GOOD OL' BATTLE!

YEAH! WE DROP EVERYTHING FOR A GREAT OL' BLOODY BATTLE!

OH DRAT THE DAY I STARTED WORKING FOR COMIC BOOKS!

BALOWM TAC TAC KA! PWEENG

Panel 3: LOOK! IT'S AN ENEMY DIVISION ALL ARMED WITH MACHINE GUNS ATTACKING IN A BANZAI CHARGE!...I THOUGHT YOU SAID THIS WAS A *SERIOUS* ATTACK!

...IT'S NOT AS BAD AS I GUESSED!... TELL YOU WHAT!... YOU TAKE 'EM ON ALONE!...I'LL COME ALONG TO HOLD YOUR COAT!

Panel 5: G.I. SHMOE! EVERY TIME I SEE YOU, YOU FIGHT WITH THE CLUBBED RIFLE! DON'T YOU THINK IT WOULD BE MORE ADVANTAGEOUS TO USE FIRE POWER OF THIS MACHINE-GUN?

...AWWW.! ALL I DO IS *BASH 'EM WITH THE RIFLE-BUTT!*

BASH

Panel 6: ...YOU SEE, THIS MACHINE GUN HAS THE QUICK-LOADING FEATURE OF THIS AUTOMATIC BLOWBACK FEED ACTION CLIP...

YOU'RE RIGHT!... I CAN READILY SEE HOW THAT AUTOMATIC BLOWBACK FEED-ACTION CLIP WOULD DEFINITELY HELP...

Panel 7: ...WHEN I *BASH 'EM WITH THE TOMMY-GUN* BUTT!

BASH

2

WE'VE DESTROYED THE ENEMY DOWN TO THE LAST MAN... AND NOW WE DESTROY THE LAST MAN!

...GAW-HEAD! HITTIM WITTA GUN-BUTT!

WAIT A MINUTE, SQUIRT! ...LOOK!

...NO YOU DON'T! ...EAT HOT LEAD!

BRADADAT

PTOW

BRA DAP

...SNEAK ATTACK! ...DRINK LEADEN DEATH!

UGH! ...I'M HIT!

POW

BRAP BA DAP

WE CANNOT DESTROY THE ENEMY DOWN TO THE LAST MAN MAINLY BECAUSE THE LAST *MAN* IS THE LAST *WOMAN!*

...GAW-HEAD! HITME WITTA GUN-BUTT!

O.K., BABY! YOU'RE ALL MINE! I GAVE YOU A CHANCE TO HITME WITTA GUN-BUTT... BUT NATURALLY, YOU HAVE IMMEDIATELY FALLEN IN LOVE WITH ME SINCE I AM BIG HERO OF THIS STORY!

YOU WANT TO SPEAK!...NO DOUBT YOU WANT TO SAY YOU ARE TIRED OF ENEMY WAY OF LIFE... YOU WANT TO WEAR LIP-STICK... YOU WANT TO SHOP IN THE A+P!... YOU WANT TO THROW POP-BOTTLES AT THE UMPIRES!... GO AHEAD, BABY!... WHAT IS IT YOU WISH TO TELL ME?

... HEY, JOE! ... YOU GOT CHEWING GUM?

3

OH BABY... THE WAY YOU ASK FOR CHEWING GUM... I GET A PRICKLING SENSATION UP AND DOWN MY SPINE!

DON'T TAKE **HIS** GUM, BABY! I'VE GOT **INDIAN** GUM WITH FREE PICTURE TICKETS IN EACH PACKAGE!

BR'RUP!

GOOD WORK, COMRADE! BY CAUSING THEM TO FIGHT EACH OTHER, G.I. SHMOE HAS FIVE BULLETS IN HIS SPINE AND FOUR BULLETS THROUGH HIS HEART! SGT. SQUIRT HAS SEVEN BULLETS IN HIS HEAD AND A BAYONET THROUGH THE GUT! I THINK THEY ARE SUFFICIENTLY WEAKENED FOR CAPTURE!

HERE, O' COMRADE COMMANDER, ARE THE AMERIKANNER SHVEINHUNT WHO HAVE BEEN CAUSING SO MUCH TROUBLE!... WE FINALLY CAPTURED THEM BY PROVOKING THEM TO FIGHT OVER A WOMAN!

THAT'S A FILTHY LIE! WE NEVER FIGHT OVER WOMEN!

G.I. SHMOE! G.I. SHMOE! LOOK AT O' COMRADE COMMANDER!

VERY GOOD, COMRADE LIEUTENANT! WITH G.I. SHMOE AND SGT. SQUIRT CAPTURED, NOTHING STANDS BETWEEN US AND WORLD CONQUEST!

AND NOW WE TORTURE YOU FOR INFORMATION! WE SHALL THRUST SHARP BURNING BAMBOO SLIVERS UNDER YOUR FINGER NAILS! WILL YOU TELL ME WHAT I WANT TO KNOW?

NO! NO!

AH! BUT WE HAVE MORE EXQUISITE TORTURES THAN THIS!... WE WILL PUT YOU ON **PERMANENT K.P.!** NOW WILL YOU TELL ME WHAT I WANT TO KNOW?

YES! YES!

WHAT I WANT TO KNOW IS...

...HEY, JOE! ...YOU GOT CHEWING GUM?

HUH!

HAVE YA?

4

5

O.K., SGT. SQUIRT! I'VE GOT INFORMATION THAT'LL CHANGE THE WHOLE *COURSE* OF THIS WAR! WE'VE GOTTA GET OUTTA HERE! FORTUNATELY, THEY HAVE MERELY HALF A DIVISION ARMED ONLY WITH LIGHT WEAPONS TO GUARD US!

HEY WAIT A MINUTE, AMERICANS...

HOW COME WE KEEP FIRING AT YOU AMERICANS AND WE NEVER HIT!

...SURELY A *STRAY CHANCE, LUCKY* SHOT IS *BOUND* TO GET YOU!

AWWW... WE'RE JUST LUCKY, I GUESS!

YAAAHOO! WATCH ME GO TO TOWN NOW THAT I'VE GOT MY FAVORITE WEAPON... A *RIFLE-BUTT!*

YAHOO! I BROKE RIFLE-BUTT TO SPLINTERS SO NOW I'LL HAVE TO USE THE NEXT BEST THING... A *CIGAR-BUTT!*

YAHOO!... WORE OUT THE CIGAR BUTT... BUT THERE'S PLENTY OTHER TYPE BUTTS I CAN STILL USE!

HOO BOY! ONLY ONE MORE ENEMY SOLDIER TO GIVE THE BUTT TO!

... HEY, SGT. SQUIRT! DIDJEVER MASH FLIES ON A SCREEN...

OW!

POK

G.I. SHMOE! G.I. SHMOE! YOU ARE KILLING AN ENEMY WITH A CANNON! I THOUGHT YOU ONLY USED YOUR *FISTS!* I THOUGHT YOU ONLY USED YOUR *GUN-BUTT!*

WELL... UNDER EXTENU-ATING CIRCUMSTACES... I'M NOT PROUD!

BOOM!

6

...CALL OUT THE RESERVES! ...CALL OUT THE RESERVES!

...IT'S AN ENEMY ADVANCE... A HUGE BANZAI CHARGE RUNNING TOWARDS US AND THE WHOLE UNITED NATIONS ARMY!

MAIN HEADQUARTERS U.N. TROOPS

WAIT! LOOK...

...CALL OUT THE M.P.'S! ...CALL OUT THE M.P.'S!

...IT'S AN ENEMY SURRENDER!... A HUGE BANZAI RETREAT RUNNING AWAY FROM... FROM G.I. SHMOE!

G.I. SHMOE! YOU AND SGT. SQUIRT HAVE SINGLE HANDEDLY TAKEN OVER THE ENEMY ARMY! I'LL SEE YOU BOTH GET A WEEK-END PASS FOR THIS!... AND NOW IF YOU WILL LEAVE THE ROOM AND ALLOW ME TO QUESTION THE ENEMY COMMANDER...

NO! I QUESTION THE COMMANDER!

NO! ME! ME! ME! ME! ME! OW! ME!

ONE MOMENT PLEASE! IT IS NOT FOR YOUSE TO QUESTION ME! YOU ARE ALL MY PRISONERS...

...FOR IF YOU LOOK OUT THE WINDOW, YOU WILL SEE THAT MY ARMY HAS TAKEN OVER YOUR ARMY, BY SUBVERSION... YOU SEE... MY WHOLE ARMY OF MEN IS ACTUALLY AN ARMY OF...

...WOMEN!

GUM? GUM? GUM? GUM? GUM?

YOU GOT GUM?

YOU GOT GUM?

GOT GUM?

YOU GOT GUM?

HEY JOE! YOU GOT GUM?

YOU GOT GUM?

HEY JOE! YOU GOT GUM?

HEY JOE! YOU GOT GUM?

HEY, JOE, YOU GOT GUM?

HEY, JOE! YOU GOT GUM?

HA HA G.I. SHMOE... SGT. SQUIRT! YOU THOUGHT YOU HAD ME AND MY ARMY PRISONER... AND NOW YOU BOTH FIND YOU ARE MY PRISONER!... TELL ME... AS YOU STAND GAPING FOOLISHLY AT ONE ANOTHER, HERE ALONE WITH ME... WHAT IS YOUR REACTION?

...OUR REACTION IS...

WEE!

WOOPS

HEY! WE GOT GUM!

FOOM!

7

...SHE'S ALL MINE!

NO! SHE'S ALL MINE!

OW!

...LISTEN O'COMRADE COMMANDER ...WE FIGURED YOU'D TRY A TRICK LIKE THIS KNOWING FULL WELL OUR CLEAN LIVING WOULD NOT ALLOW US TO FIGHT WOMEN...

...SO WE PREPARED IN ADVANCE! WE SENT A MESSAGE TO CENTRAL HEADQUARTERS TO CALL SOLDIERS TO FIGHT YOUR WOMEN!... *WE SENT A MESSAGE TO CALL OUT THE...*

...WACS!

EEK! YOU RUINED MY HAIR DO!

EEK

SQUEAL

EEEE

EEEE

I'LL MAKE YOUR SEAMS CROOKED!

OOH! I BROKE A FINGERNAIL!

G.I. SHMOE AND SGT. SQUIRT... YOU HAVE SAVED THE U.N. ARMY FROM TOTAL DESTRUCTION AND SAVED THE WHOLE WORLD! I, AS GENERAL OF THE WACS FEEL IT IS IMPORTANT TO MAKE A STATEMENT IN REGARDS TO YOUR QUICK THINKING IN CALLING THE WACS, YOUR BRAVERY AND YOUR UNSWERVING LOYALTY TO WHAT YOU THOUGHT WOULD MAKE YOU THE MOST MONEY... AND THAT STATEMENT IS...

...HEY JOE! ...YOU GOT CHEWING GUM?

8

LITERATURE DEPT.: WE HAVE ALWAYS WANTED TO COMPARE A BOOK AND THE MOVIE THEY MADE FROM IT! THE FIRST PART OF THIS FEATURE WILL BE A TYPICAL...

BOOK!

CINEMA DEPT.: WHEN A BOOK BECOMES A BEST SELLER, HOLLYWOOD EVENTUALLY MAKES A CELLULOID VERSION! THE SECOND PART OF THIS FEATURE THEN, WILL BE THE...

MOVIE!

BEFORE WE LAUNCH INTO OUR STORY, WE'D LIKE TO NOTE THAT IN UNDERTAKING THIS FEATURE, **MAD** FACED THE PROBLEM THAT **IF** WE DUPLICATED A TYPICAL MODERN NOVEL IN THIS COMIC BOOK... WE'D BE RUN OUT OF TOWN ON A RAIL!... SO, IN THE INTERESTS OF GOOD TASTE, US EDITORS HAVE EMPLOYED THE CENSORSHIP STAMP THAT WE PICTURE HERE!... WHEREVER YOU SEE THIS STAMP, YOU WILL KNOW THAT WE OF **MAD** HAVE CANCELLED PORTIONS OF PICTURES WE HAVE DEEMED IMMORAL, INDECENT AND MAINLY BAD FOR BUSINESS!

—the editors of 'Mad'

...FIRST, THE BOOK VERSION...

...WELL...I GUESS I'LL GET UP AND GET MY ©ᴍ✳#☆☆ BREAKFAST!

...LOOK AT HER SNORING THERE! ...WHY DO I HATE HER? WHAT IS THE DEEP, INTELLECTUAL, HIGHLY COMPLEX AND SUBTLE REASON THAT I HATE HER FOR?

...THE DEEP, INTELLECTUAL, HIGHLY COMPLEX AND SUBTLE REASON IS OBVIOUSLY THIS...

...IT STARTS WITH THE SYSTEM OF THINGS...NOT THE SOCIAL OR POLITICAL SYSTEM, BUT THE SOLAR SYSTEM...THE REASON BEING PHILOSOPHICAL IN NATURE!...WHEN A MAN'S ENVIRONMENT COMES UP AGAINST HEREDITY...YOU JUST DON'T HAVE A CHANCE!... THE AGGRESSION, FED BY FRUSTRATIONS, BUILDS *UP* AND *UP* AND *UP*...FIRST THING YOU KNOW... YOU'VE GOT A PERSECUTION COMPLEX! AND THEN COMES THE HATE...AND THEN COMES THE NOW AND THE NEVER NOW AND THE EVER NEVER NOW... AND ON TOP OF THAT... I HATE SNORING!

HAH! YOU ©ᴍ✳#₽#☆!! YOU FINALLY DECIDED TO GET UP!

...*WHAT DO YOU MEAN, ELLEN, BY COMING INTO A KITCHEN IN THAT KIND OF OUTFIT!*

...*WHAT DO YOU MEAN WHAT DO I MEAN BY THIS OUTFIT!* I JUST FINISHED TAKING MY SHOWER!

WHAT DO YOU MEAN WHAT DO I MEAN WHAT DO YOU MEAN!... WHAT KIND OF OUTFIT IS THAT WHERE YOU COME IN *STARK NAKED!*

IT'S PERFECTLY LOGICAL! I CAME IN STARK NAKED 'CAUSE I DIDN'T HAVE MY DRESS WHICH I LEFT HERE IN THE MIXMASTER BOWL!

CENSORED

CENSORED

©☆ᴍ☭#✳ᴍ☆XX ☲©✳ᴍ☺— #⁓☆ᴍ, ⚊⚊⁓ WHY DID I EVER MARRY HER!

...I KNOW! I'LL GO SEE MY GIRL- FRIEND ROSIE AT HER SIMPLE LITTLE APARTMENT!

slam

ROSIE IS YOUNG...FRESH! ...WHEN I AM AWAY FROM HER... HER VISION HAUNTS ME...

...A STRONG, LITHE, GRACEFUL BODY... SLEEK AND TANNED! ...SLENDER DELICATE WRISTS AND ANKLES...

OUT OF ORDER

...*AND HERE SHE STANDS... IN HER BEAUTY... THE SUBTLE BEAUTY OF A DELICATE ELBOW... OF A SHELL-LIKE EAR... AND MAINLY... WATTA BILT!*

stomp

ROSIE! ☺☆♏✳#☺ XX ఴ! WHEN I SEE YOUR RUBY LIPS LEANING HUNGRILY TOWARDS ME, I GET A YEARNING, ACHING, STOMACH TWISTING, ACHING, YEARNING, PAINING, ACHING, AND I LEAN MY LIPS FORWARD FOR **I WANT... I WANT... I WANT...**

...A ASPIRIN?

...I WANT TO KISS YOU...

...MY LITTLE ASPIRIN!

KISS SIZZLE

SLUSH KISS kiss SLUSP

CENSORED

MY DARLING... NOW THAT OUR LIPS HAVE MET IN WILD EMBRACE... NOW THAT YOUR HAIR IS DELIGHTFULLY TOUSELED... YOUR LIPS DELIGHTFULLY SHMEARED... MY EMOTIONS ARE CONDENSED INTO A WORD... WHICH IS...

...ECHH!

KLIK

O.K., ROSIE... LET THE SUCKER GO!... I'VE GOT THE PICTURE!

☺#☺X! WHAT'S THIS? A ♏✳☺# FRAME-UP?

GIMME THAT ♏☺✳~#? FILM, YOU ♏☺#ఴ☆!

uk gimme eh egh

ug **GIMME** ek UMPH

NNAAGGH...

CENSORED

(PUFF)... (PUFF)... TIRED... WHUTSIS... KITCHEN DRAWER... INSIDE AMONGST FORKS AND SPOONS... (PUFF)... **A KNIFE!**

③

END

4

...NOW, THE MOVIE VERSION...

...WELL...I GUESS I'LL GET UP AND GET MY DARNED BREAKFAST!

...LOOK AT HER SNORING THERE! ...WHY DO I HATE HER? WHAT IS THE DEEP, INTELLECTUAL, HIGHLY COMPLEX AND SUBTLE REASON THAT I HATE HER FOR?

sickness

...THE DEEP, INTELLECTUAL, HIGHLY COMPLEX AND SUBTLE REASON IS OBVIOUSLY THIS...

...SHE'S A SLOB!

Potrzebie

HAH! YOU DARNED THING! YOU FINALLY DECIDED TO GET UP!

...WHAT DO YOU MEAN, ELLEN, BY COMING INTO A KITCHEN IN THAT KIND OF OUTFIT!

WHAT DO YOU MEAN WHAT DO I MEAN BY THIS OUTFIT! I JUST FINISHED TAKING MY SHOWER!

WHAT DO YOU MEAN WHAT DO I MEAN WHAT DO YOU MEAN!... WHAT KIND OF OUTFIT IS THAT WHERE YOU COME IN IN A DRIPPING WET BATHROBE!

IT'S PERFECTLY LOGICAL! I CAN'T GET UNDRESSED IN A MOVIE SO I HAD TO TAKE MY SHOWER IN MY BATHROBE!

DASH-BLAST THE GOSH DARNED BLANKETY HECK! WHY DID I EVER MARRY HER!

...I KNOW! I'LL GO SEE MY GIRL-FRIEND, ROSIE AT HER SIMPLE LITTLE APARTMENT!

ROSIE IS YOUNG...FRESH! ...WHEN I AM AWAY FROM HER... HER VISION HAUNTS ME...

...A STRONG, LITHE, GRACEFUL BODY...SLEEK AND TANNED! ...SLENDER, DELICATE WRISTS AND ANKLES...

...THAT'S ME I'M TALKING ABOUT, YOU UNDERSTAND!

...ROSIE'S ALL RIGHT TOO, IN A PINCH!

5

ROSIE! GOSH DARNIT! WHEN I SEE YOUR RUBY LIPS LEANING HUNGRILY TOWARDS ME, I GET A YEARNING, ACHING, STOMACH TWISTING, ACHING, YEARNING PAINING, ACHING, AND I LEAN MY LIPS FORWARD FOR *I WANT... I WANT... I WANT...*

A ANACIN?

... I WANT TO DANCE...

MY DARLING... NOW THAT OUR LIPS HAVE MET IN WILD EMBRACE... NOW THAT YOUR HAIR IS DELIGHTFULLY **UN**TOUSLED...YOUR LIPS DELIGHTFULLY **UN**SHMEARED... MY EMOTIONS ARE CONDENSED INTO A WORD... WHICH IS...

HOWCUM?

NATURAL-BORN RUBY-LIPS AND DACRON, WRINKLE PROOF HAIR... WHATELSE?

O.K., ROSIE... LET THE SUCKER GO!... I'VE GOT THE PICTURE!

DARN IT! WHAT'S THIS? A GOSH-AWFUL FRAME UP?

GIMME THAT FURSHLUG-GINER FILM, YOU BLACK-GUARD!

crack

crunch

bap

(PUFF)... (PUFF)... TIRED... WHUTSIS... KITCHEN DRAWER... INSIDE AMONGST FORKS AND SPOONS... (PUFF).. *A REVOLVER!*

6

7

FROM ETERNITY BACK TO HERE!

FROM H.Q., G-2? YOU MEAN 1ST C.P. H.Q. G-2? A.R.? ...Q-G 2R M1?

...ER...CAPTAIN... THERE ARE THE REPORTS!... MORNING REPORTS... BOOK REPORTS... CAN YOU TAKE CARE OF IT?

...OH SGT... YOU TAKE CARE OF IT!

...THE CANNON REPORTS TOO, EH?...OH. SGT. ...YOU TAKE CARE OF IT!

THIS IS MY HORN MOUTH-PIECE!

...ER...CAPTAIN! THERE'S SOME-ONE WAITING OUTSIDE TO SEE YOU!...CAN YOU TAKE CARE OF IT?

...OH SGT. ... YOU YOU **YOU** TAKE CARE OF IT!

HMMM, STRANGE! SGT. WARDEN USUALLY HATES TO TAKE CARE OF THINGS FOR ME!... WHY, THEN, DID HE KISS ME?

NOW, PREWITT, I SEE BY YOUR RECORD YOU'RE A TROUBLE-MAKER!... WHY'D THEY KICK YOU OUT OF YOUR LAST OUTFIT?

...AWWW...JUST BECAUSE I PLAYED THE HORN THEY KICKED ME OUT!

...WHY? DID YOU PLAY THE HORN VERY BADLY?

...NO! AS A MATTER OF FACT, I'M AN EXCELLENT HORN PLAYER! ...CAN'T UNDERSTAND WHAT THEY OBJECTED TO!...LISTEN ... I'LL PLAY FOR YOU!

MEANWHILE ...

MY, SGT. WARDEN, BUT YOU'RE A WONDERFUL SWIMMER! ... NOW LET'S SIT HERE ON THE BEACH!

...WAIT'LL I TAKE MY TUBE OFF!

I'M GLAD YOU TOOK ME AWAY, SWIMMING... AWAY FROM MY HUSBAND, CAPT. HOMES!... SHERLOCK IS SUCH A NEUROTIC... SUCH A PHILANDERER... SUCH A... SUCH A SHNOOK!

...HOT DOG!...THE KISSING SCENE ON THE BEACH THAT YOU SEE IN ALL THE MOVIE ADS IS COMING!

OH, SGT. WARDEN...SGT. GAYM WARDEN...IT IS SO ROMANTIC HERE...ON THIS WILD ROMANTIC BEACH...**THE WAVES ROARING IN...**

...HOT DOG! ...HERE COMES THE KISSING SCENE!

...SO ROMANTIC ... IF YOU'RE **GAME**, GAYM... **KISS ME!**

2

MEANWHILE...

HEY YOU! MAJJIO! JODIE MAJJIO! WHERE ARE YOU GOIN'! CAHMERE! I WANT TO SEE YOU A MINNIT!

NYAH GIT OUTTA MY WAY, FATSO!

O.K., MAJJIO! O.K.! FELLERS LIKE YOU ALWAYS WIND UP IN THE STOCKADE...AND WHEN YOU DO...I'LL BE WAITIN' CAUSE I'M THE STOCKADE SERGEANT!

MAJJIO? STOCKADE SERGEANT? WHY'S HE CALLIN' ME MAJJIO! MY NAME AIN'T *MAJJIO!*...IT'S *SINATRA!*...HMF!...WHAT SOME PEOPLE WON'T DO TO GET AN AUTOGRAPH!

...THESE ENGAGEMENTS AT THE PARAMOUNT ARE ROUGH!

MEANWHILE...

...NOW LISTEN, PREWITT!...YOU GO ALONG WITH US, AND...WE'LL GO ALONG WITH YOU, IF...YOU GO ALONG WITH US AND WE GO ALONG WITH YOU...YOU US...US YOU...YOUYOU USUSYOU!

...BUT IF YOU INSIST ON BEING A TROUBLE-MAKER...WE WILL GIVE YOU MORE OF *THE TREATMENT* LIKE WE GAVE YOU JUST NOW!

...AND *THE TREATMENT* CAN BE PRETTY ROUGH AS YOU CAN SEE!

...OH, I DON'T KNOW! IT ONLY HURTS WHEN I LAUGH!

...NOW ANSWER ME, PREWITT!...WILL YOU JOIN THE REGIMENTAL BOXING TEAM?...*WILL YOU FIGHT?*

NO!...I WILL NOT FIGHT!...I CAN TAKE ANYTHING YOU CAN DISH OUT!

...*BUT WE CAN'T*

3

WELL, PREWITT! THIS IS IT! THE NEW SENATE CLUB! JUST LOOK AT THIS PLACE!... LOOK AT THEM BEAUTIES! ...ROWF! ARF!

FOLLOW ME, PREWITT! LET'S RESERVE ONE OF THEM BEAUTIES FOR OURSELVES! ...YESSIR! THEY SURE ARE BEAUTIES!

...THEM PING-PONG TABLES ARE SURE BEAUTIES! NOW IF WE CAN ONLY GET PAST THESE DOPEY GIRLS...

HEY! C'MON! LET'S PLAY PING PONG!

YOU!...THEY CALL YOU THE PRINCESS! THIS IS LOVE AT FIRST SIGHT! OOH I'M DYING... I'VE GOT TO BE ALONE WITH YOU... I'VE GOT TO...DO YOU HEAR!

...MY DARLING!...YOU HAVE BROUGHT US TO THIS ROOM WHERE WE CAN BE ALONE! NOW THAT WE ARE ALONE, I CAN DO WHAT I WANTED TO DO FROM THE VERY FIRST MOMENT I SAW YOU, AND THAT IS... THAT IS...

STOP THE MUSIC!

EEK! WE ARE NOT ALONE!... IT IS MRS. KIPPER, THE ONE WHO RUNS THIS NEW SENATE CLUB!...AND NOW I WILL NEVER KNOW WHAT YOU WANTED TO DO FROM THE VERY FIRST MOMENT YOU SAW ME!

...BUT I, MRS. KIPPER, AM IN REALITY, CAPT. HOMES IN DISGUISE AND MY INTRUSION IS MERELY PART OF 'THE TREATMENT'! ...I WARNED YOU 'THE TREATMENT' CAN BE PRETTY ROUGH ..

...NOW, IF YOU WANT TO BE LEFT ALONE TO DO WHAT YOU WANTED TO DO FROM THE VERY FIRST MOMENT YOU SAW HER, ANSWER ME THIS... ...WILL YOU FIGHT?

NO! I WILL NOT FIGHT!...ALSO...YOU MAY STICK AROUND IF YOU WANT TO! I WILL DO WHAT I WANTED TO DO FROM THE VERY FIRST MOMENT I SAW HER...ANYHOW...AND THAT IS... ...PLAY MY HORN?

4

MEANWHILE...

B-DUMM!!!

LISTEN!

WHAT WAS THAT BLAST?

...I THINK THEY'RE DOING SOME BLASTING DOWN AT HINKCUP FIELD!

MEANWHILE...

...YOU ASKED ME TO MARRY YOU, PRIVATE PREW PREWITT, BUT I CAN'T!

WHY, PRINCESS? WHY? WHYWHY? IS IT BECAUSE I'M A SOLDIER... A 30 YEAR MAN? (WELL I'M NOT! I'M ONLY 18.!)...IS IT BECAUSE YOU WANT TO GO HOME AND MARRY SOMEONE PROPER? IS IT BECAUSE OF THE CURRENT POLITICAL SITUATION?

...NO!...THE REASON IS MUCH DEEPER!...MUCH MORE COMPLEX, INVOLVED AND SUBTLE!/... THE REASON IS...

YES!

...IS...IS...

YES YES

...IS...I CAN'T STAND THAT FURSHLUG-GINER HORN!

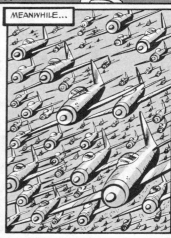

MEANWHILE...

P-L-O-PP!

EEK! THOSE PLANES DROPPING BOMBS! ...ARE THEY ENEMY PLANES DROPPING BOMBS ON THE U.S.A. ARMY IN THE OPENING PHASE OF A BLOODY WAR?

NO! THOSE PLANES DROPPING BOMBS ARE FRIENDLY PLANES DROPPING BOMBS ON THE P.V.T. PREWITT IN THE CLOSING PHASE OF 'THE TREATMENT'!

...NOW, PREWITT... WILL YOU FIGHT?

Petrobie

6

One moment please!

...The ending to this original story is wretched. So in order to make people laugh...to ease the tensions of the world...to bring joy to our readers, we have yakked up the ending of this story. We have taken the liberty of changing the former wretched ending to the present nauseating ending. Our humble apologies...

—The happy Mad editors.

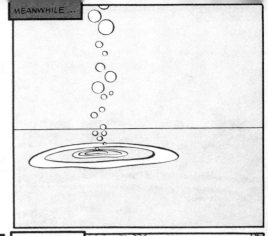

MEANWHILE...

LOOK!

THAT WAS THE BLAST!

...I WAS RIGHT!... THEY ARE DOING SOME BLASTING DOWN AT HINKCUP FIELD!

MEANWHILE...

AT LAST, PRINCESS... UNLIKE THE ORIGINAL WRETCHED ENDING TO THIS STORY... WE HAVE FINALLY GOTTEN MARRIED AND ARE LIVING HAPPILY EVER AFTER!

FOR MARRIAGE IS THE FINAL STAGE OF HAPPINESS WHERE MEN AND WOMEN FIND FINAL PEACE CONTENTMENT AND HARMONY!

SHODDOP YOU LAZY BUM!

...LITTLE DID YOU KNOW THAT THIS FINAL STAGE OF HAPPINESS WHERE YOU THINK YOU WILL FIND FINAL CONTENTMENT AND HARMONY.... IS MERELY THE FINAL PHASE OF 'THE TREATMENT'!

...NOW PREWITT, WILL YOU FIGHT?

...BUT TELL US..WHY YOU WON'T FIGHT?...DID YOU HAVE AN ACCIDENT IN THE RING?...DID YOU ACCIDENTALLY BLIND A BUDDY WHILE FIGHTING? DID YOU HAVE SOME KIND OF STRONG EMOTIONAL DISTURBANCE WHEN YOU WERE AN INFANT?... WO HOPPEN? WHY WON'T YOU FIGHT?

WO HOPPEN?...IS VERY SIMPLE WO HOPPEN!... IF YOU WILL NOTICE... NO WHERE IN THIS STORY DID I SAY I KNEW HOW TO FIGHT! THERE ARE THOSE WHO CAN FIGHT AND THOSE WHO CAN'T FIGHT.!... ME, I CAN'T PUNCH MY WAY OUT OF A PAPER BAG!

...NOT EVEN A TISSUE PAPER BAG YET!

7

WRECK OF THE HESPERUS

by H.W. LONGFELLOW

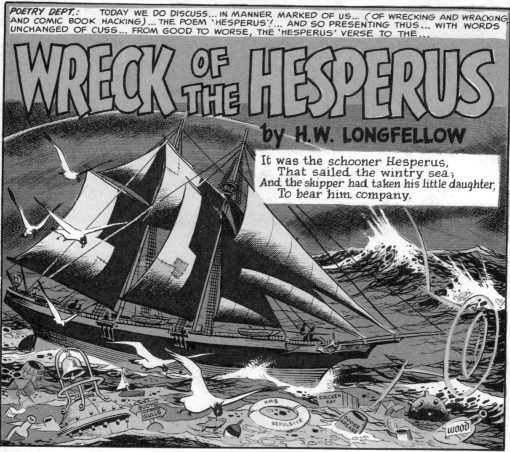

It was the schooner Hesperus,
That sailed the wintry sea;
And the skipper had taken his little daughter,
To bear him company.

Blue were her eyes as the fairy-flax,
Her cheeks like the dawn of day,

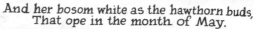

And her bosom white as the hawthorn buds,
That ope in the month of May.

The skipper he stood beside the helm,
His pipe was in his mouth;

And he watched the veering flaw did blow
The smoke now west, now south.

Then up spake an old sailor,
Had sailed the Spanish Main:

"I pray thee, put into yonder port,
For I fear a hurricane."

"Last night the moon had a golden ring,
And tonight no moon we see!"

The skipper, he blew a whiff from his pipe,
And a scornful laugh laughed he.

Colder and louder blew the wind,
   A gale from the north-east;

The snow fell hissing in the brine,
   And the billows frothed like yeast.

Down came the storm and smote amain
   The vessel in its strength;

She shuddered and paused like a frightened steed,
   Then leaped her cable's length.

"Come hither! Come hither! My little daughter,
   And do not tremble so;"

"For I can weather the roughest gale,
   That ever wind did blow."

He wrapped her warm in his seaman's coat
    Against the stinging blast;

He cut a rope from a broken spar,
    And bound her to the mast.

"O father! I hear the church-bells ring,
    O say, what may it be?"

"'Tis a fog-bell on a rock-bound coast!"—
    And he steered for the open sea.

"O father! I hear the sound of guns,
    O say, what may it be?

"Some ship in distress, that cannot live
    In such an angry sea!"

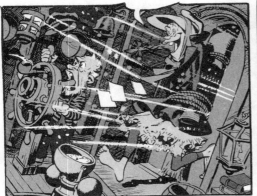

But the father answered never a word,
   A frozen corpse was he.

Lashed to the helm, all stiff and stark,
   With his face turned to the skies;

The lantern gleamed through the gleaming snow
   On his fixed and glassy eyes...

...And fast through the midnight dark and drear,
   Through the whistling sleet and snow,

Like a sheeted ghost, the vessel swept
   Towards the reef of Norman's Woe.

And ever, the fitful gusts between,
A sound came from the land;

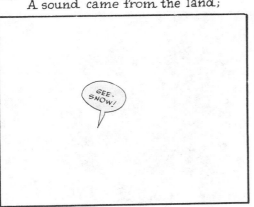

It was the sound of the trampling surf,
On the rocks and the hard sea-sand.

The breakers were right beneath her bows,
She drifted a weary wreck,

And a whooping billow swept the crew
Like icicles from her deck.

She struck where the white and fleecy waves
Looked soft as carded wool,

But the cruel rocks, they gored her side,
Like the horns of an angry bull.

Her rattling shrouds, all sheathed in ice,
With masts, went by the board;

Like a vessel of glass, she stove and sank,
Ho! ho! the breakers roared.

At daybreak, on the bleak sea-beach,
A fisherman stood aghast,

To see the form of a maiden fair,
Lashed close to a drifting mast.

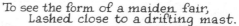

The salt sea was frozen on her breast,
The salt tears in her eyes;

And he saw her hair like the brown sea-weed,
On the billows fall and rise.

Such was the wreck of the Hesperus,
In the midnight and the snow.
Christ save us all from a death like this
On the reef of Norman's Woe!

Don Martin, who is a noted gourmet (He invented french-fried halvah), tells us about sampling strange delicacies . . .

IN A FRENCH RESTAURANT

Ecch! How dare you call zees atrocity "Roti de Porc Head, Garni"! I demand to see zee Chef . . . immediatement!

Oui, Monsieur . . . immediatement!

O.MARTIN

He said to his friend, "If the British march
By land or sea from the town tonight,
Hang a lantern in the belfry arch...

Of the Notch Church tower as a signal light,—
One, if by land, and two, if by sea;
And I on the opposite shore will be,

Ready to ride and spread the alarm
Through every Middlesex village and farm,
For the country folk to be up and to arm."

Then he said, "Good night!" and with muffled oar
Silently rowed to the Charlestown shore,
Just as the moon rose over the bay,
Where swinging wide at her moorings lay...

The *Somerset*, British man-of-war;
A phantom ship, with each mast and spar
Across the moon like a prison bar,
And a huge black hulk, that was magnified...

By its own reflection on the tide.
Meanwhile, his friend through alley and street
Wanders and watches with eager ears,
Till in the silence around him he hears...

The muster of men at the barrack door,
The sound of arms, and the tramp of feet,
And the measured tread of the grenadiers,
Marching down to their boats on the shore,

Then he climbed to the tower of the Old North Church,
By the wooden stairs with a stealthy tread,
To the belfry-chamber overhead,
And startled the pigeons from their perch...

On the somber rafters, that round him made
Masses and moving shapes of shade,—
By the trembling ladder, steep and tall,
To the highest window in the wall,

Where he paused to listen and look down
A moment on the roofs of the town
And the moonlight flowing over all.

Beneath in the churchyard, lay the dead,
In their night-encampment on the hill,
Wrapped in silence so deep and still
That he could hear, like a sentinel's tread,

The watchful night-wind, as it went
Creeping along from tent to tent,
And seeming to whisper, "All is well!"
A moment only he feels the spell...

Of the place and the hour, and the secret dread
Of the lonely belfry and the dead;
For suddenly all his thoughts are bent...

My head
is bent
too!

sqeek
sqeek

On a shadowy something far away,
Where the river widens to meet the bay,—
A line of black that bends and floats
On the rising tide like a bridge of boats.

3

Meanwhile, impatient to mount and ride,
Booted and spurred, with a heavy stride
On the opposite shore walked Paul Revere.
Now he patted his horses side,

Now gazed at the landscape far and near,
Then, impetuous, stamped the earth,
And turned and tightened his saddle-girth;
But mostly he watched with eager search...

The belfry tower of the Old North Church,
Lonely and spectral and somber still.
And lo! as he looks on the belfry height
A glimmer, and then a gleam of light!

He springs to the saddle, the bridle he turns,
But lingers and gazes, till full on his sight
A second lamp in the belfry burns!

A hurry of hoofs in a village street,
A shape in the moonlight, a bulk in the dark,
And beneath, from the pebbles, in passing, a spark
Struck out by a steed flying fearless and fleet;

That was all! And yet, through the gloom and the light,
The fate of a nation was riding that night;
And the spark struck out by the steed in his flight...

Kindled the land into flame with its heat.
He has left the village and mounted the steep,
And beneath him, tranquil and broad, and deep,

Is the Mystic, meeting the ocean tides;
And under the alders that skirt its edge,
Now soft on the sand, now loud on the ledge,
Is heard the tramp of his steed as he rides.

It was twelve by the village clock,
When he crossed the bridge into Medford town.
He heard the crowing of the cock,

And the barking of the farmer's dog,
And he felt the damp of the river fog,
That rises after the sun goes down.

It was one by the village clock,
When he galloped into Lexington.
He saw the gilded weathercock
Swing in the moonlight as he passed,

And the meeting-house windows, blank and bare,
Gaze at him with a spectral glare,
As if they already stood aghast
At the bloody work they would look upon.

5

It was two by the village clock,
When he came to the bridge in Concord town.
He heard the...birds among the trees,
And felt the breath of the morning breeze...

You know the rest. In books you have read,
How the British Regulars fired and fled,—
How the farmers gave them ball for ball,
From behind each fence and farmyard wall,

Chasing the redcoats down the lane,
Then crossing the fields to emerge again
Under the trees at the turn of the road,
And only pausing to fire and load.

So through the night rode Paul Revere;
And so through the night went his cry of alarm
To every Middlesex village and farm,—
A cry of defiance and not of fear,

A voice in the darkness, a knock at the door,
And a word that shall echo forevermore!
For, borne on the night-wind of the Past,
Through all our history, to the last,

In the hour of darkness and peril and need,
The people will waken and listen to hear
The hurrying hoof-beats of that steed,
And the midnight message of Paul Revere.

'EY JOEY! 'EY JOEY! 'EY JOEY! WA' YA WANT! WA' YA WANT! TERRY!

I GOTSHA PIDJHIN'! I FONNIM OMMY ROOF! Y'WON'M?

MY GOODNESS, GET THE POTATOES OUT OF YOUR MOUTH! ...YOU GOT MY PIGEON, YOU SAY?...O.K.! I'LL OPEN THE CAGE ON THE ROOF AN' I'LL BE RIGHT DOWN!

I'LL BE RIGHT DOWN...

YAA..

AAAH SPLAT!

THASS JOEY! ALLA TIME DOIN' THINGS THE HARD WAY!

BLEED BLEED BLEED

AWRIGHT, YOU BUNCH OF PUNCH-DRUNK EX-BOXERS, QUIT THIS SHADOW BOXING F'RA MINUTE!

NF NGF

MF! MNF!

BASH! BASH!

HNF! HMF!

THIS PUNK WAS TRYIN' TO SHORT CHANGE ME OF SOME LONGSHOREMAN RECEIPTS! THROW HIM UNDER A TRAIN!

HIYA, TERRY KID! THANKS FOR SENDING JOEY UP ON THE ROOF!

LE'S BOX!

JAB

HUH! HUF!

HNF! NF!

MFF! HF!

2

3

THEN HERE'S THAT FEATURE YOU ALL KNOW AND LOVE... BUT IF YOU THINK IT'S INTERESTING NOW...YOU SHOULD'VE SEEN IT IN THE OLD DAYS! YOU OLD-TIMERS KNOW WHAT WE MEAN!... REMEMBER WHEN THEY FIRST STARTED PRINTING IT?..'MEMBER, YOU OLD-TIMERS?..IT WAS REAL QUEER...REAL WEIRD...REAL *ECHHHH!*... YOU KNOW...LIKE PEOPLE WHO READ *MAD!*...'MEMBER YOU BUSTED-DOWN OLD-TIMERS YOU?...OF COURSE, WE'RE TALKING ABOUT

RIPUP'S

Believe It or Don't!

THE HUMAN PINCUSHION

GUNG GOHOME, Hindu Ascetic, **WALKED IN THE HOT SUN** with **50** sharp spear-like pins embedded in his flesh — to make pennance — to punish self — but mainly to help wife who was sewing new veil and needed pin-cushion!

SYMBOL OF DEATH!

SACRED SOUTH AMERICAN INDIAN SYMBOL, WHEN GAZED UPON, CAUSES DEATH WITHIN THE YEAR! Too bad if you looked.

MELVIN FURD of Banff, Vt., is a MARTIAN!

THE TALLEST MAN IN THE WORLD—

GALUSHA STURDLEY of Poontang, O. is the tallest man in the world. Note size of hand. (figure on left is not Galusha but his father, Zane Sturdley)

GALUSHA IS HAND FATHER ZANE IS STANDING UPON!

Rrrrrrrrrip.

1

... 'MEMBER? HAH?... 'MEMBER THE WAY HE'D SHOW A GUY WHO COULD STICK HIS ELBOW IN HIS EAR?... OR THE GUY WHO HANGS BY HIS EYEBALLS?...OR THE GUY WHO COULD STICK HIS ELBOW IN HIS EYEBALLS WHILE HANGING BY HIS EAR? BUT MAINLY HE'D DIG UP THESE UNBELIEVABLE FACTS YOU'D NEVER BELIEVE IN A MILLION YEARS... FULLY AUTHENTICATED, FULLY DOCUMENTED, AND APPROVED BY PARENTS MAGAZINE...LIKE FORINSTANCE...

RIPUP's — Believe It or Don't!

JOSEPH STALIN
WAS BORN IN THE BRONX!

HE WORKED HIS WAY THROUGH COLLEGE SELLING MAGAZINE SUBSCRIPTIONS, AND THEN WENT WEST TO BE A COWBOY BEFORE HE CROSSED THE OCEAN AND BECAME DICTATOR OF **RUSSIA!**

NIAGARA FALLS DOES *NOT* FALL!

It actually rises—but in such a way as to create an illusion of falling. For years, Honeymooners have believed that Niagara Falls is falling!

THE EARTH HAS 10 YEARS TO LIVE!

A comet is heading *DIRECTLY TOWARDS EARTH* and is due to smash it into oblivion in *APRIL, 1955!*

$$5+3-2=7248$$

FIRE IS A LIQUID!

Rrrrrrrip

2

...'MEMBER?... BUT THAT WAS YEARS AGO, AS YOU OLD-TIMERS... YOU BUSTED-DOWN RACKETTY OLD-TIMERS... REMEMBER!
MEANWHILE, RIPUP IS FOR MANY YEARS, GONE FROM THE SCENE! NEVERTHELESS, "BELIEVE IT OR DON'T" CONTINUES...
BUT SOMEHOW, IT'S NOT THE SAME!... SOMEHOW...SOMEWHERE... SOMETIME... SOMEHOW... SOMEWHERE... IT IS DIFFERENT!...
THE *EUCHHH* IS GONE!... YOU SEE... EUCHHH HAS BEEN REPLACED BY YECHHH!... LIKE FORINSTANCE...

RIPUP's —— Believe It or Don't!

RENFREW ZETS FELL FROM A 50 STORY WINDOW-
AND LIVED!

Fortunately, there was a fire escape outside the window.

HE ALWAYS READS SIDEWAYS!

Eddie Ptung reads his Chinese language newspaper up and down instead of left to right!

CALF BORN WITH LETTER 'O'!

A calf owned by Elmer Smurd was born with the letter 'O' on its side — or it might have been a 'Q'— or it could even be a face — then again it could be a crooked egg —

SERUTAN
spelled backwards is
NATURES

OPTICAL ILLUSION

Sent in by Robert Hall
JACKET SEEMS TO TURN INSIDE-OUT, YET STAYS OUTSIDE-IN AND VISA-VERSA! (And why not? It's a reversible!)

3

PSYCHOLOGY DEPT.

You know how every once in a while you stop suddenly in the middle of flapping the lower lip, and you wonder if maybe you're crazy? Well, you don't have to wonder any more. Now you can be sure. Because, today, high-priced psychiatrists have fool-proof tests which can prove you're a fool. Like, f'rinstance, there's the famous Rorschach Test, where you look at these interesting ink blots and tell the psychiatrist what they look like to you . . . and then he tells what you look like to him. The only trouble with that test is . . . it costs about forty or fifty dollars. Which brings us to the purpose of this next article:

Now, as a service to those of you who have stopped suddenly in the middle of flapping the lower lip and wondered, MAD saves you money, eliminates the middle-man, and allows you, in the privacy of your own home, to find out once and for all if you're crazy. So don't be chicken. Go ahead. Take . . .

MAD'S INK BLOT TEST

Directions: These ink blots were scientifically designed by a psychiatrist friend of ours who gave up his practice after he suffered a nervous breakdown from listening to his patients' constant complaining. Study each blot for a moment and let it suggest something to you. Then see if it matches the analysis below each blot. Hey . . . no cheating!

IF this ink blot looks to you like a stork delivering twins, then you are obviously emotionally immature, since any grown-up knows that storks don't bring babies.

IF this ink blot appears to be a bartender loaded with two kegs of whiskey, then watch out. Your subconscious mind indicates that you are a potential alcoholic.

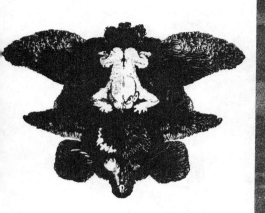

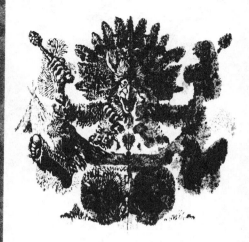

IF this blot resembles a baby on a bear skin rug, then you are emotionally inhibited. Let yourself go, man! A *babe* on a bear skin rug is what you *should* be seeing!

IF this blot suggests an American Indian pounding a war drum, then you obviously have repressed hostilities. You'd like to beat up somebody named Tom . . . *twice.*

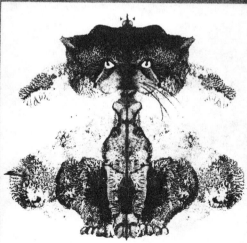

IF this ink blot bears a likeness to two swordsmen engaged in an affair of honor, battling to the death, beware! Your reaction shows you have a duel personality.

IF this blot looks like a squatting cat, you're definitely crazy! Not 'cause you see a squatting cat. You're crazy to spend good money on trash like MAD magazine!

**Don't kill the goose that lays golden eggs
—Dean Martin

The Trash Can Tam

Garbage can lid balancing would develop air of great poise, and be useful during heavy hailstorms.

MAD HATTER DEPT.

Have you noticed lately that women's hats seem to resemble bowls, pans, and other receptacles found around the house? Well, Basil Wolverton noticed it, and figured that women could save

Mad

The Crystal Chignon

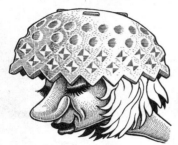

Sparkling cut-crystal fruit bowl could adorn the head of gal who considers herself a peach.

The Frying Pan Fez

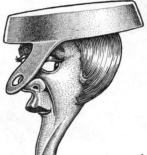

Frying pan would be ideal for lady tourist traveling in places where coconuts fall from trees overhead.

The Teapot Turban

Teapot dome affair would provide protection for delicate or broken nose.

The Colendar Cloche

Ventilated colander would be just the thing for that hot-headed type dame.

The Wash Tub Wimple

Wash tub would be unexcelled for concealing moles on chin, and would also serve as boat in event of flash flood.

millions of dollars per year by simply wearing the original items instead of expensive copies. Besides being as smart, they'd be far prettier. Here, then, are Basil's suggestions for stylish

Hats

The Biscuit Pan Boater

Square-headed woman would welcome square-shaped biscuit pan, especially on cold winter days when hot biscuits could be left in.

The Cookie Tin Capote

Cookie tin would be perfect for gal wishing to preserve that "just graduated" look.

The Saucepan Shako

Saucepan could be worn to show that wearer's husband has deserted her to join the Foreign Legion.

The "Mr. John"

This item might be worn with satisfaction by woman who is proud that ancestors fought in Trojan War.

Strangely Believe It!

PICTURES BY WALLACE WOOD

CONTRARY TO POPULAR OPINION,

WAVING A RED FLAG

AT A **BULL**

DOES **NOT** IRRITATE HIM!

ACTUALLY **COWS** ARE THE ONES WHO GET IRRITATED WHEN A RED FLAG IS WAVED AT THEM.

The reason a BULL gets mad when a RED FLAG is waved at him is because he dislikes being mistaken for a COW.

POST NO BULLS

KEEP OUT

ARMAND K. FRECHETTE

A **FUR TRAPPER** from GRANDEBOUCHE, Canada,

TRAPPED A **SINGLE MINK** WORTH **$8000.00**

IT WAS DRAPED OVER THE BACK OF A CHAIR AT THE STORK CLUB.

Although a pound of **SALAMI** and a pound of **LIVERWURST** weigh **EXACTLY THE SAME,** THREE POUNDS of **CHOPPED LIVER** weighs more than both put together.

ARTHUR K. LIMBISH a little known **COMEDY WRITER** MEMORIZED THE TAG LINES FOR OVER **930,000** JOKES THE REASON ARTHUR IS A LITTLE KNOWN COMEDY WRITER IS HE NEVER LEARNED THE SET-UP LINES.

JOE MILLE

THE FANTASTIC ODDS OF

10,000 TO ONE

WERE LEVELED AGAINST "FIREBRAND" WINNING THE EPSOM DOWNS DERBY STEEPLECHASE IN 1938

AXOLOTL DAILY BLEK
SATELLITE IMPOSSIBLE SAYS RUSSIAN SCIENTIST

Daily Tout and Tipster

"FIREBRAND" WAS A GARTER SNAKE.

ALTHOUGH THE **MOON** IS ONLY **ONE 49TH** THE SIZE OF THE **EARTH**, IT IS **FURTHER AWAY!**

A MAN TRAVELLING ON FOOT FROM **TOKYO,** JAPAN, TO **SAN DIEGO,** CALIFORNIA

... WILL DROWN BEFORE HE GOES A HUNDRED MILES!

THE INDIGNANT HUSBAND

INFERIOR DECORATION DEPT.

Ever notice how that floral-patterned paper you were so crazy about when you picked it starts to *drive* you crazy after it's up a few *months*? That's because the pattern had no practical purpose. We believe a wallpaper design should have a practical purpose. That's why we've designed these practical patterns ...purpose being to drive you crazy after they're up a few *days!*

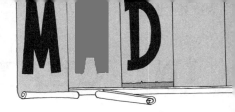

FOR PEOPLE WITH SMALL ROOMS

FOR EX-URBANITES WHO MISS THE CITY

FOR ACCOUNTANTS

FOR EX-CONVICTS

FOR GETTING RID OF GUESTS

WALLPAPER

FOR BATTLING COUPLES

FOR CONFUSING BURGLARS

FOR CROSSWORD PUZZLE FANS

FOR PEEPING TOMS

PICTURES BY BOB CLARKE

THINGS TO MAKE & DO DEPT.

PAPER DOLL PAGE

PRESENTING PAT & PETE PAPERDOLL AND THEIR PCLOTHES

CUT OUT CAREFULLY ON HEAVY OUTLINE

DRESS PAT PAPERDOLL FOR GOING OUT IN THIS BLACK STYLE EVENING DRESS

FLASK FOR PETE PAPERDOLL!

23 SKIDOO

FOR VARIETY DRESS PAT PAPERDOLL IN THIS TACKY STYLE WORK DRESS WITH MATCHING HAT

CUT OUT IRON FOR PRESSING FOLDED CLOTHES

THIS IS NOT A PAPER TAB— BUT CIGARETTE PAPER FOR ROLLING YOUR OWN HAIR TO BE WORN WITH EVENING DRESS—OVER LEFT EYE OR RIGHT EYE . . . OR BOTH EYES

DRESS PETE PAPERDOLL IN THIS SPORT JACKET AND WESKIT STYLE LETTING HIS UNDER- WEAR SERVE AS BERMUDA SHORTS

DRESS PETE PAPERDOLL IN SLACKS WHICH ARE STILL HANGING ON HOOK HERE AND NEED TO BE UNFOLDED

CIGARETTE HOLDER TO GO WITH PAT'S EVE- NING DRESS

THIS IS A BIKINI BATHING SUIT, NOT AN EXTRA TAB!

AND NOW INSTEAD OF DRESSING PAT PAPERDOLL, HOW WOULD YOU LIKE TO UNDRESS PAT PAPERDOLL?

FOR DRY CLEANING PAPER CLOTHES USE SOAP ERASER

DRESS PETE PAPERDOLL IN EVENING DRESS STYLE JACKET

TABS

CUT OUT BOX OF EXTRA TABS

CUT OUT SCISSORS FOR CUTTING OUT CUT- OUTS!

INSTRUCTIONS: To you grownups . . . Here at the end of our magazine, now that your whole attitude towards life has shifted as a result of reading the past fifty-five pages . . . what could be more appropriate than paper dolls for you to cut out. You might try pasting Pete and Pat onto a sheet of cardboard for stiffness, before cutting them out. You might even paste them onto a thin sheet of plywood for real stiffness and cut them out with a coping saw. Then again, a sheet of tempered steel, trimmed with a gas torch would make the ideal backing.

PICTURES BY WILL ELDER

Watch for our next issue. Perhaps we will then show you how to play the interesting game called FLAP THE LOWER LIP, another MAD time and mind killer.

YEMEN

Once again, let's take a look at the insidious plots being hatched in the rivalry between

A FAIRY TALE

A TONE FOR OUR SINS DEPT.

WRITER & ARTIST: DAVID BERG

We all take the telephone for granted ... until we get the bill at the end of the month. That's when we realize a phone is something we keep paying for, but never get to own. Which is why AT & T tells us:

"It's fun to phone!" It *is* fun—for *them!* All kidding aside, though, a phone can be a real convenience ... if you're looking for a convenient way to go crazy! You'll see what we mean as the Editors present

A MAD LOOK AT

THE TELEPHONE

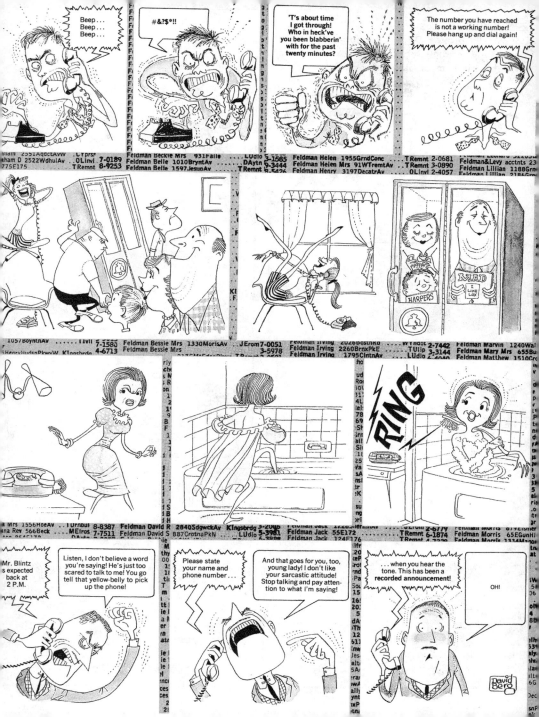

Don Martin proved Darwin's theory in reverse, 'cause they certainly made a monkey out of him when he tried impressing the natives there as

THE GOOD DOCTOR IN AFRICA

For the Sportsman

"Tarheel State"
10-S-NE-1
N. CAROLINA '61

Here's another installment of that friendly rivalry between the man in black and the man in white, both dedicated to the "cause" . . . of outwitting each other as —

Our educational systems have a sneaky little gimmick (as far as the kids are concerned) called "Open School Week"—or "Open School Night"—in which the parents of the students are invited to come in and discuss their sons' and daughters' progress and problems with their teachers. As champions of justice, we believe that turnabout is fair play, and business organizations should invite children of parents to come in and discuss their Daddies' and Mommies' progress and problems with their bosses. In short, they ought to have

OPEN OFFICE WEEK

ORGANIZATION ENTERPRISES CORPORATION, INC.
12345 Conformity Way   Businessville, U.S.A.
TOgetherness 2-2222

October 26th 1961

Dear Children:

Every year at this time, ORGANIZATION ENTERPRISES CORPORATION, INC., invites the offspring of our employees to visit our offices. This year, we have designated the week of October 30th 1961 as "Open Office Week."

Your Daddy's Department Head is looking forward to meeting you personally, and discussing your Daddy with you. Should you have any further questions concerning how he is getting along, I will also be available to talk things over with you during that week.

Hoping to see you soon, I remain,
Yours truly,

E. J. Organization
Chairman of the Board

P.S. Naturally, this invitation is also extended to those children whose mommies work for us, too.--EJO

ARTIST: WALLACE WOOD   WRITER: GARY BELKIN

WELCOME CHILDREN

What a nice welcome! I understand the Daddies made all the decorations **themselves!**

Yes, my Daddy was **complaining** how he had to stay late painting signs!

I really don't know why we bother even **coming!** They **always** tell us that he's doing well!

Let **me** do the talking with his Department Head. You know how **emotional** you become whenever we discuss Daddy's intrapersonal relationships!

Our Daddy promised to raise our **allowances** if we didn't come!

But our Mother promised **she'd** raise them if we **did!**

Ever since his **fifth divorce,** I've had the feeling that my father doesn't work well with others.

THE ESCALATOR

THE BIG BAD WALL

ARTIST: WALLACE WOOD

Hi! Welcome to another unrehearsed Imperial Margarine Test! We've spread two crackers—one with the "expensive spread," and one with new Imperial—and we're going to stop someone now and see if she can tell the difference!

SOUND FAMILIAR? YOU'VE PROBABLY SEEN THIS AD ON TV LOTS OF TIMES. IT'S ONE OF THOSE "COMPARISON TESTS." EVER NOTICE THAT THESE TESTS ARE ALWAYS PRE-RECORDED ON VIDEO TAPE OR FILM? WANNA KNOW WHY THEY'RE NEVER MADE "LIVE"? WELL, JUST WATCH THE RESULTS OF . . .

SOME NEV

THE IMPERIAL MARGARINE TEST WE NEVER GOT TO SEE #1

Pardon me, Ma'am. I wonder if you would mind making the Imperial Margarine Test!

You mean like they do on Television?

Yes. . . .

OH, YOU DON'T KNOW HOW LONG I'VE WAITED FOR THIS!! Ever since six months ago, when you first started showing the test on TV, I've wanted to do it!

As a matter of fact, I've shopped ten hours a day in different supermarkets, looking for you!

Oh, really? That's a compliment, but. . . .

You know my grocery bill is over $4000 a week!

$4000. . . .!!

Well, you just can't spend ten hours a day in a supermarket and not B U Y something. . . .

I guess that's true. . . .

I'm wanted in five states for not paying my grocery bill!

Well, to. . . .

The "A&P" has my picture on a wanted poster!

That's terribl—

I owe "Piggly Wiggly Markets" $6000. . . .

I wish I could help, but. . . .

Fortunately, I have $2000 worth of empty deposit bottles to return!

Yes, well, if we could proceed with. . . .

Have you ever made this test in Murray's Kosher Delicatessen on Delancy Street?

I don't think so, but. . . .

I figure I'd spent ten lost hours in that place!

Look, lady — you've waited six months to make this test! Can we do it N O W ?

I'd love to . . . only I'm on a "fat-free" diet!

TV ADS WE
ER GOT TO SEE

ARTIST: JACK RICKARD
WRITERS: DICK DI BARTOLO, WITH AL JAFFEE

THE IMPERIAL MARGARINE TEST WE NEVER GOT TO SEE #2

ardon me, Ma'am. I wonder if you would ind making the Imperial Margarine Test!

Oh, yes! **God, yes.** . . .

r . . . we're on television, Ma'am. . . .

Pictures that fly through the air and come out of little boxes in living rooms across the nation! The inventive genius of man!!

Y-yes. Now, one of these crackers has been spread with the "expensive spread.". . .

The "expensive spread.". . . .?

You know. Like **Mother** used to churn?

I'm glad you **said** that! There aren't many of us left today who **remember** Mama! You and I **think alike!**

ok — would you taste his cracker?

For **you**, my love, I would go to the end of the Earth!

And now, eat this cracker, please!

Do not say "please!" **EXPECT** it of me! We know each other well enough!

Now, would you please tell us which is better?

Anything but **that**, my precious! Who am I to condemn one man's product, and praise another's! Free enterprise must **survive!** The very future of Mankind **depends** upon it! Four score and seven years ago. . . .

THE IMPERIAL MARGARINE TEST WE NEVER GOT TO SEE #3

Pardon me, Ma'am, I wonder if you would mind making the Imperial Margarine Test. . . .

Oh, one of those **quiz shows!** How wonderful! I **love** to win prizes . . . and fame and fortune!

This isn't **exactly** a quiz game!

Don't be modest! Go ahead and ask me the first question. . . .

Now I've spread one of these crackers with Imperial Margarine, and the other with the high-priced spread. . . .

Oh, what a beautiful sterling silver knife! **Thank you!**

Er . . . you're welcome! Now, would you taste this cracker. . . .?

Sure. . . .

And now this one?

Uh-huh!

Now, which one do you think was the **high-priced spread?**

Do I get into an isolation booth?

No . . . you just answer!

No "thinking music" to build suspense?

NO! Which do you think was the high-priced spread?

This one! My opening bid is 79¢!

Now let's see if you guessed right! This is Imperial! I'm afraid you guessed **wrong**, Ma'am!

Oh, no. . . .

But don't let that bother you! Almost **everybody** guesses wrong!

Then I win these two beautiful **plates?** And this lovely **box of crackers**. . . .?

So remember, folks. . . . whether you're home or on vacation — be sure to keep Imperial in your refrigerator!

A home? A vacation? And a refrigerator? All for me?? And I always said these tests were phony!!

Ma'am. . . . you haven't won —

And this gold tie clasp for my husband! — With this matching key chain and watch! — And these cuff links, too! You quiz game MC's have hearts as big as all outdoors!

THE IMPERIAL MARGARINE TEST WE NEVER GOT TO SEE #4

ARTIFICIAL DISSEMINATION DEPT.

Every once in a while, we get to wondering just what kind of thinking goes into the creation of some of the absurd product-names that are advertised today. Namely, what these names they've come up with have to do with the purpose of the product beats us! So we've dreamed up our own MAD version of 5 Madison Avenue "Brain-Storming Sessions" which resulted in—

THE BIRTH OF A

MADISON AVENUE B

THE HOUSEHOLD CLEANSER

Gentlemen, our client has come up with a **new household product** designed to clean out sinks, tile, porcelain, and mainly the consumer's pocketbook! We've got to think of a **catchy name** for it! Something **new** and **different**!

How about "Mr. Whiz"?

I've got it! "Mr. Quick"!

I like "Mr. Spotless"!

"Mr. Sheen"!

"Mr. Gallagher"!

Hold it! **Hold it!** This is getting us nowhere! What **we** need is a **fresh** point of view! Smedley—ask that **window washer** to come inside . . .

THE UNDERARM DEODORANT

Men—we've got to create a brilliant name for our client's new **spray deodorant** . . . so I've decided to try something **different** this time. Namely, we're going to stay in this sealed room, **inhaling its fragrance, in hopes that it will inspire us** . . .

Okay Charlie . . . open up that valve . . .

"We knew GEORGE RAFT when he was just a Floater."

Sounds like a great idea, T.B.!

Here it comes! No, shout out your immediate impressions—

Coff-Coff . . . What do you think of "Misty"?

Gasp . . . "Heaven Scent"?

Choke! How about "Cloud"?

Keep trying— *Cough-Cough!!* We'll get it!

RAND NAME

ARTIST: GEORGE WOODBRIDGE WRITER: WALTER FARLEY

What happened? Where did he go?

When I opened the window, I knocked him off the ledge! H-he's falling . . . **Straight down** . . . Boy, look at him **travel!** Just like a . . . like a . . .

By George, Smedley— That's **IT!**

...We knew HOWARD FAST when things were slow.

Gakk! Choke! "Cloud" is okay with me! I **like** it!

Please, T.B.! **Gagg!** Let's use "Cloud"!

I know it's—**Gasp**— tough, men . . . but we **still** haven't got it. Keep . . . **Gasp** . . . trying!

You . . . you gotta make him **stop it**, T.B.! I can't **stand** it anymore! Tell Charlie to—

That's it, Finster! That's it!

THE HAND SOAP

THE BOURBON WHISKEY

THE NATIONAL MAGAZINE

"Palm-Onion"?

"Palm-Cherry"?

Sir—not to change the subject, but I have looked around and—

Perkins! I get the distinct impression that you're not **with** us completely in this brainstorming session! Just what's **bothering** You?

Sir . . . I get the distinct impression that we better **forget** this brainstorming session before it's **too** late! Mainly because that **volcano** there is about to erupt all over this clean, clear, sweet-smelling tropical island, covering us all with . . .

By George, you've **got** it, Perkins!

Lava

The Hand Soap

"Sheven Roses"?

"Shixteen Roses"??

Arnold! What's going **on** here! You're supposed to be working . . . not getting stoned with those drunken employees of yours! **Get** out of here! All of you! **GET OUT** . . .

See! Wha'd I tell you! My wife don' approve of drinkin'! She's nuthin' but an ol' . . . an ol'—

Thash it, A.A. . . . **Thash** it!

OLD CROW

KENTUCKY STRAIGHT BOURBON WHISKEY

"Everywoman's amily Argument"!!

"The Reader's Gobbledegook"!!

"U.S. News and Halavah"!!!

What kind of a magazine would make a great Madison Avenue talent like him go off the deep end . . .?

Look! He's waving a piece of paper . . .

It says, "This new magazine will be devoted to Humor & Satire! It's main stock-in-trade will be to make fun of—" Oh, no! Get this!! "—MADISON AVENUE ADS!"

No wonder That's enough to drive **any** advertising man . . .

BUILD UP YOUR EGO WITH **MAD**

500   500

500   30   500

G.WOODBRIDGE

A VISIT TO THE COUNTRY

And now, Antonio Prohias introduces a new "twist" to that friendly rivalry between the man in black and the man in white . . . mainly, a woman in gray!

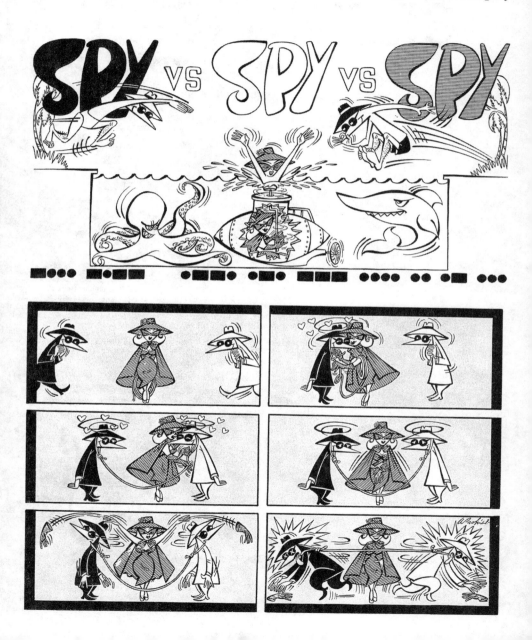

The next time you look at a newspaper picture, just remember one thing: Every newspaper has an editorial policy. Unfortunately, the policy is usually to give the readers sex and sensationalism. But sometimes there are other reasons for publishing a particular photo, like f'rinstance it's a good chance to attack some public figure the publisher hates, or con

SEEING ISN'T AL

WHEN YOU LOOK AT

NEWSWORTHY "ARRIVAL" SHOTS ARE ALWAYS GOOD FOR CIRCULATION ·······························

Daily Bugle Photo No: _1_ Comments:
Several luminaries arrived at N.Y. International Airport today. BOAC brought Dr. Albert Schweitzer, here to reveal his new-found cure for malaria, rated as the top medical achievement in the past five years.

Daily Bugle Photo No: _2_ Comments:
General Charles De Gaulle arrived on KLM flight #45. He will attend several testimonial dinners, confer with Maurice Chevalier, visit the French Embassy, make a speech, and take English lessons from Genevieve.

Daily Bugle Photo No: _3_ Comments:
TWA brought Pulitzer-Prize-winnin poet Robert Frost, who is en-rout to Washington D.C. to donate his manuscripts to the Smithsonian, a then go to the White House and re nursery rhymes to Caroline Kenned

THE PAPER IS SEARCHING FOR TEAR-JERKING SENSATIONALISM ·······························

Daily Bugle Photo No: _1_ Comments:
Car driven by Philo Gribbish is slightly dented after running into tree outside home of Mr. and Mrs. Sidney Witherspoon of this city.

Daily Bugle Photo No: _2_ Comments:
Gribbish explains to passerby that he swerved to avoid hitting a pair of rollerskates, but ran over them anyway, and then struck the tree.

Daily Bugle Photo No: _3_ Comments:
Holding one of the skates, Gribbi berates little Bobby Witherspoon, 5, for leaving the skates in the street, and causing his accident.

ersely, to publicize someone the publisher would like to see get ahead. What the newspaper does, therefore, is to print photos that don't really tell the whole story. Which brings us to this article. When you study the following photographs (with accompanying comments) which were available and then see the one that was finally published, you'll understand why we say

WAYS BELIEVING
NEWSPAPER PHOTOS

ARTIST: WALLACE WOOD
WRITER: FRANK JACOBS

···········SO THEY SELECT THIS ONE

Daily Bugle Photo No: _4_ Comments:
ia Quicklime arrived from the
toum Film Festival where she
named 4th best actress in a
orting role for her portrayal
beach nymph in MGM's "The Bad
th of Sidney Finsternisherman."

Daily Bugle Photo No: _5_ Comments:
Soviet Premier Nikita Khrushchev
arrived by Russian MIG en route to
a speech before the U.N., a summit
conference with President Kennedy,
and another harangue with the State
Dept. about getting into Disneyland.

LOOK WHO'S ARRIVED!

Today's featured arrival at N. Y.'s
International Airport is starlet Gloria
Quicklime, still radiant from her vic-
tory at the Khartoum Film Festival.
Gloria sure adds a touch of class to
the local scene.

········ SO IT PRINTS THIS PHOTO

Daily Bugle Photo No: _4_ Comments:
y yells back at Gribbish that
s now missing his other skate.
bish tells him it's most likely
l under the car--to look for it.

Daily Bugle Photo No: _5_ Comments:
While Bobby wriggles under car to
find skate, Gribbish sadly mulls
over damage to car and fact that
his insurance lapsed week before.

GRIM AFTERMATH

"Tried to avoid accident, but swerved
too late!" sobs motorist Philo Gribbish
as he sadly fingers the rollerskate of
five-year-old Bobby Witherspoon (lying
under car). Gribbish's car went out of
control in street outside boy's house.

THE PAPER HAS A GRUDGE AGAINST A POPULAR SINGER ·····················

Daily Bugle Photo No: _1_ Comments:
Before entering plush El Humidor
club with his wife, singer Billy
Hamster buys bouquet of orchids
from poor, needy flower-seller.

Daily Bugle Photo No: _2_ Comments:
In lobby, Hamster is thanked by
Boy Scout Leader for his $25,000
personal check to aid the Over-
Age Boy Scout Pension Fund drive.

Daily Bugle Photo No: _3_ Comments:
At table, Hamster greets 3 clergy
men who thank him for his support
of inter-faith activities and his
promotion of religious tolerance.

HERE ARE PHOTOS OF A POLITICIAN THE PAPER IS TRYING TO DEFEAT ················

Daily Bugle Photo No: _1_ Comments:
Reform Candidate for Mayor, Harvey
Elkblight begins his campaign with
a sidewalk tour of city's downtown
area, shaking hands with voters
and giving his views on main issues.

Daily Bugle Photo No: _2_ Comments:
Despite the heat, Elkblight moves
along his route, stopping before a
dry cleaning store to symbolically
point up his dedication to cleaning up the corruption in our city.

Daily Bugle Photo No: _3_ Comment
He attacks vice, gambling, ille
sale of liquor, cheap dance-hal
the large number of bars, rigge
pinball machines, etc. as both
temper and the temperature soar

HERE ARE PHOTOS OF A POLITICIAN THE PAPER IS TRYING TO RE-ELECT ···············

Daily Bugle Photo No: _1_ Comments:
Mayor Frank Grafter starts off his
re-election campaign by making the
usual deals with local Party Bosses.

Daily Bugle Photo No: _2_ Comments:
Continues busy re-election campaign
schedule by conferring privately
with Racketeers about needed funds.

Daily Bugle Photo No: _3_ Commen
Awards several municipal contra
to questionable Construction Fi
to insure their loyalty and sup

.... SO IT PLAYS UP THIS PICTURE

Daily Bugle Photo No: __4__ Comments:
While his wife freshens up in the Ladies' Room, Hamster obliges the couple at the next table who have asked him to autograph their menu.

Daily Bugle Photo No: __5__ Comments:
Alone at last, and oblivious to everyone around, Hamster and his lovely wife exchange soft words and knowing looks of two people in love.

Hamster "Plays" Off-Key When He's Not Singing Off-Key

Singer Billy (*But, I'm happily married, I tell you!*") Hamster nestles up to an unidentified admirer in the Goldfish Room of the plush EL HUMIDOR CLUB.

.... AND HERE'S THE ONE THEY PRINTED

Daily Bugle Photo No: __4__ Comments:
lkblight pauses for breath, removes at and loosens collar as temper-ture hits 90°. "This is nothing ompared to how hot I'm making it r my opponent!" he quips slyly.

Daily Bugle Photo No: __5__ Comments:
Candidate Elkblight ends sidewalk tour by stating that a vote for him is a vote for sane, clean, upright, honest City Government. As crowds cheer him, his prospects look good.

CANDIDATE FOR MAYOR IS CAUGHT OFF-GUARD

Harvey Elkblight, candidate for Mayor, was caught by our alert photographer in an unguarded moment outside a bar today. Looks like the Reform Candidate may need to do some reforming himself.

.... SO IT DOESN'T PRINT ANY OF THEM BUT PULLS OUT A MORGUE SHOT FROM 1948

ily Bugle Photo No: __4__ Comments:
ds meeting with assorted Civic ups and makes promises that he no intention of keeping at all.

Daily Bugle Photo No: __5__ Comments:
Ends his campaign with his one and only public appearance at a super market where he kisses 795 babies.

Mayor Confident Of Victory

Handsome and popular Frank Grafter, Incumbent Mayor seeking re-election, poses confidently for photographers. "The people will return me to office to continue serving them!" he smiled.

GREAT OAFS FROM LITTLE ACORNS GROW DEPT.

Every proud parent thinks his kid is a genius, and almost every little thing the brat does is taken as a sure sign of some extraordinary ability or talent that will surely manifest itself in later life. If, however, the little tyke does **not** fulfill his parents' hopes, it isn't because **he** failed, but rather because his **parents** failed. Mainly, they failed to **interpret** those early signs **correctly!** F'rinstance, there are some parents who thought their children would become great artists and writers. You can imagine their shock when their offspring ended up as members of the MAD Magazine staff. With this in mind, here are some other case histories which show ...

HOW PARENTS GUESS WRONG ABOUT THEIR KIDS' FUTURE CAREERS

ARTIST: BOB CLARKE   WRITER: DON REILLY

THE "PREDICTION"

YEARS LATER

THE "PREDICTION"

YEARS LATER

THE "PREDICTION"

YEARS LATER

THE "PREDICTION"

See how our little Basil spends hours on end **stacking his blocks!** Someday, he's going to be a successful **builder!**

YEARS LATER

THE "PREDICTION"

Have you noticed how Clyde loves to **pour stuff** in and out of old jars and bottles? Betcha it means he's a natural-born **chemist!**

YEARS LATER

THE "PREDICTION"

The way Zelda loves to **scribble in her little pad** all the time makes me feel that she's destined to be a **great writer** someday!

YEARS LATER

... and a cheeseboiger wit' all d' trimmin's ...

THE "PREDICTION"

Heh-heh! There's little Fenwick— **"hamming it up"** with that **old straw hat** again! He's a **"born entertainer"** if I ever saw one, the li'l ham!

YEARS LATER

ON A SUMMER'S AFTERNOON

One of the popular best-sellers of the past year has been a charming little book by the creator of "Peanuts," Charles M. Schulz, called "Happiness Is A Warm Puppy." Using his "Peanuts" characters, Mr. Schulz explores the little things of childhood that

MISERY I

Misery is a classmate screeching nails on a blackboard.

Misery is an overcoat that has to last for two seasons.

Misery is moving.

Misery is your ball down the sewer.

Misery is a sister.   **M**isery is having to share.

Misery is landing on *Boardwalk* with a *hotel,* just when you've gotten enough money to afford a house on *Ventnor Avenue.*

Misery is an ice cream pop falling off the stick.

Misery is a knot in your hair.

bring happiness. For example: "Happiness is walking on the grass in your bare feet," "Happiness is three friends in a sand box ... with no fighting," "Happiness is a bread and butter sandwich folded over," etc. Which is all very well if you remember childhood being full of happiness. We at MAD have the distinct recollection of childhood being pretty miserable. So here is our version of how the rest of the comic strip kid-characters would show the other side of the coin in this MAD children's book called . . .

S A COLD HOT DOG

ARTIST: BOB CLARKE   WRITER: LARRY SIEGEL

M isery is the skinny end of your tie sticking out.

M isery is a left-handed kid sitting next to you, whose paper is impossible to copy from, during a test.

M isery is eating a peanut butter sandwich with braces on your teeth.

M isery is no skate key.

M isery is finding your pet goldfish floating.

M isery is the first snowfall of Winter— and you have a cold.

M isery is getting lost at the beach.

M isery is a piece of birthday cake with no flower.

M isery is Milk of Magnesia.

$\mathbb{M}$isery is having to change
out of a wet bathing suit
under a towel at the beach.

$\mathbb{M}$isery is being dressed up
and waiting an hour before
the rest of the family is
ready to go out.

$\mathbb{M}$isery is getting clothes
instead of toys
for Christmas.

$\mathbb{M}$isery is a wet kiss
on the face by an
aunt with a mustache.

$\mathbb{M}$isery is having to eat
the watery part of a
loose soft-boiled egg.

$\mathbb{M}$isery is coming home from the beach
and sitting on hot plastic auto seat
covers wearing nothing but swim trunks.

$\mathbb{M}$isery is a
tongue-depressor.

$\mathbb{M}$isery is finding a
squashed banana in
your school lunch bag.

Misery is buying five baseball gum cards and getting five Marv Throneberrys of the New York Mets.

Misery is coming home with a rip in your best suit.

Misery is a roll of damp caps.

Misery is trying on clothes.

Misery is when your parents won't let you keep a kitten you found.

Misery is crayons left out in the sun.

Misery is a sun-burned back, and then not being able to reach the good spots when it starts peeling.

Misery is walking in the grass in your bare feet— and then discovering you're in a cow pasture.

Misery is a rectal thermometer.

The characters in the comic strips do things that their real-life counterparts can only dream of doing. That's why we enjoy them so much. Through them, we can escape into a far more exciting and interesting world than the mundane one we live in. So even though they act completely unbelievable, we accept comic characters as if they were real living people. Which is why we feel it'd be such a shock . . .

IF COMIC STRIP CHARACTERS BEHAVED LIKE ORDINARY PEOPLE

ARTIST: WALLACE WOOD   WRITER: AL JAFFEE

If PEANUTS
behaved like real-life children

If DICK TRACY
behaved like an ordinary cop

If SUPERMAN
behaved like any normal guy

 BANG!!   BANG!!

I WAS SICK YESTERDAY!

MY MOMMY'S GONNA BUY ME A DOLL HOUSE IF I REMEMBER TO ALWAYS WIPE MY NOSE!

I GOT A HOLE IN MY KNEE!

SO WHAT! I'M ALMOST 5 YEARS OLD!

SLURP SLURP SLURP

Y'KNOW WHAT I'D LIKE! I'D LIKE A GREEN SKY!!

GUESS WHAT I'M GONNA GET FOR MY BIRTHDAY!?!

SLURP

SCHLITZ

WANT YOU TO GO IN THERE AND GET HIM OUT, TRACY!

WHY ME? WHY IS IT ALWAYS ME? AM I THE ONLY GUY ON THE FORCE? WHY CAN'T MAGGIO OR COHEN OR KELLY DO SOME OF THIS DISTASTEFUL STUFF ONCE IN A WHILE?

CHIEF

CAUTIOUSLY, TRACY ENTERS...

N-NO FUNNY S-S-TUFF, NOW! TURN AROUND S-SLOWLY AND K-KEEP TH-THOSE...

YECHHHH!

MUCOUS-FACE GOT AWAY WHILE TRACY WAS HEAVING, CHIEF!

#@!!*♏?!!

URP BRECHH!

JESTER GOLDBRICK

LOOK! HOW HORRIBLE!!

AN ARMY OF KILLERS WITH GUNS, KNIVES, AND BOMBS -- HEADING FOR CITY HALL!!

THIS IS A JOB FOR...

TELEPHONE

..SUPERMAN!

NOT TONIGHT IT AIN'T! I GOT A HEAVY DATE!!

TELEPHON

If POGO characters behaved like real animals

If MANDRAKE THE MAGICIAN had true-to-life talents

WHY YOU STAND THERE LOOKING STUPID, MANDRAKE? WHY YOU NOT **GESTURE HYPNOTICALLY** AND **FIX** TIRE?

BECAUSE, LOTHAR, YOU IDIOT, I CAN HYPNOTIZE **YOU** INTO THINKING THE TIRE IS FIXED!

AND I CAN HYPNOTIZE **NARDA** INTO THINKING IT'S FIXED!

POW!

If B.C. characters acted like real cavemen

NKZBLK BRN FGNKLKMIG!

ZKUNG GLP ARG KLNT!

OOGA LNK ZBRTMIL?

GZZ!

If BRINGING UP FATHER was about a real couple

If DENNIS THE MENACE had parents with normal patience

Enough is enough!!

THE FIRE
at the
ART MUSEUM

SHIPWRECKED

In answer to the sex polls conducted by *Cosmopolitan, Redbook,* and *Playboy,* a few months ago *Mad Magazine* surveyed *our* readership in the form of a questionnaire inserted in every 4 out of 5 issues (it figures—*you* got the one out of 5 with *no* insert, right?). Well, the figures have been tabulated! We are pleased to present the exciting results of...

THE MAD READER'S

SEX SURVEY

ARTIST: BOB CLARKE   WRITER: LARRY SIEGEL

How Did You First Learn About Sex?

¼% **Parents**

¾% **Religious leader**

½% **Teacher**

½% **Doctor**

98% **From a fat kid in the schoolyard named Marvin, who had acne and breathed hard and giggled a lot—and was 99-44/100% wrong.**

What Was The First Thing That Came To Your Mind When You Saw This Inkblot?

16%   I didn't know ball point pens leak.

31%   That's a nice hour glass, but I prefer a digital watch.

20%   It looks like my brother in San Francisco.

22%   Big deal. I can make a locomotive with Silly Putty.

11%   Rack and pinion steering. I just love cars!

What Is Your Most Exciting Sexual Fantasy?

18%   Being alone on a desert island with a Pac-Man game and 9,000 quarters

31%   Being hit very slowly in the mouth by Brooke Shields with a deep dish pepperoni pizza

22%   Rolling around naked in a field of answers to a math exam final

16%   Spending a weekend on a trapeze with Charlotte Rae (my fantasies need a lot of work).

13%   Making out once with my wife before I die—if I ever get married. I'm very insecure.

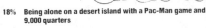

How Old Were You When You Had Your First Sexual Experience?

- 17%* Nine or under
- 60% 10–20
- 11% 21–40
- 7% 41–80
- 5% Over 80
- 0% Over 80 who lived to be 101 after having sex
- 100%* 16–20 year-olds who said they were nine or under to impress friends and frat brothers and still haven't had any sex.

Whom Do You Usually Consult With Your Sexual Problems?

- ¼% Parents
- ¾% Religious Leader
- ½% Psychiatrist
- ¼% I write to "Dear Abby" (as "Confused From Sheboygan")
- ¼% I write to Ann Landers (as "Confused From Dear Abby")
- 98% Marvin in the schoolyard (some people just never learn)

How Do You Feel About S&M?

- 14% Didn't know what S&M is
- 31% Said they liked the letters B, J, and F much better
- 15% Thought S&M stood for spaghetti and meatballs
- 21% Confused S&M with M&M
- 19% Said they never eat candy during sex

What Do You Find To Be The Sexiest Feature In A Partner?

- Eyes 5%
- Lips 6%
- Teeth 3%
- Chin 8%
- Arms 2%
- Left Shoulder Blade 9%
- Right ear lobe 6%
- Patella 11%
- Pulmonary Artery 21%
- Mesenteric Vein 9%
- The Empty Area Between Legs 20%*

*LEARNED ANATOMY FROM KEN AND BARBIE DOLLS

What's Your Initial Reaction To This Porno Movie Scene?

- 15% How come there's no night light in this bedroom?
- 31% Does that silly lady who broke the ceiling mirror know she's going to have seven years hard luck?
- 20% The man in the dress could go to jail if he rips off that "Do Not Remove" tag from the mattress
- 18% Doesn't the man with the whipped cream know it's not kosher to mix dairy with meat?
- 16% I don't think that man truly loves his tennis shoes. He's probably just trying to make his bedroom slippers jealous!

DON MARTIN IN AN
ITALIAN RESTAURANT

And now, Mr. Prohias offers another installment in his contention that truth is never all black nor all white—but merely shades of gray. He calls it . . .

GOOD GRIEF DEPT.

Charles M. Schulz, the creator of "Peanuts" has a warm, happy secure way of looking at things. In his "Happiness Is A Warm Puppy", he told us about the things in childhood that make us happy. MAD, in the belief that childhood is more miserable than happy, answered Mr. Schulz with its parody, "Misery Is A Cold Hot Dog". Now, Mr. Schulz has another best-seller called "Security Is A Thumb And A Blanket," which reveals the things in childhood that make us feel secure, like: "Security is having a big brother." and "Security is a candy bar hidden in the freezer." Once again, MAD takes exception. All we remember of childhood are the things that made us feel "INsecure", like . . .

Insecurity is being a tall 11-year-old.

Insecurity is eating something with a big dog watching.

Insecurity is having a father who's an accountant.

Insecurity is examining a fire cracker that didn't go off.

Insecurity is a helium-filled balloon.

Insecurity is being the odd kid in a choose-up game.

Insecurity is when they start surveying your favorite vacant lot.

Insecurity is being the first to hand in a test paper.

INSECURITY
IS A PAIR OF
LOOSE SWIM TRUNKS

ARTIST: BOB CLARKE   WRITER: FRANK JACOBS

Insecurity is a hole in
both your front pockets.

Insecurity is moving into
a new neighborhood.

Insecurity is coming home alone
from a horror movie.

Insecurity is holding a baby.

Insecurity is bringing a sealed
note home from your teacher.

Insecurity is when the
ferris wheel stops and
you're at the top.

Insecurity is being the last
to hand in a test paper.

Insecurity is going by yourself
for the first time.

Insecurity is your ball
bouncing into traffic.

Insecurity is waiting for the thermometer to come out.

Insecurity is going into a strange store with a deposit bottle.

Insecurity is your sister getting chicken pox before Christmas vacation, and you never had it

Insecurity is sleeping in the upper bunk the first night at camp.

Insecurity is trying not to look guilty when accused of something you didn't do.

Insecurity is your mother and father arguing downstairs.

Insecurity is going downtown and seeing two Santa Clauses.

Insecurity is running an errand with a 10-dollar bill.

Insecurity is a tough kid approaching your sand castle

DON MARTIN

alone in a washroom FOR THE FIRST TIME

Do you worry about walking through tough, strange neighborhoods? Ar you concerned that muggers may attack you? Well, let's face it . . how many people are actually attacked by muggers these days? On th other hand, there are far more painful and insidious attacks visite upon every adult and teenager today. We're talking about the attack

MAD'S SNAPPY ANSWERS

ARTIST: PAUL COKER

At Weddings...

In Hospitals...

O THOSE OLD CLICHÉS

WRITER: STAN HART

At Family Reunions...

At Funerals...

Antonio Prohias is a famous Cuban artist whose anti-Castro cartoons have appeared in such publications as Bohemia (largest circulation of any Spanish language magazine), the daily *Prensa Libre* (Free Press) *El Mundo,* and the Sunday *Oveja Negra* (Black Sheep). He has won the "Juan Gualberto Gomez" award (the equivalent of our Cartoon Society's "Ruben") six times. On May 1st, three days before Castro henchmen took over what remained of Cuba's free press, Prohias fled to N.Y. stone broke. Once here, he came directly to MAD. Among the things he showed us was this captivating cartoon-sequence of friendly rivalry called

SPY vs SPY

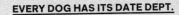

WHAT IS A

WRITTEN BY ARNIE KOG

Between the time a boy starts dating and the time he gets married, he is guaranteed to come across a creature called a "Blind Date." Blind dates come in an assortment of sizes and shapes . . . all ridiculous.

Blind dates are found everywhere. Their names appear in discarded address books, and their numbers on telephone booth walls. Blind dates are arranged by everyone, including agencies, relatives, and guys who—up until you see what they've stuck you with—were your best friends.

It's a pity on blind dates: Popular girls belittle them, popular boys ignore them, parents console them, Dear Abby advises them, beauty parlors con them, teachers pass them, nature fails them, and spray deodorants protect them . . . sometimes.

A blind date is Neatness with a run in her stocking, Primness with mustard on her chin, Shyness with a loud voice, Poise with her slip showing, Femininity with a hint of a mustache, and Hysteria in gym bloomers.

A blind date is Yogi Berra in pedal pushers, Irene Ryan in a Bikini, Fred Gwynne in a shift, Shirley Booth in stretch pants and Dan Blocker in hip-huggers. She is the girl across the street who looks like the boy next door.

A blind date is never a show girl, a model, a cheerleader or a farmer's daughter. She is always a nurse's aid, somebody's clunky cousin from out of town, or a member of the Girls' Field Hockey Team.

BLIND DATE?

ILLUSTRATED BY SERGIO ARAGONES

A blind date is a composite: She has the gender of Elizabeth Taylor, the figure of Richard Burton, the hairdo of Dr. Zorba, the elocution of Casey Stengel, the charm of an untipped waiter, the facial expression of Alfred E. Neuman, and the aroma of the Pittsburgh Steelers' locker room during half-time.

A blind date likes nice-looking boys, night clubs, moonlight walks, little compliments, some attention and lots of respect. She doesn't particularly care for insults, laughing out loud when you first meet her, introducing her to your friends as an April Fool joke, taking her to Supermarket Openings, spending Prom night at a Carvel Stand, asking her to split the check, or taking her to Lovers' Lane . . . and then leaving her there.

When you take out a blind date, you can't win. Who else can ruin your evening just by showing up? Who else laughs out loud during the newsreel? Who else wears Vicks Vap-O-Rub for cologne? And lipstick on her teeth? Who else puts on galoshes to go surfing? Who else still has diaper rash at 17? Who else has a measurement of 38-25-38 . . . on her leg?

Might as well face it . . . blind dates are losers and rejects. They are a plague and a blight. They are funny-faced, scatter-brained, double-chinned, wax-eared, pigeon-toed, hairy-legged, hang-nailed, pot-bellied, baggy-eyed, knock-kneed, baby-fatted, gum-chewing, time-consuming things.

But, at the end of the evening, when you take her home, and she turns softly to you and shakes your hand and slams the door in your face . . . you shout after her the words that millions who have dated blind dates have shouted before . . .

"CAN I SEE YOU AGAIN NEXT SATURDAY NIGHT?"

MAD ISSUES 101–200

"DAYS OF TRIUMPH, NIGHTS OF TURPITUDE"

WRITERS AND ARTISTS: SERGIO ARAGONES NEAL BARBERA GILBERT

What does the term "Affluent Society" mean to you? Aw—go ahead! Take a guess! Nobody will laugh! You're among friends! What? Is that what you think it means? HA-HA! (If you learn nothing else from this article, you have just learned not to trust your friends!) Now, here is—

THE MAD SUBURBAN PRIMER

A CHILD'S-EYE VIEW OF "THE AFFLUENT SOCIETY"

Lesson 1.

THE HOUSE

See the beautiful big house.
It is a very expensive big house.
Its owner can afford to be very proud.
In fact, pride is all that its owner can afford now!
The house is peaceful and quiet.
That's because no one in the suburbs ever stays home!
Father is out playing golf.
Mother is out playing cards.
And the children are sleeping at Grandma's house
Back in the city.
The only sound in the house
Is the pitter-patter of little feet.
The house is being robbed by a small burglar!

ARTIST: BOB CLARKE   WRITER: STAN HART

Lesson 3.

JUVENILE DELINQUENCY

There is much juvenile delinquency in the suburbs.
Parents are always shocked to find their children
In a Police Station.
They don't even recognize them.
That's because they haven't seen them for 6 months!
Parents never know why kids go wrong.
"I've given her everything," one mother says.
"A mink stole, a sport car, a charge account,
Formal parties, a vacation in Europe . . ."
"What more," the mother cries,
"Can a girl of 9 want?"

"The trouble is
Our youngsters don't do anything constructive,"
The mothers complain to each other.
The problem preys on their minds.
They discuss it every day among themselves.
Right before their Mah Jongg games.

Lesson 2.

THE LESSONS

Children in the suburbs are kept very busy.
They are forced to take many lessons.
Lessons on how to dance.
Lessons on how to act and speak.
Lessons on how to play musical instruments.
What does the suburban child learn at these lessons?
He learns that he is pleasing his parents!
Too bad he cannot take lessons
On how to be a child!

Suburban children must be a credit to their parents.
They must not lie.
They must not cheat.
They must not steal.
Poor suburban children.
They are so unprepared for the adult world!

Lesson 4.

FUN AND GAMES

In each suburban community,
There is one indispensible man.
Is it the Mayor? No! The Clergyman? No!
It is the Caterer.
Without the Caterer, there would be no parties.
Then husbands and wives
Would have to talk to each other.
They would really get to know each other.
So you see, the Caterer holds the family together!

There are always parties in the suburbs.
There are teenage parties,
And there are grownup parties.
There is wild dancing and wild kissing
And plenty of liquor and plenty of drunks.
And the grownup parties are even more fun!
The grownups play games.
These games cause lots of laughs.
These games also cause lots of divorces!

Lesson 5.

DIVORCES

There is a lot of confusion in the suburbs.
Sometimes a child does not know
Where his next father is coming from.
That's because there are a lot of divorces
In the suburbs.
When parents get divorced,
They sign visitation agreements,
The Father will see the children
On Wednesdays and Saturdays.
That's one more day than he sees them now!

He will take them to shows and ball games.
He will become their pal.
He isn't their pal now.
He will give them big allowances,
And he won't come around
Threatening to take it away when they are bad.
Mother and Father will play a game.
The game will be called
"Let's See Who Can Be Kinder To The Children."
Divorces must be a good thing!
It makes people into such good parents!

Lesson 7.

HOUSEHOLD HELP

See the woman hiding in the bushes.
She is a kidnapper.
She is trying to kidnap
Her neighbor's maid.
A maid is very important in the suburbs.
She is the child's second mother.
The first mother
Is the nurse.

Some people have this problem solved.
They bring a young girl over from Sweden
To be their maid.
It sounds like a very clever idea
Thought up by a very clever husband.

Some maids are a problem.
Some maids stay on the telephone for hours,
Or sleep all afternoon,
Or drink.
This keeps the woman of the house
    so busy checking her maid
That the woman has no time
To stay on the telephone for hours,
Or sleep all afternoon,
Or drink.

Lesson 6.

PARENTAL SUPERVISION

In the suburbs, some parents
Try to teach their children real values.
One youngster has a newspaper route.
His mother beams with pride
As she drives him on his rounds
In her Cadillac.

Someday, he will have enough money
To put himself through Medical School
And become a Doctor.
His mother will beam with pride
As she drives him on his rounds
In her Cadillac.

She deposits the money he makes in the bank.
Last week, he made $4.80.
Sometimes she adds to it
To make the deposit a round number.
Last week, she added $95.20.
She wants him to know what it feels like
To earn his own money.

Lesson 8.

WHY THE SUBURBS?

"Why do people move to the suburbs?" you ask.
"We do it for our children!" the parents answer.
That's why they buy a big $50,000 house—
Because what child could possibly be happy in less!
That's why they join an exclusive Country Club—
Which doesn't allow dogs or children!
That's why they hire gardeners to fix the lawn
So it looks pretty—
Too pretty for children to play on!
That's why they build finished basements—
So the children can't play there either
Because they might scratch the fancy bar
Or scuff the grownups' pool table!

KEEP OUT

Isn't it wonderful to be a child in the suburbs?
Think about all the poor children in the slums.
They live in such terrible homes
That they can sit in the living room
Any time they want!

SUCCESS STORY"

WRITER: DEAN NORMAN

LICKING THE PROBLEM DEPT.

Everyone profits by using the U.S. Mails. Everyone, that is, except the U.S. Post Office Department, as their yearly deficit will attest. So we here at MAD have come up with a solution to this problem —mainly, *advertising!* Stamps are seen by millions of people daily, and the only messages that come through are things like "It's the 100th Anniversary of Groundhog Day" or "Celebrating the Bi-Centennial of the Founding of the U.S. Fertilizer Industry." These ridiculous "Commemoratives" bring nothing but the few pennies that the public pays for these stamps. What we suggest is that the Post Office Department get out of the red and into the long green by selling space for

POSTAGE STAMP ADVERTISING

ARTIST & WRITER: AL JAFFEE

STAMP ADS COULD BE US

Standard Post Office Dept. stamps could become highly desirable advertising spaces for certain companies because of their clever "message tie-in" value:

For some advertisers, the "TV Story-Board" technique could be particularly appealing. Here's an example of an effective "TV Story-Board" stamp strip:

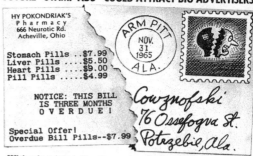

"STAMP ADS" ARE ALREADY IN USE ON A SMALL SCALE

STAMP OUT POSTAGE STAMPS
Pitney-Bowes Postage Meter Corporation

NORTH ARGH
OCT 36 '65
N.A.
P.B. METER 7490

US POSTAGE =05

Mr. Mel Haney
11 Veeblefetzer St.
Frammis, Ill.

Some "stamp advertising messages" already appear on mail. They are the messages printed by Postage Meters. But the profits from these all go to the Independent Meter-Maker.

FUTURE "STAMP ADS" COULD ATTRACT BIG ADVERTISERS

HY POKONDRIAK'S
P h a r m a c y
666 Neurotic Rd.
Acheville, Ohio

Stomach Pills ..$7.99
Liver Pills $5.50
Heart Pills $9.00
Pill Pills $4.99

NOTICE: THIS BILL
IS THREE MONTHS
O V E R D U E !

Special Offer!
Overdue Bill Pills--$7.99

ARM PITT
NOV.
31
1965
ALA.

Cowznofski
76 Ossefogva St.
Potrzebie, Ala.

With ads printed directly on stamps, the U.S. Government would reap huge profits, and public would be treated to a respite from those idiotic, meaningless commemoratives.

D IN MANY EXCITING WAYS

Advertisers could split the costs by participating in sheets of stamps the way sponsors do with "Special TV Shows." This would be especially effective when the products relate well to each other.

Happy Hunting Lodge
MOOSEDROPPING, VT.

McGREGOR SPORTSWEAR
REMINGTON FIREARMS
HARTFORD ACCIDENT INSURANCE COMPANY
WINCHESTER AMMUNITION

Myron Bloodthirsty,
27 Blastum Place,
Catskill, Ga. 67890

Other stamps, sold on rolls, could be used one at a time . . . or all at once to create amusing "teaser" effect that their road-sign counterparts produce:

EMPTY BEER CANS — ON THE ROAD — ARE UGLY, MANY SAY— — BUT AT NIGHT — REFLECTING BRIGHT — THEY SAFELY GUIDE THE WAY! — Burma Shave

1¢ UNITED STATES POSTAGE

Everyone would collect odd-shaped stamps. A double-purpose could be served by producing them, since it is an ideal way to promote company trade-marks:

The largest volume of mail sent out by business organizations contains bad news for the public . . . mainly bills. To offset the bad feeling created by this necessary evil, bill-senders could use special stamps like these, that feature fun and entertainment, and make the recipient forget his troubles:

THE SYNDICATED CARTOON STAMP

Famous Comic Characters could be used on stamps to get laughs. Value of such Public Relations to Bill-Mailers would be so great, they'd willingly use costly denominations for ordinary 5¢ letters.

THE ONE-PANEL GAG CARTOON STAMP

Popular magazine cartoonists would submit fresh gags for each month's new issue of these hilarious stamps.

THE CONTINUITY SERIAL-STORY STAMP

Customers would look forward to each month's installment, and might even make unwanted purchases just to be sure of having a bill mailed to them.

On the local level, Postmasters would be authorized to accept small orders for special printings of stamps containing personal messages. For example:

ANNOUNCEMENTS

Stamps like these could be used as extra reminders of gifts due, etc. Excellent for notices of Engagements, Marriages, Births, Deaths, Divorces, Re-Marriages, etc.

ELECTIONEERING

Politicians couldn't resist this publicity gimmick, and P.O. Dept. would make money instead of losing it on all these free-loaders who can now mail their letters free.

SALES GIMMICKS

Small "Mail-Order" outfits would find the personalized stamp a real boon with its easily-clipped-out coupon. (Note: Coupon is glueless on back for easy removal.)

FUN AND GAMES

Huge teenage market could be created with personal "Do-it-yourself" gag-type stamps. Besides profit for P.O. Dept., kids would also be forced to learn to write

IN THE
OPTOMETRIST'S WAITING ROOM

A MAD LOOK

AT BATMAN

ARTIST & WRITER: SERGIO ARAGONES

SLURG!!   SLURG!!

SUPERMAN IS CLARK KENT

TOLL
25¢

TONIGHT
GALA
COSTUME
PARTY

TONIGHT
GALA
COSTUME
PARTY

ARAGONÉS.

What was once upon a time nothing more than a delightful comic strip has become, in the past few years, a business organization that could someday rival General Motors! We're talking, of course, about that $20-million industry called "Peanuts"! As this fantastic new enterprise branches out into more Books, more Newspapers, more TV Specials, more Dolls and Sweatshirts and Records and Off-Broadway Shows and so forth, Charlie Brown and his gang continue to be real, honest, sincere and endearing people. Nevertheless, we at MAD are worried. After all, Charlie Brown and his gang are practically "Human"! So it's only a matter of time before terrible things start happening to them. All we'd like to know is:

WILL SUCCESS SPOIL CHARLIE BROWN?

ARTIST: JACK RICKARD   WRITER: LARRY SIEGEL

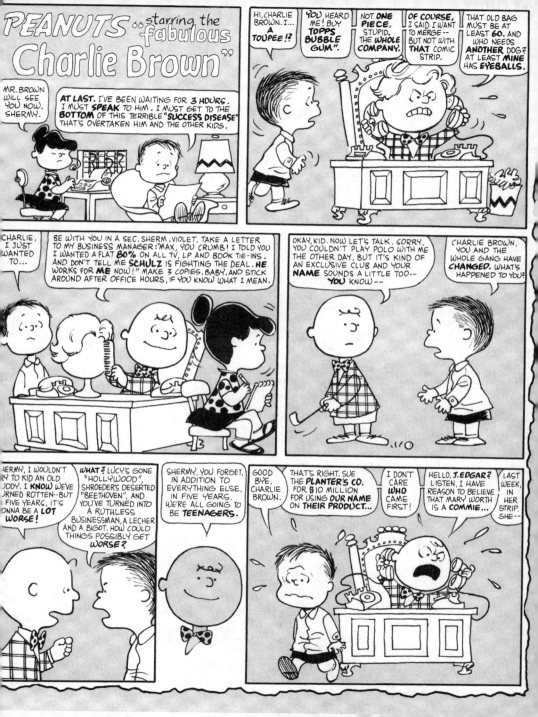

THE LIGHTER SIDE OF

Autumn is Harvest Time!

We've nursed the crop through wind and hail and drought . . . and now it's time to reap the fruits of our Summer's labors!

All set? Let's go . . .

Look at you! You're spoiled rotten by modern electronics! Here it is, a brisk Autumn day, and you're sitting in the comfort of a steam-heated living room, watching a football game on a television set!

When I was a boy, I bundled up warm and I went out to the stadium . . . and I enjoyed a football game in the healthy, nippy Autumn afternoon weather!

Okay! Okay! You made your point, Pop! I'm going . . .

Poor fallen leaf!
You have had your day in the sun!
But now, in Autumn, you must die
In a flash of brilliant cold fire!
Ah—even in death, you are beautiful
In salmon and scarlet and yellow!

Alright, already, Mr. Poet! Stop with the free verse—and make with the rake!

Crummy, rotten salmon and scarlet and yellow leaves! I need you like a hole in the head!

Looks like we got our first Autumn cold snap.

Yea
I'r
freez

AUTUMN

WRITER & ARTIST: DAVID BERG

...ck ...at!

It's blackmail, that's what this Halloween business is! **Blackmail!** I wonder what would happen if, just once, I **refused** to give in to it?

Trick or treat!

TRICK!!

WAAA!

D-d-don't cry, kids! I-I was only **kidding!** Here! Here— take the **whole bowl** of candy!

You can't buck the **system!**

Before we eat, I'd like to say a few words about "Thanksgiving"! Too often, we **forget** the real idea of this holiday! Now is the time when we should **count our blessings!**

We may not be **wealthy** . . . but as long as we have our **lives** and our **health**, we are indeed **very rich!**

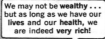

Yes, I would say that **everybody** at this table has a **great deal** to be thankful for!

Except the **turkey!**

So am I! Neither of us are **dressed** warm enough! It's all because of that **darn undependable Telephone Weather Forecasting Service!**

Did **they** goof again? Boy, they **never** get it right! Why do you even bother to **call** them?

It's a little **game** I play! I like to see how **far off** they are every time! So before I left, I dialed them, and that stupid recorded voice said, "The temperature will drop to 40 degrees by noon today"!

Huh? But they were **right!** Why didn't you **take along** some warm clothes?

Because I **never believe** them!

Autumn is the time for **burning leaves!**

Mmmm—I just **love** the smell of it!

How many times have I told you not to smoke that foul-smelling **pipe** in the house!!

But I thought you **loved** the smell of burning leaves!?

Who **you** voting for?

Stanley Muggwump!

Ahh, he's a **bum!** I'm voting for **Alvin A. Bushkin!**

What **are** you, some kind of **ignoramus?** Bushkin is a **Republican!**

Well, so am **I** —just like my **father**—and his father before him! My family's **always** voted Republican!

That's **typical,** conservative, "status quo" thinking! I'm for **progress!** That's why **I** vote **Democratic!**

Oh, yeah! You think you know **everything,** just because you go to **school!**

Oh, yeah! We know a heckuva lot more than yo Wanna make something ou of it?

Look at that **Roger Kaputnik!** Here it is—Autumn . . . he's just brought his wife back from their **Summer Vacation** . . . and already, he's getting set for their **next** trip!

And look at **you!** You never take me **any** place! It's like we're **stuck** here, with our roots down so deep, they'll **never** come out! I feel that **life** is passing me by!

Are you putting up the **Ski Racks** already?! We haven't unpacked from our **Summer Vacation** yet! Why can't we stay put for a change—like the **Bookbinders** over there!?

We're always going somep! We're always running—run —running! We're never in one place long enough to g roots and **take hold!** I fe that **life** is passing me by

Mmmm! **I love** Autumn—because that's when I go shopping for **Winter Clothes!**

I got **three dresses** and a **Winter coat!**

As a friend, George— tell the **truth!** How do you like them?

I would say they are absolutely **gorgeous!** They are tasteful, stylish, and expensive-looking!

SO DO ME A FAV DON'T SHOW TH TO MY WIFE!!

Panel 1: Look at that long line of idiots—waiting for us to winterize their cars!

Panel 2: People! I swear, there's nobody dumber than people! They never **think** ahead!

Panel 3: Here we are, two months into **Autumn!** That's **two months** when they could've had their cars Winterized! But, **no!** It's always **tomorrow!** I'll do it **tomorrow!**

Panel 4: Then comes the **first freezing day,** and every car for miles around charges in for **Anti-Freeze,** all at the same time! And they want it done right **away** . . . if not sooner!

Panel 5: So—er—after you're finished with them, you can put some Anti-Freeze in **my** car, too!

Panel 1: Gee! It's Indian Summer!

SCORE HIGH OR DIE!

BAN THE BOMB

BAN THE BOMB

TODAY THE WORLD TOMORROW NOTHING

Panel 2: Yeah! Just **yesterday,** I was freezing—and **today,** it's so warm, I feel like going in for a swim!

Panel 3: I wonder why we **call** it "Indian Summer"?

Panel 4: That's a good question! It's probably due to our **collective** guilty consciences!

Panel 5: First we pushed the Indian off his **land!** Then, we **slaughtered** him! Then, we broke every **treaty** we ever made with him! And now, we call him the "**Noble Redman**"!

Panel 6: What's **that** got to do with **Indian Summer?**

Panel 7: How should **I** know? I'm no philosopher!

Panel 1: Gee, I **love** Autumn—when **School starts** and I buy all new **pens** and **pencils** and **notebooks** and **looseleaf books** and reams of nice clean spotless looseleaf **paper!**

Panel 2: Hey, Mom! Doesn't **that** look **boss?**

Panel 3: Yes, but didn't you tell me you have **homework?**

Panel 4: Yup!

Panel 5: Then why aren't you **doing** it?

Panel 6: **WHAT!? AND MESS UP ALL THIS NICE CLEAN SPOTLESS PAPER??!!**

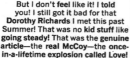

Panel 1: C'mon! Summer's over! It's Autumn—time to meet new girls!

Panel 2: But I don't feel like it! I **told** you! I still got it bad for that **Dorothy Richards** I met this past Summer! That was no **kid** stuff like **going steady!** That was the **genuine article**—the real McCoy—the once-in-a-lifetime explosion called **Love!**

Panel 3: So what if she lives way the heck up in New Rochelle! **Distance** doesn't make any difference when **Love** slugs you in the gut! So, you **see!** I just . . . **can't** . . . get . . .

Panel 4: . . . my . . . mind . . . off . . .

Panel 5: . . . whatever the heck her name was!

DAVE BERG

Parents and teachers are forever screaming about what kids are reading today. They say that children are exposed to too much "trash" such as Comic Books and Horror Stories and MAD! But for some strange reason, they never point their fingers at the worst Children's Literature of all—"Mother Goose." Just pick up any collection of Nursery Rhymes and you will quickly see how horribly written, badly rhymed and poorly metered they are. The whole trouble with Nursery Rhymes is that the folks who wrote them were "amateurs"! Obviously, the "professional touch" was sorely needed. So let's take a look at what we'd have...

IF FAMOUS POETS HAD WRITTEN "MOTHER GOOSE"

ARTIST: JACK RICKARD   WRITER: FRANK JACOBS

If RUDYARD KIPLING had written
JACK AND JILL

You can talk of blood 'n gore
When you're in a shootin' war
And the enemy is chargin' for the kill—
But if you're likin' slaughter
Then you oughta haul some water
Like that brave and fearless couple, Jack and Jill.

Well, they had a pail to fill
When they climbed that craggy hill
And they never thought that soon they
    would be dead;
But Jack he took a fall
And he bounced just like a ball
Till he landed in a gulley on his head.

He hollered, "Jill, Jill, Jill!
I'm a-lyin' at the bottom of the hill!"
But poor Jill had plunged as well,
And they died right where they fell.
You've a lot more guts than I have, Jack and Jill.

If OGDEN NASH had written
THE OLD WOMAN WHO LIVED IN A SHOE

I've often wondered whether we
Should allow an old woman to raise a lot of children in a
shoe under conditions which can only be described as
leathery.

If HENRY WADSWORTH LONGFELLOW had written
LITTLE MISS MUFFET

By the house of Mother Hubbard,
Near the fabled Pumpkin Eater,
Sat the hungry one, Miss Muffet,
On her tuffet sat Miss Muffet,
Eating curds and whey for supper;
(She was tired of eating chicken
And could not afford a pot-roast.)
But behind her loomed a creature,
Not the cat who plays the fiddle,
Not the three blind mice a-running,
Not the sheep Bo Peep lost track of,
But a single icky spider
Who sat down beside Miss Muffet,
Though he had no invitation.

"Eek! A spider!" cried Miss Muffet,
When she saw the icky spider,
And she jumped up from the tuffet
And ran down the dirt road screaming
Past the house of Mother Hubbard,
Past the fabled Pumpkin Eater,
Never ever looking backward
At the single icky spider
Who remained there on the tuffet
Where the curds and whey were sitting,
And who tasted them, despised them,
Found them lacking in nutrition,
Then departed from the tuffet
While the curds and whey just sat there,
Turning sour in the sunshine,
Smelling awful in the sunshine,
Looking ecchy in the sunshine,
While the neighbors held their noses,
And I really am not certain
That this poem is an improvement.

If EDGAR ALLAN POE had written
OLD KING COLE

Hear the call of Old King Cole—
Old King Cole!
What a frantic, fearful craving fills his morbid soul!
Hear him moaning, moaning, moaning
For his pipe and for his bowl,
Like the dreaded, deadly groaning
Of some ghoul that is intoning
From its ghostly, graveyard hole!
Hear him plea, plea, plea
As he calls his fiddlers three!
Ah, what horrifying hunger fills the terror-troubled soul
Of King Cole, Cole, Cole, Cole,
Cole, Cole, Cole—
Of the bleak and blackened soul of Old King Cole!

If WALT WHITMAN had written
HUMPTY DUMPTY

O Humpty! O Dumpty! You've had a fearful spill,
You've tumbled from the stony height,
    you're lying cold and still;
Your shell is cracked, your yolk runs out,
    your breath is faint and wheezy;
You landed as a scrambled egg, instead of over easy;
    The king has sent his steeds and men
    To mend you if they can;
        I pray that they did not forget
        To bring a frying pan.

If **ROBERT W. SERVICE** had written
LITTLE BOY BLUE

A bunch of the cows were mooing it up
    in the cornfield, so they tell;
And down in the meadow a big flock of sheep
    were raising a bit of hell;
There wasn't a way on that God-awful day
    of stopping that crop-wrecking crew—
'Cause under a haystack, flopped out on his back,
    lay that gold-bricking Little Boy Blue!

The folks from the farm, they all cried with alarm
    on that sad but sunny morn;
Each one of them knew he could save all their crops
    if he'd only blow his horn;
But none of them dared or especially cared
    to waken him from his snooze;
'Cause Little Boy Blue was as drunk as a skunk
    from a bottle of two-dollar booze!

If **WILLIAM BLAKE** had written
LITTLE JACK HORNER

Horner! Horner, on the sly,
In thy corner, eating pie!
What immortal, gastric force
Makes thee hungry as a horse?

    Horner! Horner, greedy bum,
    Sticking in thy grimy thumb!
    What cheap, greasy luncheonette
    Taught thee such bad etiquette?

        Horner! Horner, full of crumbs,
        Always eating pies with plums!
        Why not pumpkin, peach or mince—
        Or, better still, a cherry blintz?

If **JOYCE KILMER** had written
JACK SPRAT

I think that I have never seen
A platter that was licked so clean
As that one licked with fork and knife
By Jack Sprat and his hungry wife;
Betwixt the two, they've made a deal
That puts an end to beef and veal;
Lean is shunned by Mrs. Sprat,
But only Jack can eat no fat.

If **CARL SANDBURG** had written
TOM, TOM, THE PIPER'S SON

Pig Stealer for the World,
Law Breaker, Snatcher of Hogs,
Son of a Piper and the Nation's Swine Handler;
Sneaky, rotten, under-age,
Big Shot of the Pork Grabbers:
They tell me you are wicked, and I believe them,
    for I have seen you seize a pig and go
    running down the street.
And they tell me you are crooked, and I answer:
    Yes, I have seen you eat a pig and then
    go free to eat again.
And having answered, I have to ask myself:
    Why do I waste my time writing a poem
    glorifying a Pig Stealer, Law Breaker,
    Snatcher of Hogs, Son of a Piper, and
    the Swine Handler of the Nation?

IN THE HABERDASHERY

POLL-TAXED DEPT.

It is impossible to pick up a newspaper these days without reading a
some ridiculous new "Opinion Poll." Thanks to Gallup, Neilsen,
ris, Trendex and so on, America has become a "survey-happy" nation.
we at MAD feel this is a dangerous trend. (Well, to be exact, 67
feel it's a dangerous trend; 10.5% feel it's okay; and 22% couldn't

If Polls And Surveys Ha

CHRISTIAN RELIGION TO BE ABANDONED

ROME, 97 A.D.—Disciples and followers of the religion known as "Christianity" have decided to drop all plans for further developing their unusual creed. Recent public opinion polls conducted in Rome, Damascus and Alexandria show a heavy "No" response to the new idea.

Of those polled, 73% were opposed to the Christian doctrine; only 9% were in favor; and 18% had "no opinion". In view of the public reaction, leaders of the Christian faith now feel there is no hope that their ideas will ever win wide acceptance.

They polled a Preview Audience, and only 7% liked it. 34% hated it, 41% found it depressing, and 18% fell asleep. Obviously, it was a bomb!

OPENING SOON

A New Play By
William Shakespeare

"HAMLET"

Production Cancelled

advance ticket holders may
apply at box office for refunds

Globe Theatre
Bankside-London

Mr. President! The Japanese are bombing Pearl Harbor! The Pacific Fleet is in ruins, and thousands of Americans have been killed!

Mr. Secretary, give the order to mobilize at once!

Yes, sir! We mobilize the Army, the Navy, the Air Corps, the Coast Guard and the Marines?

No, Stupid!

We mobilize the Public Opinion Poll-Takers! Nobody's sticking his neck out around here until we can spot a National trend!

Been Used Through History

ARTIST: GEORGE WOODBRIDGE   WRITER: SY REIT

Dear Neighbor—   April 10, 1775

Tired of tension? Fearful of the future? If so,
you may be interested in "Operation Redcoat"—
an exciting new Service Organization now being
set up to alert Massachusetts residents if and when
the British troops should appear in this area.

DO YOU WISH TO BE AMONG THOSE NOTIFIED?

We hope so! Please indicate your preference
by filling out the attached card and returning
it to us:

tear on dotted line

es, I am interested in "Operation Redcoat". Wake me up
henever the British are sighted, even if it is the middle of
e night .... ☐

es, I am interested in "Operation Redcoat", but do not wake
e up after ...........P.M., or before ............A.M.   ☐

o, I am not interested in "Operation Redcoat" ....☐

am undecided. Please send me additional information about
Operation Redcoat" (I understand that this will

e in any way)

AME

DDRESS

TO: Paul Revere, Concord, Mass.

FROM: The Sons of Liberty, Boston, Mass.

Paul—
No soap! We mailed out hundreds of these cards
and only got a 3% return. You'd better sell the horse
and forget the whole thing!
                                               Bill Dawes

Fourscore and seven years ago, 62% of our forefathers—
with 10.4% disagreeing and 27.6% abstaining—brought
forth upon this continent a new nation, conceived in
liberty and dedicated by 63.2% of its citizens—with
9.8% against and 27% "don't knows"—to the proposition
that all men are created equal. Now, 78% of us—with
9% remaining neutral and 13% showing marked Southern
sympathies—are engaged in a great civil war . . .

Sorry, boys, but the results of the poll are in. Of the
500 adults polled here in Liverpool, 72% think your hair
is ridiculous, 81% think your music is terrible, and 91%
think that any group with an idiotic name like "The Beatles"
hasn't got a chance! So if you want my opinion, you'll give
up the idea of making it big in Show Biz!

POTRZEBIE POLLS, INC.

Mr. William M. Gaines   April 5, 1952
E.C. Publications, Inc.
New York City

Dear Mr. Gaines:

We have completed the Opinion Poll you re-
quested. As per your instruction, 5,672
people were asked how they felt about your
plans to publish a new satire magazine to
be called "MAD".

Our sampling included educators, scientists,
Congressmen, psychiatrists, business tycoons,
advertising agency executives and other
members of the so-called "Establishment".

Amazingly, the vote by this distinguished
group was 100% SOLIDLY OPPOSED to the magazine you are planning. Never in my years
as a pollster have I run into such unanimous
nausea and total repugnance to an idea.

Sincerely yours,

Sturdley Twinch

Sturdley Twinch, Pres.

MAD

INTEROFFICE MEMO

TO: THE EDITOR   FROM: THE PUBLISHER

Al--
looks like we're on the right track!
Let's start those presses rolling!
                                        Bill

IN A FANCY RESTAURANT

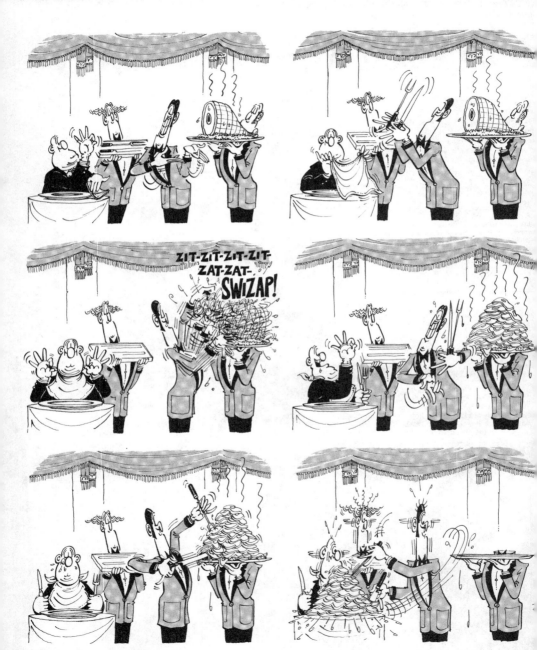

HERE WE GO WITH MAD'S VERSION OF THE TV SERIES THAT STARTS OFF EACH WEEK LIKE THIS:

Good evening, Mr. Phelts. Thank you for pushing the **"message"** button. When you hear this week's **assignment,** you'll be sorry you didn't push the **"Coke"** button. Mainly because this is another—

MISSION:
RIDICULOUS

A valuable roll of **microfilm** has been stolen from the laboratory of **Dr. Demetrius Emo, the famous microfilm-maker.** Your job is to **recover** that film, rush it over to a drugstore to be **developed,** and then turn it over to the **U. S. I. A.** All we know is that the film is somewhere in the state of **Maine,** it is so **valuable** that you and your team will be **killed** the minute anyone learns you are trying to retrieve it, and that you have only **52 television minutes** left to do the job. So get going!

ARTIST: MORT DRUCKER   WRITER: DICK DE BARTOLO

usual, at the end of this message, ...s recording will **discreetly destroy** ...tself. So, step back! Bye, now . . .

That Coke machine just **blew itself up!** Isn't that the most **suspicious** thing you've ever **seen**!?

Not really! They once got an assignment from a **hydrant** on High St. which **dissolved itself** immediately afterward!

This is the state of Maine—

How come it says "Texas"?

To confuse anyone **watching!**

It **must** work! I'm confused!

TEXAS

Now, we are all going to Maine for this assignment. But to avoid suspicion, we **won't travel together.** Bowling, you'll go by **plane** . . . Blarney by **train** . . . Synonym by **bus** . . . and I'll grab a **cab.** Synonym, did you get the **tickets?**

I got them, but the travel agent sure was **suspicious** about four friends going to **one** destination **four** different ways.

I'll have Billy, the fifth member of our team, **take care** of him and meet us here in El Paso . . .

Is that anywhere near **Portland?**

Idiot! That **IS** Portland! Now—in order not to attract attention, we will rendezvous in three days in the phone booth in the lobby of the Portland Hilton. Good luck!

TEXAS

Here we are . . . and the fare is **$3,466.75.** You know, this is the most **suspicious** thing I've ever heard of . . . taking a **cab** from **Los Angeles** to **Maine!** What **are** you, some kind of **secret agent?**

No, I'm some kind of **secret nut!**

THE Portland HILTON HOTEL

TAXI

SID ASCHER MOTEL

Cigars . . . cigarettes . . . clues! Cigars . . . cigarettes . . . clues!

Why, **Synonym!** What a **fantastic** disguise!

You have no idea **HOW** fantastic . . . considering I'm **not** Synonym! I'm **Billy,** the strong man of this team! We couldn't find an empty phone booth, so sign the hotel register with a phony name and come up to room 1313 . . .

Welcome to the Portland Hilton, Mr. Smith . . . **MR. SMITH!?** You're the **fourth** person to sign "Mr. Smith" in the last **ten minutes!** That's the most suspicious thing I've ever **seen!**

What's so **suspicious?** It's a **family reunion!**

Yeah, but **two** of the four **Mr.** Smiths were **women!**

"That's the most **suspicious** thing I have ever **seen**!"

"**What!?** Me, walking around in a **sheet**?"

"No—you, walking around! Because I **killed** you and **took the microfilm** less than an **hour** ago!"

"So it was **YOU** with the **knife**!"

"Yes, and now it's **me** with the **GUN**! Ta-ta!"

BLAM!
BLAM!

"Speak to me! Are you **okay**?"

"Certainly! I was wearing my **bullet-proof underwear**! Now that we **know** everything, signal Bowling and Synonym to **intercept** that nogoodnick, Nogoodnick, in the lobby!"

"Hey, Bowling! Synonym! Try to intercept that nogood—"

"**Don't YELL** down! Use the secret **Flower-Phone**!"

"Bowling? Synonym? **Report,** please—"

"Hey, I don't hear anything but a **buzzing** sound!!"

"That's a **bee** you hear! The **OTHER** vase is the Flower-Phone, you idiot!"

"Bowling? This is Blarney! There'll be a **man** coming into the lobby any moment. You'll know him by his **medium height, checkered suit,** and **smoking revolver.** He has the **microfilm** in his **attache case,** so use the **"switch ploy"** on him!"

"**Got** you, Blarney! Use the **"switch ploy"** on him . . ."

"Look, Emma—a man talking to a **flower vase**! Isn't that the most **suspicious** thing you've ever **seen**?"

"**Why?** The flower vase is **answering** him, isn't it?"

"Here he comes! Okay—go to work . . ."

"Er—pardon me. sir . . . do you have change for a **Series E Savings** bond?"

"No, I'm sorry!"

Victims of "Cliche Conversation"... unite! You have nothing to lose but your utter boredom! Yes, here's your chance to strike back! Unfortunately, you will probably end up with nobody talking to you once you start using:

MAD'S "CLICHI

"CONVERSATION" KILLERS

AT A REUNION PARTY

ARTIST: GEORGE WOODBRIDGE   WRITER: STAN HART

THE SMARTEST APE IN CAPTIVITY

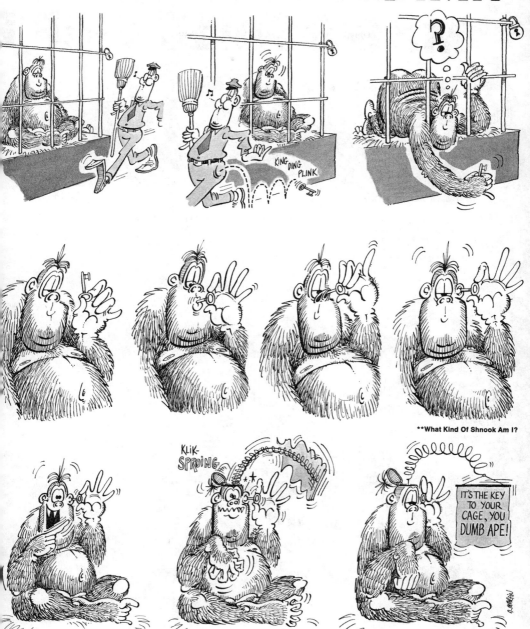

Quite a few issues back (MAD #82, to be exact!), we pointed out that progress brings change, but tha
sometimes the change isn't all for the better. Man often forgets to look back to see how far he's pr

MAD'S FOLLOW-UP

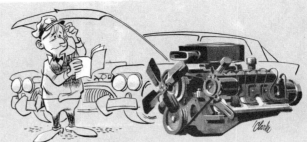

The old fashioned car engine consisted of a few inexpensive parts which ran trouble-free for years, but only delivered a ridiculous top speed of 50 mph.

The modern, high-compression, supercharged, dual-carburetored V-8 car engine is in constant need of expensive replacement parts and repairs, despite its original cost of ten times the old-fashioned car engine. But its high horsepower delivers a top speed of over 130 mph! Too bad most highways only have a top speed of 50 mph.

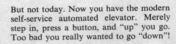

Recognize this man in uniform? He is an elevator operator. Better make that "he *was* an elevator operator." Yes, time was when you had to depend on him for service.

But not today. Now you have the modern self-service automated elevator. Merely step in, press a button, and "up" you go. Too bad you really wanted to go "down"!

The old-fashioned wrist watch
merely gave the correct time

The modern wrist watch gi
the day, date and moonpha
while showing elapsed tin
sounding an alarm, and s
plying a stop-watch. If you
really observant, you may
able to pick out correct tin

ssed. **Which is what this next article is all about. It's also exactly what the article in MAD # 82 all about, which gives you an idea of how progress can really take a beating. At any rate, here's**

PORT ON PROGRESS

ARTIST: BOB CLARKE   WRITER: DICK DE BARTOLO

Picnics were often ruined in the past when you had the old-fashioned cans of beer and no one brought a "church key".

Modern pull-tab beer cans eliminate need for can openers entirely. Now picnics are often ruined because no one brings bandages for fingers cut by those metal pull-tabs.

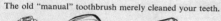

The old "manual" toothbrush merely cleaned your teeth.

Today's streamlined electric toothbrush cleans your teeth with thousands of power strokes per minute . . . unless, of course, you forget to plug it in, or they turn off your electricity, or you want to use it away from an electric power source, or you short-circuit the thing and nearly electrocute yourself by dropping it into a basin of water.

Those ridiculous "prop" planes took over 11 hours to fly from N.Y. to California, and you had to carry your own luggage!

Today's modern jet planes whisk you from N.Y. to California in just over 5 hours . . . a full 6 hours or more before your lost luggage finally shows up.

Can you recall when washing the dishes took you a time-consuming 15 minutes and used up about 2¢ worth of soap?

Compare that with using the modern electric dishwasher, which can usually be loaded with dirty dishes in half-an-hour, and only costs about 50¢ per wash (when you've averaged in the initial investment of several hundred dollars, plus costs of installation, plumbing, repairs, electricity, and about 2¢ worth of detergent per wash.)

Remember this stuff? It was called cash! People would carry 20 or 30 or 50 dollars worth of it . . . then lose it, and be out all that money.

Here is the modern man's wallet. Notice—no cash! Just dozens of convenient (but bulky) credit cards. And if he loses them, he's not out one penny . . . not until the end of the month, that is, when he receives bills for $23,589.37—charged by the guy who found his wallet.

Remember when you had to carve a turkey with that tedious back and forth motion using an old-fashioned plain knife?

Today, with a modern vibrating electric knife, you merely have to guide it as it effortlessly slices through a turkey, and accidentally slices through its own power cord.

Before television, if a person wanted to be entertained, he'd have to go to the movies—which in those days were nothing more than trashy, poorly written dull melodramas.

Today, thanks to television, a person merely has to turn a knob to be entertained in the comfort of his own home.

ONE NIGHT ON SKULL ISLAND

If **Poe's "THE RAVEN"** Were Written By **Joyce Kilmer**

I think that I shall never hear
A raven who is more sincere
Than that one tapping at my door
Who's ever saying, "Nevermore;"
A raven who repeats his words
Until I think I'm for the birds;
A raven who, I must assume,
Will dirty up my living-room;
A raven fond of bugs and worms
With whom I'm on the best of terms;
Let other poets praise a tree—
A raven's good enough for me!

THE MAD POETR

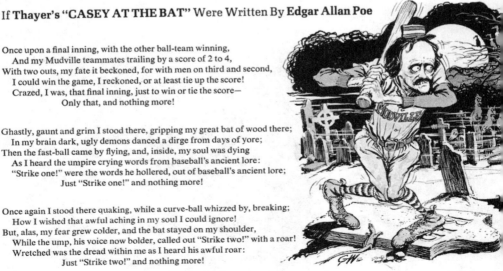

If **Thayer's "CASEY AT THE BAT"** Were Written By **Edgar Allan Poe**

Once upon a final inning, with the other ball-team winning,
  And my Mudville teammates trailing by a score of 2 to 4,
With two outs, my fate it beckoned, for with men on third and second,
  I could win the game, I reckoned, or at least tie up the score!
  Crazed, I was, that final inning, just to win or tie the score—
        Only that, and nothing more!

Ghastly, gaunt and grim I stood there, gripping my great bat of wood there;
  In my brain dark, ugly demons danced a dirge from days of yore;
Then the fast-ball came by flying, and, inside, my soul was dying
  As I heard the umpire crying words from baseball's ancient lore:
  "Strike one!" were the words he hollered, out of baseball's ancient lore;
        Just "Strike one!" and nothing more!

Once again I stood there quaking, while a curve-ball whizzed by, breaking;
  How I wished that awful aching in my soul I could ignore!
But, alas, my fear grew colder, and the bat stayed on my shoulder,
  While the ump, his voice now bolder, called out "Strike two!" with a roar!
  Wretched was the dread within me as I heard his awful roar:
        Just "Strike two!" and nothing more!

If **Kilmer's "TREES"** Were Written By **John Masefield**

I must go up in a tree again
 and sit where the bullfinch warbles;
Where the squirrel runs up and down a limb
 and the owl has lost his marbles;
And the squawks and hoots and chirps and squeaks
 that all the birds are making
Fill the air around so I can't hear
 the branch beneath me breaking!

I must go up in a tree again,
 from where people look like ants,
And all I ask is a branch that's smooth
 so I won't rip my pants;
And a dozen bugs running up my leg,
 and the sap so sticky,
And the cooing doves and the screaming crows
 making messes icky;

Y ROUND ROBIN

ARTIST: GEORGE WOODBRIDGE   WRITER: FRANK JACOBS

Praying for some god to guide me, hope, I feared, would be denied me
While the tell-tale heart inside me beat upon some distant shore;
Then the change-up came by, looming, and I swung, my fate now dooming,
While the umpire's call came booming, and it chilled me to the core;
Ghostly was the call he thundered, chilling me right to the core—
Just "Strike three!" and nothing more!

If **Masefield's "SEA FEVER"** Were Written By **Carl Sandburg**

Fish Tank for the World,
Shark Breeder, Maker of Waves,
Lousy with Herring and the Nation's Saltcellar;
Briny, bottomless, undrinkable,
Home of the Big Flounder:
They tell me you are stormy, and I believe them;
    for I have crossed you on a tramp steamer
    and have lost my lunch at the poop rail.
And they tell me you are messy, and my reply is:
    Yes, it is true I have swum in your surf and
    have emerged yecchy, with seaweed.
And having answered, I ask myself: Why am I not
    writing a poem about Chicago instead of a poem
    about the Fish Tank for the World, Shark Breeder,
    Maker of Waves, Home of the Big Flounder, and
    Saltcellar to the Nation?

If **Carl Sandburg's "CHICAGO"** Were Written By **Rudyard Kipling**

You can talk of Mandalay,
Of Calcutta or Bombay,
    Where the heat'll make a fuzzy-wuzzy fry;
But if to drink you're driven
And don't give a damn for livin'
    Then you oughta hit the road for windy Chi.

It's a town where hoods and thugs
Like to send a dozen slugs
    Right through a copper pretty as you please;
Where the breezes blow like hell,
And that awful stockyard smell
    Is enough to bring a blighter to his knees.

For it's Chi! Chi! Chi!
Guns are shootin' and I'm just a passerby!
Though your buildings may be pretty,
You can keep your bloomin' city
'Cause I'm headin' back to Injia, windy Chi!

If **Longfellow's "THE MIDNIGHT RIDE OF PAUL REVERE"** Were Written By **Ernest Lawrence Thayer**

It looked extremely rocky for the Colonists that night;
The British were attacking with no hope of help in sight;
So, with villages in danger from the enemy so near,
They had to send a warning, and they called on Paul Revere.

There was ease in Paul's demeanor as he climbed upon his mare;
There was pride in Paul's expression as he sat so tall and fair;
And then the horse grew skittish, and she gave a sudden jump,
And Paul fell from his saddle, landing smack upon his rump.

With a smile of Yankee courage, Paul rose smartly to his feet,
And once again upon the saddled mare he took his seat;
But as he gripped the reins, she made a sudden turn around,
And once again Paul plummeted onto the dusty ground.

The smile has vanished from Paul's face, his eyes burn with a glare;
He grips the bridle fiercely as again he mounts the mare;
And now he tells the horse to gallop, in an urgent tone,
And now the air is shattered as the horse takes off—alone;

Oh, somewhere in this war-torn land the people safely know
That Redcoats are invading, taking captives as they go;
And somewhere people are prepared to flee the British force
But there's no hope for New England—
    Paul Revere can't ride a horse!

If Kipling's "GUNGA DIN" Were Written By Clement Clarke Moore

'Twas the night of the battle, and all through the slaughter,
Not a creature was stirring—we all needed water;
The canteens were slung on the sand-dunes with care,
In hopes that old Gunga Din soon would be there;
When what should appear to our wondering eyes
But a skinny brown native—oh, what a surprise!
I cheered with delight as he crossed a ravine,
For I knew right away that it was Gunga Din!
His garment was merely a cute little rag,
And he brought along with him a big water bag!
Then he went right to work in a manner quite shocking—
He shunned our canteens and instead filled each stocking!
It all seemed so senseless and, making things worse,
I knew there was something quite wrong with this verse!
I remarked, "What a strange thing to do in a war!"
And he said, "That's because you are Clement Clarke Moore;
"I'm confused by your verses, so rhythmic and rippling—
"Please write about Christmas, and give me back Kipling!"

If Moore's "THE NIGHT BEFORE CHRISTMAS" Were Written By Robert W. Service

A bunch of the boys were whooping it up
    on a Christmas Eve one year,
All full of cheap whiskey and hoping like hell
    that St. Nick would soon appear,
When right through the door and straight out of the night,
    which was icy and cold as a freezer,
Came a broken-down sled, pulled by eight mangy dogs,
    which were whipped by an old bearded geezer.

His teeth were half missing, and flapping his frame
    was a tatter of red-colored clothes;
He was covered with snow from his head to his toe,
    and an icicle hung from his nose;
The miners all cheered when the geezer appeared,
    and the poker game stopped in mid-bet;
Each sourdough smiled like a young, happy child
    at the thought of the gifts he would get.

They pushed him aside and went straight for his bag
    to be sure that they'd all get their share;
And, oh, how they cried when they found that inside
    there was nothing but old underwear;
So they plugged the old geezer, which was a great shame,
    for if anyone there had been sober,
He'd have known double-quick that it wasn't St. Nick,
    'cause it only was early October!

If Service's "THE SHOOTING OF DAN McGREW" Were Written By Henry Wadsworth Longfellow

Listen, my children, and I'll tell you
Of the valiant death of Dan McGrew;
With a patriot's pride he made his stand
While foes assailed his native land
And threatened to tear down
    the red, white and blue!

When the struggle for freedom
    lay hanging in doubt,
He cried to the bartender, with a fierce shout—
"One if it's whiskey, and two if it's beer!"
He drank like a man who had nothing to fear,
While brave men around him
    were all passing out!

At last, the dread enemy came into view,
And a cowardly bullet cut down Dan McGrew;
How the hopes of a nation
    were shattered that night!
And yet men could say as they took up the fight—
"A bullet achieved what no rotgut could do!"

When "Frozen Foods" were first introduced, the innovation was greeted by housewives with w cries of joy. But all that has changed. Today, "Frozen Foods" are looked upon as a housewife "cop-out"! Today, if a housewife serves her family "Frozen TV Dinners" or other Frozen Dish it means she's lazy and she lacks imagination. In short, when the family sees "Frozen Food

MAD'S FRO
THAT FAKE

MAD'S FROZEN
BURNT VEGETABLES

CONTENTS: One pound of burned carrots-and-peas, plus one packet of carrot-scrapings and empty pea pods, plus one miniature spray can of "CHAR-SMELL".

INSTRUCTIONS: Thaw burned carrots-and-peas and heat in saucepan for 5 minutes. Sprinkle carrot scrapings and empty pea pods liberally around sink, spray "Char-Smell" around kitchen to simulate odor of burning, and serve family while sobbing, "—after all my hard work!"

the table, it knows that dear old Mom has spent the afternoon watching the "Boob Tube" or [pl]aying "Mah-Jongg" or picketing the local School Board. However, thanks to MAD's inventive [ge]nius, we can now offer Mom a solution. Now she can enjoy the convenience of Frozen Foods and [sti]ll maintain the status of a woman who does her own cooking! All she has to do is start using

ZEN FOODS
OUT FRESH

PHOTOGRAPHY: BY IRVING SCHILD   WRITER: SY REIT

MAD'S FROZEN "LEFTOVERS" MEAL

CONTENTS: 4 dry chicken wings, 3 partially-gnawed drumsticks, 2 slices of soggy pot roast, 1 over-cooked lamb chop, assorted ham fragments, half of a baked potato, and 1 shriveled tomato.

DIRECTIONS: Heat contents of package in 350° oven for 15-20 minutes, [re]move and place on platter, and bring to table while making cheery [c]omments like: "Waste not . . . want not!" or "It's a sin to throw out [p]erfectly good food!" or "Think of all the people starving in India!"

NOTE: TOP OFF THIS DELICIOUS "LEFTOVERS MEAL" WITH A PACKAGE OF "LEFTOVERS DESSERT". CONTAINS: TWO SLICES OF CONGEALED PEACH PIE, 1 STALE "HOMEBAKED" BLUEBERRY MUFFIN, HALF A CUPCAKE, 3 BROKEN ASSORTED COOKIES, AND A CUP OF PARTIALLY-EATEN CHOCOLATE PUDDING.

MAD'S FROZEN NON-RISING
"HOMEBAKED" CAKE

CONTENTS: One three-layer chocolate cake, guaranteed to remain flat and soggy; and one plastic container of special "runny sauce".

INSTRUCTIONS: Thaw cake at room temperature. Pour special "runny sauce" over top, and while serving, apologize for failure of cake to rise. Also apologize for consistency of icing. Spend balance of meal brooding unhappily over "what went wrong?"—and at the same time, impressing family with all the hard work that goes into baking a cake to begin with. Wind up blaming Husband for everything, pointing out that he's too cheap to replace crummy old kitchen stove.

MAD'S FROZEN
"NEVER AGAIN"
CHICKEN SALAD

CONTENTS: Three pounds of quick-frozen chicken salad, PLUS one packet of "Kitchen Mess" containing assorted carrot greens, radish tips, celery stalk tops, etc. PLUS two pre-bloodied Band Aids.

INSTRUCTIONS: Thaw chicken salad at room temperature and place in salad bowl. Scatter contents of "Kitchen Mess" packet all over counter tops to give the impression of lengthy preparation. Place pre-bloodied Band Aids on fingers to simulate chopping cuts, and serve salad while complaining about "...all the work involved!" Repeat "Never again! Never again!" frequently. For added effect, at end of meal, look at empty salad bowl and say something like "Boy, you work all day to make it, and it goes in two minutes!"

ANOTHER GREAT BANK ROBBERY

A BOY and his CHEMISTRY SET

Almost every magazine other than MAD (Yes, there *are* magazines other than MAD!) runs an annual "READER SURVEY" in which they ask a couple of dozen questions to find out more about their readers. MAD has never run such a survey because, as you know, our readers come last and we really don't care to know anything about you. Frankly, we're not interested in anyone stupid enough to buy this trash magazine. However, just in case you've never had the opportunity to fill out one of these dumb things, hurry up and mail us

MAD'S FIRST ...AND PROBABLY LAST... READER SURVEY

NAME_____ ADDRESS_____

CITY _____STATE_____PHONE NO. _____

1. HOW DID YOU FIRST HEAR ABOUT MAD MAGAZINE?
☐ Friend   ☐ Relative   ☐ Stranger   ☐ Strange Friend or Relative   ☐ Other

2. HOW DO YOU RATE THE CONTENTS OF MAD MAGAZINE?
☐ Excellent   ☐ Really Excellent   ☐ Truly Excellent   ☐ Really Truly Excellent   ☐ All Of The Above

3. WHAT IS THE POPULATION OF THE TOWN OR CITY IN WHICH YOU LIVE? _____

4. HOW DO YOU RATE THE EFFECTIVENESS OF THE POLICE FORCE IN YOUR TOWN OR CITY?
☐ Good   ☐ Fair   ☐ Poor   ☐ Yecch   ☐ The Keystone Cops Did a Better Job

5. WHAT ARE YOUR HOBBIES? _____

6. DO YOU COLLECT: ☐ Stamps   ☐ Rare Coins   ☐ Anything Else of Value _____
PLEASE GIVE DETAILS

7. WHAT KIND OF CAR DO YOU DRIVE?_____WHAT YEAR & MODEL IS IT? _____
WHERE DO YOU KEEP THE KEYS FOR IT?_____

8. WHAT ARE THE NAMES OF THE BANKS WHERE YOU KEEP YOUR MONEY?
a._____
b._____
c._____

SIGN YOUR NAME HERE: _____

9. WHAT KIND OF VALUABLE ELECTRONIC EQUIPMENT OR OTHER EXPENSIVE THINGS DO YOU OWN?
Color TV ☐   B&W TV ☐   Stereo System ☐   Tape Recorder ☐   Portable Radio ☐   Binoculars ☐
Wristwatch ☐   Digital Calculator ☐   Other_____
PLEASE GIVE DETAILS

10. DO YOU LIVE ALONE?_____WHEN ARE YOU OUT?_____
WHEN DO YOU GO ON VACATION? _____
HOW MUCH CASH DO YOU KEEP IN YOUR HOME OR APARTMENT?_____
EXACTLY WHERE IN YOUR HOME OR APARTMENT DO YOU KEEP IT?_____

11. WHAT KIND OF LOCK DO YOU HAVE ON YOUR DOOR? _____

12. PLACE YOUR KEY IN THIS BOX AND TRACE THE OUTLINE OF IT:

THANK YOU VERY MUCH FOR YOUR HELP. PLEASE NOTIFY US IF YOU MOVE, IF YOU CHANGE YOUR WORKING HOURS, OR IF YOU CHANGE YOUR VACATION PLANS.

WRITER: DICK DE BARTOLO

GREAT
NON-VIOLENT
GUNS!

Idiot! Use mine! It's got a **silencer** on it!

I'm sorry it has to **end** like this, Arthur . . .

HAWKS DOVES

MAJOR HAWKS

ARTIST & WRITER: AL JAFFEE

PRIVATE DOVES

ONE DAY IN THE GARDEN OF EDEN

ORDURE OF THE DAY

ARTIST: PAUL COKER, JR.   WRITER: RONNIE NATHAN

It's true, as we've heard wise men say,
That every dog must have his day,
In cities, though, each day we rue
How many dogs have had their do.

The streets are spattered all through town
With beagle beige and boxer brown;
Though litter we're taught not to strew,
Still every dog's allowed his do.

The tree-lined parks give off a scent
Of, mainly, canine excrement,
Which clings to him who wears the shoe
That steps where dogs have had their do.

In playgrounds where the toddlers crawl,
And ball fields where boys bat the ball,
Too often what will spoil the view
Are spots where Spot has stopped to do.

Our cities will soon go to seed
With droppings from the pedigreed,
From cocker, collie, Kerry blue,
And other curs who can and do.

It's not man's best friend who's at fault,
No, it's his master we must halt;
Our neighbor who expects us to
Love him and love his doggie-do.

The city's for the birds unless
We clear its grounds of hounds that mess,
And curb, instead, pet-owners who
Care little where their dogs make do.

Let's have them, like good parents, toil
At cleaning up their puppy's soil,
Removing every tell-tale clue,
Or we'll go to the dogs with do.

Go to your local newsstand, pick up a newspaper, and what's the first thing that hits you in the eye? The newsdealer, dummy—because you didn't pay for the paper! But the *next* thing will be all those scary head-lines about "law and order" and "crime in the streets"! Incidentally, we can't figure out *why* there's so much fuss about "crime in the streets"! Isn't that where it *belongs*? Where *should* we have crime, for Pete's sake—*inside our houses*? Anyway, violence in America is becoming a serious problem. Everyone agrees that something must be done to curb all the crime, rioting, and other forms of mayhem. But we here at MAD think that the Establishment is going about it *all wrong*. Instead of trying to *suppress* violence, the powers that be ought to find a nice safe *outlet* for it. Let's face it, people *need* ways to express their anti-social urges. And everyone *has* these secret urges. So why not channel them harmlessly by setting up a special area where folks can get *rid* of these terrible impulses and natural aggressions in *completely safe and acceptable ways*? How would this work? Well, why not join us as MAD escorts you through uninhibited, satisfying . . . . .

ARTIST: GEORGE WOODBRIDGE
WRITER: SY REIT

HAWKS DOVES

MAJOR HAWKS

ARTIST & WRITER: AL JAFFEE

PRIVATE DOVES

THE HUNTERS

TV... AS VIEWED BY

A Crosseyed Rhino

A Rabid Dog

A Bug In A Rug

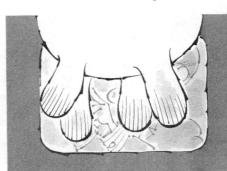

A Newborn Calf

A Baby Kangaroo

An Amused Ant

THE ANIMAL WORLD

ARTIST:
PAUL COKER, JR.

WRITER:
PAUL PETER PORGES

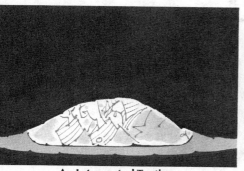

An Introverted Turtle

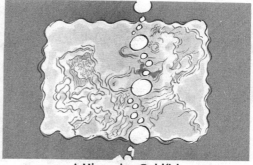

A Hiccuping Goldfish

A Housebroken Giraffe

A Curious Termite

A Bored Bat

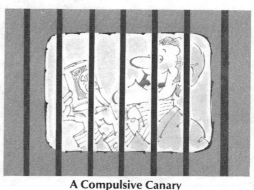

A Compulsive Canary

Are you reading a magazine? Are you reading MAD Magazine? Are your reading the introduction to this article? Then you know what "Stupid Questions" are, because we just asked three of the stupidest! Are you sick and tired of being asked stupid questio Would you like to put them down? Then this art (by Al Jaffee) is for you! So were the first articles on the very same subject (by Al Jaf

MORE SNAPPY ANSWER

TO STUPID QUESTIONS

ARTIST & WRITER: AL JAFFEE

ARE YOU COOKING SOMETHING?

No, I've decided to turn our kitchen into a Sauna Bath!

No, I'm burning pots!

No, I'm drawing a hot bath for a chicken!

Does the reader write his snappy answer here?

No, he writes "The Lord's Prayer" here! He writes his snappy answer on the head of a pin!

ARE YOU TAKING THE GARBAGE OUT?

No, I'm taking our dinner out! I put the garbage in our refrigerator!

No, I'm taking my wife out! But she's shy, and this is the only way she'll go anywhere!

No, I'm taking this picnic basket out! Anytime you're hungry, feel free to dig in!

After he fills in the balloon, what happens?

He hangs on and tries for an altitude record!

ARE YOU DIGGING A FOXHOLE?

No, I've got a three-day pass, and I'm digging a tunnel home to Chicago!

No, I'm building a swimming pool to relax in during those pleasant moments between mortar attacks!

No, I'm digging a final resting place for idiots who ask stupid questions! By the way, how tall are you?

After he's finished, should he mail them in?

Yes, to the proper Mental Health authorities!

A "SNAPPY ANSWERS TO STUPID QUESTIONS" OFFICE SAGA

IN AN ITALIAN RESTAURANT

Hey, gang! Here we go with another MAD "Hate Book," those
little literary gems calculated to help you feel better by

THE MAD CAR-OWN

DON'T YOU HATE...
... being the only one caught speeding when
you were just going as fast as everyone else.

DON'T YOU HATE...
... getting into the "Exact Change Only" lane, and ending
up behind a guy who finds he hasn't got the exact change.

DON'T YOU HATE...
... when something happens the day after
you let your comprehensive insurance expire.

DON'T YOU HATE...
...the nauseating smell of gasoline that wafts forward
to tell you that they've over-filled your tank again.

DON'T YOU HATE...
..."One Way" and "No Turn" signs that take you miles out of your way.

DON'T YOU HATE...
... bumpers that are higher than yours.

ERS HATE BOOK

ARTIST & WRITER:
AL JAFFEE

DON'T YOU HATE . . .
. . . repair shops that always have to *order* the part you desperately need.

DON'T YOU HATE . . .
. . . finally getting into that moving lane only to find that it abruptly stops . . . and your old one moves from then on.

DON'T YOU HATE . . .
. . . a convertible top that invariably fails to operate whenever there's a sudden cloudburst.

DON'T YOU HATE . . .
. . . lending your car to someone . . . and after it's returned, the engine makes a strange sound you've never heard before.

DON'T YOU HATE . . .
. . . car radios that fade out at critical moments.

DON'T YOU HATE . . .
. . . finding a vacant space where you parked your car.

DON'T YOU HATE...
. . . strange noises that always disappear the minute you take your new car back to the dealer . . . and re-appear again right after you leave!

DON'T YOU HATE...
. . . having to go to the bathroom on one of those new treeless, bushless, exitless super-highways.

DON'T YOU HATE...
. . . hearing the unmistakable sound of a failing engine when you're right smack in the middle of the worst section of town.

DON'T YOU HATE...
. . . people who carelessly track whatever they stepped into right into your brand new car.

DON'T YOU HATE...
. . . know-it-all mechanics who insist that it's perfectly okay to do exactly the opposite—or use other parts—than what the manufacturer of your car specifically recommends.

DON'T YOU HATE...
. . . people who let kids eat in your new car.

DON'T YOU HATE...
. . . two cars that take up three parking spaces.

DON'T YOU HATE...
. . . glimpsing your car keys in the ignition just as you're slamming the locked car door.

DON'T YOU HATE...
... getting a flat tire in the middle of nowhere when you're dressed to the hilt.

DON'T YOU HATE...
... lending someone your car with a full tank of gas —and having it returned with exactly two drops left.

DON'T YOU HATE...
... your new car's air conditioner that conks out during the first heat wave ... reminding you of how the heater conked out during the first cold wave.

DON'T YOU HATE...
... being trapped between two huge trucks ... and having to go miles beyond your turn-off.

DON'T YOU HATE...
... forgetting where you parked your car in a 10,000 car parking lot.

DON'T YOU HATE...
... finding a strange new puddle in your garage.

DON'T YOU HATE...
... gas station attendants who act like they're doing you the biggest favor in the world when they finally get to you.

DON'T YOU HATE...
... returning to your car the next morning just as the last faint glimmer of light fades from your headlights.

The big corporations have always depended upon "Planned Obsolescence," the calculated rapid breakdown i acceptable design and performance of their products to keep their coffers filled. Planned Obsolescence boost sales and profits by insuring quick replacement of worn-out or outmoded items. Recently, consumer crusader

PLANNED OBSOLESCENCE

TOILET PAPER

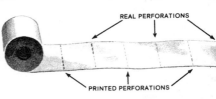

REAL PERFORATIONS

PRINTED PERFORATIONS

Careful examinations have disclosed that perforations alternate between real ones and phony ones. Phony ones are only printed on. Thus, when consumer gives normal yank, five feet of tissue cascades onto floor. Since consumer never suspects real reason, he vows time and again to be more careful next time. Of course, tissue on floor is discarded...and roll goes fast that way

SOAP

FADE

NEWLY UNWRAPPED

REAL SOAP OUTER CRUST

REAL SOAP INNER SLIVER

FAST EVAPORATING SOAP COMPOUND

2 DAYS LATER

5 DAYS LATER

Most bars of soap will turn into slivers in about 5 days whether soap is used or not. This is due to presence of "fast evaporating soap compound"—located between normal outer crust and inner sliver—which is dissolved by air.

NUTS AND BOLTS

A

B

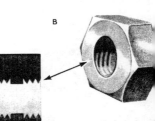

Many ordinary nuts and bolts are virtually useless. For example, threads on bolts (A) are manufactured so that they cannot work with any ordinary nuts...

...and threads o nuts (B) come to a end halfway inside

like Ralph Nader have been exposing the despicable practice of Planned Obsolescence in the automobile and appliance fields. But the use of Planned Obsolescence in less spectacular, but no less important products that the average consumer cannot do without, has been totally ignored. And so, to fill the gap, here's a MAD report on

IN EVERYDAY PRODUCTS

ARTIST & WRITER: AL JAFFEE

PENCILS

Investigation shows how lead is placed in many pencils today, and the kinds of points you get when you sharpen them.

GOOD BAD GOOD BAD GOOD BAD GOOD

Note that every other point is bad. As a result, when the consumer sharpens pencil, he keeps doing it until he gets a good point. Thus, he uses up this pencil twice as fast as a well-made one, and the sharpener is usually blamed.

ZIPPERS

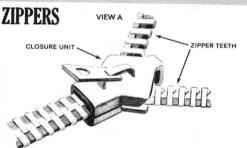

VIEW A

CLOSURE UNIT

ZIPPER TEETH

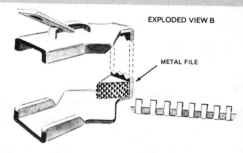

EXPLODED VIEW B

METAL FILE

The zipper is so foolproof that it could be made to last forever. But what good would that be? So, as in exploded view (B) above, we see how a carefully placed metal file in every closure unit goes to work on the zipper teeth as it moves up and down over them, wearing them out quickly. This causes gapping, jamming and—best of all—*replacing!*

ELECTRICAL UNIT PULLCHAINS

EXHAUST FAN
PULLCHAIN

LAMP SOCKET
PULLCHAINS

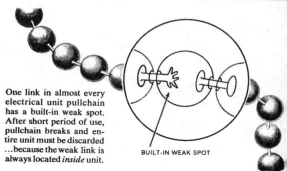

One link in almost every electrical unit pullchain has a built-in weak spot. After short period of use, pullchain breaks and entire unit must be discarded ...because the weak link is always located *inside* unit.

BUILT-IN WEAK SPOT

TEABAGS

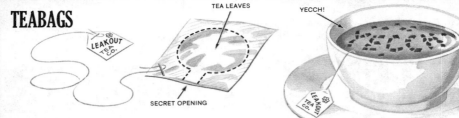

Many teabags are made with secret openings that are cleverly concealed to prevent discovery by inspection. These openings are sealed with a non-toxic glue that dissolves in hot water.

When secret opening is unsealed, tea leaves escape into the water, and unwary consumer is forced to dump it out and start all over with a new tea bag.

NAILS

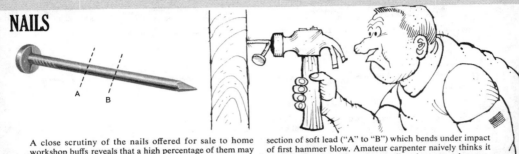

A close scrutiny of the nails offered for sale to home workshop buffs reveals that a high percentage of them may look normal but are actually manufactured with a ¼ inch section of soft lead ("A" to "B") which bends under impact of first hammer blow. Amateur carpenter naively thinks it is his bad aim, pulls out bent nail and uses another one.

MATCHES

Many matches when struck, spark, sputter and then go out. User thinks match is wet and takes another one! Actually, match has been treated with a flameproof chemical! A box of 50% bad matches like these gets used up mighty fast.

PLAYING CARDS

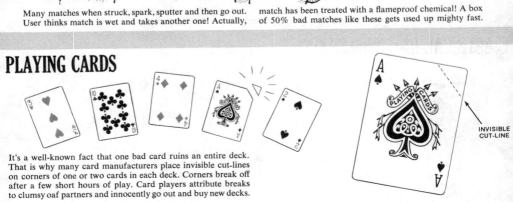

It's a well-known fact that one bad card ruins an entire deck. That is why many card manufacturers place invisible cut-lines on corners of one or two cards in each deck. Corners break off after a few short hours of play. Card players attribute breaks to clumsy oaf partners and innocently go out and buy new decks.

ADHESIVE TAPES

TAPE COATED WITH REGULAR ADHESIVE

TAPE COATED WITH SPECIAL ADHESIVE

First three feet of most adhesive tapes are coated with the normal adhesive and unrolled easily. But after that, a special adhesive is used which has been designed to stick best to tape itself. This makes it virtually impossible to remove more than one inch of tape at a time, and the disgusted consumer, thinking it's just old, buys new roll.

STAPLES

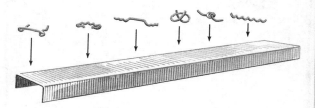

Most bars of staples look perfectly innocent. But every third staple is actually made of soft, inferior wire that can't penetrate even one sheet of paper. It simply turns into one of the grotesque shapes shown and is discarded.

CIGARETTES

Most new long cigarettes actually burn down more quickly than old shorter types, thanks to specially-developed tobacco.

A   B   C

TOBACCO BETWEEN "A" AND "B" IS REGULAR SLOW-BURNING KIND

TOBACCO BETWEEN "B" AND "C" IS SPECIALLY-DEVELOPED NEW TYPE (IMPREGNATED WITH PARTICLES OF GUN POWDER) WHICH BURNS DOWN IN A SPLIT SECOND SO CONSUMER QUICKLY LIGHTS UP ANOTHER ONE.

FACIAL TISSUES

Alternate sheets of many brands of facial tissues have been specially die-cut to create a built-in failure feature.

TEAR·E·Z TISSUES

CENTER SECTIONS OF ALTERNATE FACIAL TISSUE SHEETS ARE HELD IN PLACE BY FOUR TINY FIBERS.

WHEN A SPECIALLY DIE-CUT SHEET IS USED, IT IS TOTALLY INEFFECTIVE AND EMBARRASSING, CAUSING CONSUMER TO QUICKLY GRAB FOR ANOTHER TISSUE.

ONE EVENING IN SPAIN

A Witch's Tale

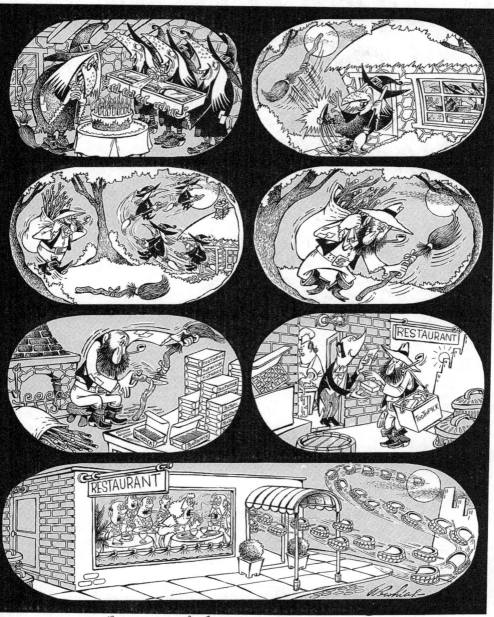

ONE NIGHT IN A RESTAURANT

ON A SAFARI

ARTIST & WRITER: ANTONIO PROHIAS

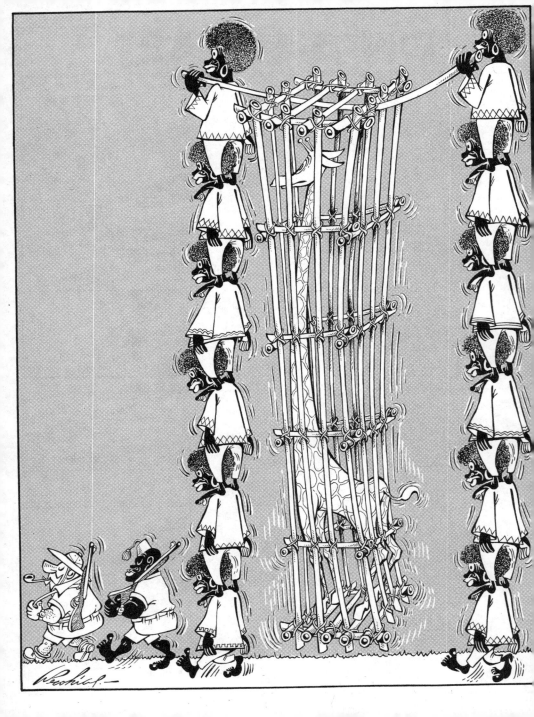

IN A SPECIALIST'S OFFICE

A MAD LOOK AT... THE GAS

SHORTAGE

ARTIST:
PAUL COKER, JR.

WRITER:
PAUL PETER PORGES

What's with parents, anyhow? Why can't they ever talk about what *you* want to talk about? Why won't they ever let you off the hook? Why, if you do one thing wrong, is it a life sentence without any possibility of pardon? What's this introduction about, anyway? We'll tell you: Parents are the ones responsible for "The Generation Gap"! Is there any doubt? Hands, please! Three . . . four . . . five . . . okay! Here's why: Whenever you tell them something, no matter how important it is to you, it becomes nothing more than a lead-in for them to zap you with a criticism. Right? Hands, please! Seven million . . . eight million . . . nine million . . . okay! In other words, parents are the acknowledged masters of the "non-sequitur" . . . which is Latin for . . . "saying what *they* want, no matter what *you* say to them!" Understand? Hands, please! None . . . okay! Here's what we mean by . . .

PARENTAL NON-SEQUITURS

ARTIST: PAUL COKER, JR.   WRITER: STAN HART

WHAT YOU SAY TO YOUR PARENTS:

Great news, Mom! I just got a **full scholarship** to **Harvard University!**

WHAT YOU HOPE THEY WILL SAY:

Just think! An **Ivy Leaguer** in the family! I'm so happy, I could **cry!**

WHAT THEY WILL PROBABLY SAY:

Sure . . . you can get into an **Ivy League School** . . . but you can't even keep your **room** clean!!

WHAT YOU SAY TO YOUR PARENTS:

I've decided to join the **Peace Corps!**

WHAT YOU HOPE THEY WILL SAY:

That's **really touching** . . . my **little** girl devoting her life to helping those **less fortunate** than herself!

WHAT THEY WILL PROBABLY SAY

What are **you** going to teach the Zambians? How to stay on the phone for hours and run up **big bills?!?**

I plan to become a **Nuclear Physicist!**

I'm—I'm so **happy!** If only your **Great Grandfather** were alive to hear this!!

I never heard of a Nuclear Physicist who won't go to her **Uncle Al's house** for a **visit** at least **ONCE** a month!

Guess what?! That aptitude test I took says I'll make a fine **Doctor!**

I tell you, Ida, if **anyone** can find a **cure** for **Cancer**, it'll be my **Sheldon!**

A **Doctor?!?** You think they'll let you become a **Doctor** when they find out how you **tease** your **Sister?!?**

I just saved **four people** from a **burning building!**

God, we're **proud** of you! You always **were** a good boy . . . never thinking of **yourself** . . . always thinking of **others!**

Sure, you can save some **strangers!** But do you ever help **ME** with the **dishes?!**

WHAT YOU SAY TO YOUR PARENTS:

Someday, I'm gonna be the **President** of the United States . . . !

WHAT YOU HOPE THEY WILL SAY:

Son . . . I know you'll make a **fine** President . . . and you'll usher in "**The Great American Century**"!

WHAT THEY WILL PROBABLY SAY:

That's **all** we need . . . a President who won't eat his **vegetables**!!

WHAT YOU SAY TO YOUR PARENTS:

My **picture's** gonna be in the **paper**! They took it when I hit a **home run**!

WHAT YOU HOPE THEY WILL SAY:

Our **hero**! He's a **born Big Leaguer**!

WHAT THEY WILL PROBABLY SAY:

They should take a picture of you **wetting your bed**! Then they'd know what a big shot you **REALLY** are!!

WHAT YOU SAY TO YOUR PARENTS:

I'm going to be a **Poetess** . . . like **Edna St. Vincent Millay**!

WHAT YOU HOPE THEY WILL SAY:

And you **will**! You're so **sensitive** . . . so **aware** of the **true** meaning of life!

WHAT THEY WILL PROBABLY SAY:

You'll make **some Poetess** with your **face breaking out** from all the junk you eat!

ONE BUSY DAY IN A HIGHWAY RESTAURANT

PEANUTS.

ADDING A NEW WRINKLE DEPT.

Charles Schulz, the creator of "Peanuts", is headed for disaster! He's making the same mistake the creators of "Little Orphan Annie" and "Dondi" and a hundred other cartoonists have made! He's not letting his characters grow up! So, wise up, Charlie Schulz! If you want to stay up there on top, study these samples of future daily strips you could be doing—

IF THE CHARACTERS IN "PEANUTS" AGED LIKE ORDINARY PEOPLE

ARTIST: BOB CLARKE   WRITER: FRANK JACOBS

at the age of 19

LUCY, I'D LIKE TO ASK YOU--

DON'T *BOTHER* ME, CHARLIE BROWN! I'M LATE FOR THE *CAMPUS WOMEN'S LIB RALLY!* DOWN WITH THE TYRANNY OF THE *MALE ESTABLISHMENT!* UP WITH *WOMEN'S RIGHTS!*

PIGPEN, MAYBE YOU'D WANT TO--

NOT NOW, CHARLIE BROWN! I'M CONDUCTING A ONE-MAN *FILTH-IN* AGAINST *LEVER BROTHERS!* DOWN WITH *POLLUTING DETERGENTS!* UP WITH *NATURAL DIRT!!*

SOMEHOW, I FEEL THIS IS *NOT* THE TIME TO ORGANIZE A *PEP RALLY* FOR THE *FOOTBALL TEAM!*

I'D *LOVE* TO, BUT IT'S *TOO UNCOMFORTABLE* IN THE WOODS WITH ALL THOSE *ROCKS* AND *PEBBLES* AND *ACORNS* AND *POISON IVY* AND *THINGS!*

DON'T GET UPTIGHT, VIOLET! WE'LL BE *VERY* COMFORTABLE!

WHY DO YOU THINK I *STILL* CARRY AROUND THIS *BLANKET?!*

POT PARTY!

PEANUTS...at the age of 65

THEY DEDUCTED THE COST OF THE WATCH!!

ZZZZZ!

There's a hit movie making the rounds that advertises itself as "The Greatest Adventure Story Ever Told!" Well, we may not exactly agree with that, but we will admit it's "The DUMBEST Adventure Story Ever Told!" We're referring, of course, to the movie about that man who had a simply unbelievable life! And that's how we feel about it! We simply don't believe it! But we do know one thing! It was so nauseating, so disgusting, so stomach-turning . . . that we bought, but never got to eat our

PICORN

ARTIST: ANGELO TORRES   WRITER: DICK DE BARTOLO

We don't assign anyone "Swamp Duty" until he's had a **thorough Medical Examination!** But I can tell merely by **looking** at you men that you're all in **great shape!**

If those two are in **GREAT** shape, I'd sure love to see what you consider to be in just **GOOD** shape!

I could **SHOW** you, but we just **buried** 'em this **morning!**

This sure is some crocodile-infested, mosquito-laden, God-forsaken, dismal hell-hole of a place . . . **isn't it?!?**

Well, **EVERYBODY** loves it at **first!** But **you'll** soon change your mind!

Did some convict go **mad** . . . and now they're **chasing** him with those **butterfly nets?**

No, they're chasing **REAL BUTTERFLIES!** The guards make **extra money** selling them to me! I pay **twenty cents a ton!** Here! Take a net and **try** it! See if you can **catch** a few million!

Thanks! I know where I can catch **plenty!** On the **French Riviera!**

See you guys around . . .

For trying to **escape,** you have been assigned to this **Maximum Penalty Prison!** Here, we will **break** you, both **physically** and **mentally!** You'll be **starved—degraded**—until you develop **cobwebs** in your brain . . . and **butterflies** in your **stomach!**

Can I be **excused** from that last part? I already have one on my **chest!**

They **won't** break me! There's **plenty** I can do in this cold, damp, smelly, tiny unlit cell! I can **walk** a lot! I can **think** a lot! I can **exercise** a lot! And mainly, I can **CRY** a lot!

Here is your first meal . . .

A moldy, rancid potato . . . and half a dead mouse?!? Is the food **ALWAYS** like this?

No! Lucky for you it's **Bastille Day!**

Boy! I've been here for **seventeen months,** and my **mind** is still as sharp as a tack!

It's a good thing I've got my **wits** . . .!

And my **doggie** . . .!

And my **froggie** . . .!

And my **dollie** . . .!

And my **goo-goo** . . .

Life, as everyone knows, is full of GOOD NEWS and BAD NEWS. Sometimes the GOOD NEWS turns into BAD NEWS. Sometimes the BAD NEWS tu... into GOOD NEWS. And sometimes the GOOD NE...

THE MAD "GOOD NEW

ARTIST: GEORGE WOODBR...

GOOD NEWS is being given a new, rare tropical fish for your tank.

BAD NEWS is discovering that its favorite food is other tropical fish.

GOOD NEWS is finding out that you a... your date share many common intere...

GOOD NEWS is asking for a cuddly Teddy Bear for your birthday, and getting it.

BAD NEWS is that you're turning 18.

GOOD NEWS is sliding into secon... base, and being called "Safe!"

GOOD NEWS is being thrown a surprise party by your wife.

BAD NEWS is figuring out that you're the one who still has to pay for it.

GOOD NEWS is going through an en... winter without once getting sick...

ich was the BAD NEWS, turns into BAD NEWS
ain. And sometimes . . . well, you get the idea.

This ends the introduction, which is GOOD NEWS,
and brings us to the following article, which is

BAD NEWS" BOOK

WRITER: FRANK JACOBS

BAD NEWS is discovering that one of your common interests is girls.

GOOD NEWS is conscientiously dieting to lose forty pounds.

BAD NEWS is succeeding . . . but in all the wrong places.

BAD NEWS is remembering you had six live caterpillars in your back pocket.

BAD NEWS is finding out there's no Santa Claus.

GOOD NEWS is realizing that it doesn't make any difference.

BAD NEWS is you're a hypochondriac.

BAD NEWS is finding out your Dad is an Accountant.

GOOD NEWS is finding out your Dad is Joe Namath's Accountant.

50

BAD NEWS is coming home at night and discovering you've been burglarized.

GOOD NEWS is calculating that your Insurance will cover the entire loss.

BAD NEWS is finding the unmailed premium in your jacket pocket.

BAD NEWS is going out with a female friend and being spotted by your Wife.

GOOD NEWS is discovering that she's out with a male friend.

BAD NEWS is noting she's having a much better time than you are.

BAD NEWS is being sent to bed without any dinner.

GOOD NEWS is finding out that dinner is a broccoli and eggplant casserole.

BAD NEWS is your Mother worried about you getting hungry . . . and sneaking a plate up to your room.

GOOD NEWS is getting GOOD NEWS.

STOCKS GO UP

BAD NEWS is getting more GOOD NEWS . . . which bothers you because you know you're now due for BAD NEWS.

STOCKS GO WAY UP

GOOD NEWS is finally getting BAD N . . . which relieves your mind beca you know you're again due for GOOD

STOCKS DOWN

BAD NEWS is a building going up on your favorite vacant lot.

GOOD NEWS is finding out it's going to be an Ice Cream Parlor.

BAD NEWS is discovering the place has a fancy name and charges $1.75 a scoop.

BAD NEWS is meeting up with a mugger.

GOOD NEWS is finding you've only got three dollars in your pocket.

BAD NEWS is discovering that three dollars is a big insult to a mugger.

GOOD NEWS is settling down at your TV set to watch your favorite comedy.

BAD NEWS is finding it's pre-empted by Cinton explaining his economic policies.

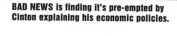

GOOD NEWS is discovering that you're getting twice the laughs.

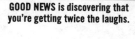

BAD NEWS is continuing to get BAD NEWS instead of the GOOD NEWS you It you were due after the BAD NEWS.

GOOD NEWS is continuing to still get BAD NEWS, which is GOOD NEWS because you know you're now really due for some GOOD NEWS.

BAD NEWS is trusting in cycles.

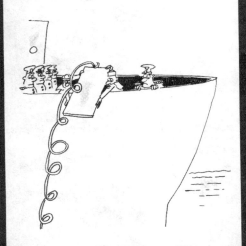

AL AT SEA

ARTIST AND WRITER: DON EDWING

ONE FINE DAY DURING THE CIVIL WAR

Here comes Bianco in with a play from the bench!

Okay, Bianco! What's the message . . . ?

The break is at Midnight! Pass it . . .

Cut that dialogue out, Man! This isn't a CLICHE PRISON MOVIE!

It's MORE than that!

Yeah! It's a CLICHE FOOTBALL MOVIE!!

OBSCENE MACHINE

Mr. Crude . . . the halftime score is embarrassingly close! Just what do you think you're doing out *here?

Playing my heart out for the crowd! Do you realize there are more spectators jammed into those grandstands today than all the people who saw "The Man Who Loved Cat Dancing"!

Mr. Crude, you will now proceed to LOSE this game . . . by 21 points!! I don't like being made a fool of! I had EIGHT YEARS of that playing opposite Eva Gabor in "Green Acres"!

I can't do that, Warden! The men trust me! They're irrepressible rejects from society—loveable misfits who are counting on me to lead them to Victory . . . to give them one small moment of dignity and pride and—

You'll dump this game, Crude . . . or you're looking at 20 years of hard labor!

Come to think of it, what do I need with a bunch of cutthroats, goons and sadists! But if I DO shave points, Warden, you gotta protect my men from VIOLENCE!

From the Guards?

No, themselves—when they want to kill me!

OBSCENE MACH

I think Crude sold us out!

How can you tell?

Well, he's thrown seven straight interceptions, he's fumbled six times . . . and he's calling our plays from the huddle!

What's wrong with that?

It's THEIR huddle he's calling them from!!

Looks like Crude is THROWING THE GAME!

So?! What are they gonna do to him . . . put him in Prison?! He IS in Prison!!

Our guys are gettin' KILLED out there, Crude! What kind of deal did you make?!?

Why, he double-crossed me! When I get through with him, he's gonna be the most humiliated Warden in the country!

You gonna go out there and lead the Team in a spectacular comeback?!

Worse! I'm gonna use my Show Biz connections to make sure Johnny Cash never does a concert in this Prison!

Okay, now I'm ready to lead a spectacular comeback! I'll play until I redeem myself!!

There ain't enough time for that!

Yeah! Some of us are only "LIFERS"!

GESUNDHEIT!

Anyway, we don't stand chance with Bigdunce as their Middle Linebacker! He's really creaming us!

Okay! **Before** we start our touchdown drive let's **amuse** ourselves while the clock is ticking away **precious** seconds! Let Bigdunce come through! We'll form a "V" Formation!

Don't you mean a "T" Formation?!

No, I mean a "V" Formation . . . for "VASECTOMY"!

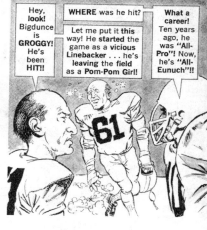

Hey, look! Bigdunce is GROGGY! He's been HIT!!

Let me put it **this** way! He **started** the game as a **vicious** Linebacker . . . he's leaving the field as a Pom-Pom Girl!

WHERE was he hit?

What a career! Ten years ago, he was "All-Pro"! Now, he's "All-Eunuch"!!

We've called you to the sidelines because Pat O'Brien isn't doing these movies any more! So I'm gonna make the speech that he would have made!

Fellow Teammates . . . Jocks . . . Sex Maniacs . . . and other lovers of Sports! We're **four points behind**, we're on the **one yard line**, and there are **three** seconds left! We've come too far to go back! So let's win this one for **Carefaker, Scarbooboo** and **Groanville!** I know you don't trust me because I once threw a game **years** ago—and I almost threw one today! But I'm begging! Let's win **THIS ONE!**

He **can't** break the **habit!** With that **SPEECH,** he just threw the **PICTURE!!**

You made it! You made it, Crude!!

Quick! Le'me up! I want to see the game films of this in the **Warden's** Secretary's Office . . .

Well, Warden! We lost! There goes your **Power Theory!** And **LOOK** . . . they're mobbing **Crude!** He's a **HERO!!**

He's a **NOTHING,** Clobber! And he's going to have 20 years in solitary to relish this empty victory!

Well . . . at least he'll always be remembered as a **really fabulous FOOTBALL PLAYER** . . .!!

You're wrong, Clobber! I'm afraid . . . no matter **WHAT** that man does for the rest of his life . . . he'll always be remembered for only **ONE THING!** He can never erase his **PAST!** Look . . . it's **come back** to haunt him **again!!**

A
COLLECTION OF MAD

X-RAYvings

ARTIST: BOB CLARKE   WRITER: DON EDWING

History has recorded the famous words uttered by famous men . . . words that we all know well. Bu did it ever occur to you that maybe the other people present didn't just stand around applaudin

ZAPPERS THAT H

ARTIST: GEORGE WOODBRID

...STORY FORGOT

...TER: ALEN ROBIN

Pollution Alert

ARTIST & WRITER: SERGIO ARAGONES

CRIME

THE LIGHTE

SUBTLETY

FORESIGHT

R SIDE OF...

ECONOMICS

PREPAREDNESS

RESPONSIBILITY

THERAPY

PRAYER

Dinosaurs were **extinct** for millions of years! Of course, movies like *Jurassic Park* created a **new interest**! But like any **fad**, in time it **fades out** and **interest wanes**!

But **fear not!** They are currently **filming** the *Jurassic Park* sequel and **dinosaurs** will **rise up** from **extinction** once more!

FINANCES

I **guess** you could **call** it an **identity crisis**!

DKNY

GUCCI

I'm **absolutely broke**!

But you had a **small inheritance**! What **happened**?

I **acted** like I had a **LARGE inheritance**!

HOT DOGS

CHIVALRY

Daddy is!

Miss, is that **creep** bothering you?

Absolutely not!

Do you **mind** if **I do**?

THE OFFICE

Hey, guys! If they **increase** the **minimum wage**, does that **affect** those who make **more** than the **minimum wage**?

Even if it does, it **wouldn't affect** your **salary, Tom!**

Really? How come?

You do **minimum work!**

CONCERN

Mr. Korn, your **son Maxwell** is very **bright**, but he's constantly **clowning around!** He'll do **anything** for a **laugh** and despite being sent to **detention**, he continues to **disrupt** the **class!** And for **me personally**, that's **not** the **worst of it!**

Good grief, Mr. Charney! What's worse?

He has a **perfect attendance record!**

DOCTORS

I **don't** like this, Kaputnik! Your **blood pressure** is **much too high!**

You've got **yourself** to **blame** for that, **Doctor!**

You shouldn't have **told me** my **cholesterol level** was **up** before you **took it!**

ONE DAY IN A RUN-DOWN SHACK

In recent years pollution has been on everybody's mind. Which may be why so ma of us have dirty minds. But while we've at least managed to cut down a bit smog, factory smoke, and industrial wastes in our waterways, nobody has yet fou a cure for one of the strangest, most prevalent forms of pollution in history graffiti. Everywhere you look—in rest rooms, subways, on building walls—you s those same stupid, usually obscene messages scrawled. And nobody seems to kn

MAD'S "NICE

Here I sit ~~broken~~ HAPPY hearted,
~~paid my dime and only~~ ~~wind~~
TALKS ON MIDEAST PEACE HAVE STARTED

LOOKING FOR THE TIME?
~~OF YOUR LIFE?~~ CALL ME 7 1212
~~WANDA 555 8210~~
PLEASE THE WEATHER? WE 6 1212

~~Don't~~ throw ALL cigarette butts
in our bowls —
~~We don't~~ ~~in your~~ ashtrays!
THE SURGEON GENERAL HAS DETERMINED
THAT CIGARETTE SMOKING IS DANGEROUS
TO YOUR HEALTH — AND WE'D HATE TO
LOSE A NICE PERSON LIKE YOU!

PRESIDENT
FORD'S
SUC~~KS~~ CES
CAN BE ATTRIBUTED TO
HONESTY, DECENCY AND A
STRONG BELIEF IN DEMOCRA
GOD BLESS AMERICA

FOR A FANTASTIC
JOB, SEE ~~CLARA AT~~
~~BRUNO'S MASSAGE PAR~~
TO IT THAT YOU FINISH
YOUR EDUCATION.

NO MATTER HOW YOU SHAKE AND YOU DANCE
~~THE LAST DROP ALWAYS FALLS IN YOUR PANT~~
YOU'LL NEVER BE OUT OF STEP TO AN ELTON JOHN NUMBER

what to do about it. Why not uplift it? Why not make graffiti more positive, more inspiring? Let graffiti help people improve themselves and the world they live in! And here's how it can be done: Instead of trying to erase or rub out wall garbage, simply rewrite it so that it says something worthwhile. For instance, here is a typical rest room wall with its typical obscene scrawls. But notice how much better and heart-warming it is after we rework it with a marking pencil and turn it into...

GRAFFITI

ARTIST:
BOB CLARKE
WRITER:
LARRY SIEGEL

THIS IS A TEEPEE ~ IS IT ANY WONDER
FOR ~~YOU TO PEEPEE~~ MANY OF US WOULD
~~NOT A WIGWAM~~ LIKE TO FIND
~~TO BEAT YOUR TOM-TOM~~ BETTER HOUSING
FOR AMERICAN
INDIANS?

STAND ~~CLOSE~~
UP FOR AMERICA
STOP
COMMUNISM!
~~BRAGGING!~~

OUR AIM IS TO KEEP
AMERICA STRONG
~~THIS BATHROOM CLEAN~~

Man's ambition must be directed ~~small~~
~~to write his name on a bathhouse wall.~~

VOTE
YOUR ~~AIM~~ WILL HELP

toward improving the plight
of the disadvantaged!

IN CASE OF ATOMIC ATTACK
~~DUCK UNDER THIS URINAL~~
~~(IF HASN'T BEEN HIT YET.)~~

SAVE AMERICAN
~~want the~~ WILD~~EST~~
~~night of your~~ LIFE ~~?~~
smokey ~~pot and shoot dope~~
says: ~~at KANG HÉZ PLACE~~
"ONLY YOU CAN PREVENT
FOREST FIRES!"

WE SHOULD CANCEL OUR GRAIN EXPORTS
TO RUSSIA, HAVE HENRY KISSENGER SEND
BREHZNEV A VERY STRONG LETTER, AND
EVERYTHING WILL TURN OUT JUST FINE!

HAWKS & DOVES

MAJOR HAWKS

ARTIST & WRITER: AL JAFFEE

PRIVATE DOVES

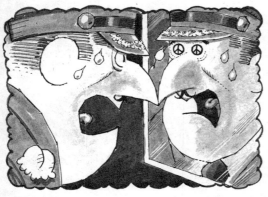

Here we go with MAD's version of TV's latest Hit Show in which two guys develop a close relationship while driving around in a car, fighting crime. It's sort of an up-dated, realistic rip-off of "Batman and Robin" called . . .

HARSKY & STUTCH

ARTIST: ANGELO TORRES   WRITER: LOU SILVERSTONE

Listen, mister . . . I'd advise you to come clean before my partner **really loses his temper!**

TALK, YOU @#$%! AND YOU HAVE THE RIGHT TO HAVE AN ATTORNEY PRESENT DURING QUESTIONING!!

But I **AM** an Attorney! *Gasp!* I'm here to see a **CLIENT!!**

What's going on in here?! Sounds like somebody's getting **killed!**

It's **nothing**, Captain! We're just advising this citizen of his rights!

Could you send in a **Stenographer?**

Does he want to make a **confession?**

No . . . his **Last Will** and **Testament!**

ou guys ve got to down on e rough ff! We've n getting lot of nplaints ately!

You mean from the **Police Brass** . . .?

No, from the **TV Critics!** Better go easy on the **violence,** or you might find yourselves **transferred!**

You mean back to pounding a **beat** . . .?!

Even **worse!** They might switch you to the **Family Hour!**

The **Family Hour!?!** That would mean **no more bloody fights** or **fatal shootouts** or **wild car chases!**

We'd end up with only a **fifteen-minute program!!**

We'll try to be **good boys,** Captain!! **Right, Harsky . . .?**

You bet, Captain! Hey . . . smell my **flower!**

Harsky, that gag is **older** than the **Crime Plots** we use on this show! But if it'll make you happy . . .

YAIIIEE!! I'm **blind**!! I **can't see**! Harsky, some day, you're going to go **TOO FAR**!

I filled it with **MACE**! Funny, eh?

It sounds like Captain Dopey is **losing** his **sense** of humor!

Here . . . Captain! Sit on **this**! You'll be more comfort- able!

Man, that "Whoopee Cushion" gets 'em every time! Hah-hah!

The D.A. here has a **special** job for you clowns! Anthony Saluggi, the ex-Mafia **boss**, is **turning** State's evidence, and **you** two will have to **escort** him from the **hotel room** where we've got him stashed, to the **Courthouse**!

But that's only **across** the **street**! Why **us**?! We ain't no **School Cross- ing Guards**!

Because this is a **Key Witness** . . . an you're my **best men**!

These are your **bes men**? The Police Dep is in **worse shape** than I thought!!

BRAFFP!!

Man . . . **you** call that **PO-LICE** work?! Escortin' some **jive dude** to a **Courthouse**?!

Like, I call that "**Baby Sittin'** "!

Hello, **Boss**! I just got the **word** . . .! Saluggi is gonna **testify** **TODAY**!

Are you **sure**?

Why do you think I **EAT** in this **dump**?! Harsky and Stutch **always** tell **Buggy Hair** what their assignments are!

I'll arrange for the "**Hit**"!

I'd like a room with a **fantastic view**, please!

Sorry . . . but all the rooms that overlook the **Massage Parlor** are **full**! The only **vacancy** we have over- looks the **Courthouse**!

By a very strange coincidence, that is **exactly** the view I want . . .!

That makes you a **Courthouse freak**, or a **Hit Man**! How long will you stay?

Just a few hou Hey!! Be caref with that **lugga** It might go of

That **cinches i** You're a **COUR HOUSE FREAK** No **fool**, I . . .

C'mon, **Turkey**! Get in the **car**! We're going **bye-bye**!

But . . . the **Courthouse** is only just **across** the **street**! Why not **walk** him?

We figure maybe a little **drive** will lend some **excitement** to this nursemaid job you saddled us with!

What's so **exciting** about a ride around the **block**?!?

Who said anything about driving around the **block**?!?

SCREEEECH!

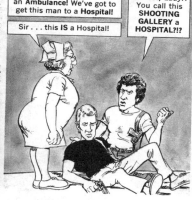

As if pictures like "Earthquake" and "Jaws" and "Towering Inferno" aren't scary enough, Hollywood has now devised a new type of film that shows how terrible life will be like in the future . . . if you're lucky enough not to be crushed to death, bitten to death or burned to death! Here's MAD's version of tomorrow's spectator sport:

ROLLE

This is the **ultimate game** . . . combining the most brutal, violent aspects of all sports! That's progress!

Some progress! They've re-invented "**The Roller Derby**"!

We have evolved to a **higher form of Civilization** . . . in which the **Government** is run by the large Corporations!

Right!! By the way . . . what **year** is this?

1976!

This movie will demonstrate how **individuality** is **destroyed**, and people are made into **MINDLESS CONFORMISTS**!

Gee! A whole picture about **America's school system**?!

I'll smash your **face**, stomp on your **windpipe** and crush your **skull**!

You're a **cruel, vicious person**!

Yeah . . . and I'm the most **sympathet**[ic] character in the movie!

GO HOUSTON

RBRAWL

ARTIST:
ANGELO TORRES

WRITER:
STAN HART

oonface . . . as head of e **Energy** Corporation, ave something to **say** to you! Tonight, you lled five and crippled seven others for life!

at's right, Sir . . . !

Let me say **this** . . . if you're **not** going to **TRY**, then **get off the team!**

Did we sustain any **injuries?**

Just **Klutzzy** over here!

What happened?

He tried to crack his **knuckles** with his **glove** on!

Jonathick . . . you are the **greatest!** Pure **poetry!** I just **adore** your **marvelous** form!

On the **Roller Rink?**

Even more, in the **SHOWER ROOM!**

Watch that stuff! I'm not that kind of **guy!**

Provincial clod!

I've been sent by e **Corporation** as a **RESENT** to you for twelve years of edicated service!

y'd they send **you?**

They thought you might enjoy **ME** more than sleeping with a **gold watch!**

I'd rather have my **Wife!** But the **Corporation** took her **AWAY** from me!

Forget about her! Here! Take one of these **Sex Pills!** They completely duplicate the mood for **Marital Love-Making!**

Do they **really** work?

Come here, Baby!

Not tonight! I have a **headache!**

Wow! They really **DO** work!

ey! Let's
ay a wild,
zy game
ke "Pin
he Tail
n The
onkey"!

What's so
wild about
that?!?

Nahhh!
I'd
rather
set
fire
to a
tree!

Yeah!
Let's
set
fire
to
some
trees!

We'll use
a REAL
DONKEY!!

This
is
FUN!

But . . . isn't it
WRONG to do this?

Nahh! Everyone does it!

Everyone?!

Sure! Look!

ell me,
nathick
. . why
o you
ate our
poration
ife so
ch . . . ?

Because it's cold and empty! I want
to know what it was like in 1975,
for example! Today, when a powerful
Corporation Exec wants your wife,
he just takes her away from you . . .
and you can't do anything about it!

THAT's what it was like!

So you
refuse
to
retire,
eh?

I'll retire
only if you
give me some
concessions!

Jonathick, you drive
a hard bargain! But
if it's a concession
you want, then it's a
concession you'll get!

I didn't mean THIS
kind of concession!!

PEANUTS

ey've changed
he rules for
ight's game!
here will be
substitutions
no time outs!
't you worried?

No . . . I
just never
learned the
meaning of
the word,
"fear"!

Gee, Jonathick,
you never learned
the meaning of
so MANY words!
Exactly what DO
you know . . . ?

Something
that no
one else
in the
country
knows . . . !

What's
that . . . ?

The
capital
of North
Dakota!

Remember, men, this is
the Semi-Final! I want
each of you to go out
there and KILL!! And
if you can't do that,
then do the next best
thing! GET KILLED!!

I DON'T WANT TO
DIE!! I DON'T
WANT TO DIE . . . !

Where's
your team
spirit?

Oh . . . !
Gee, I'm
sorry!!

Stop slouching!!

Pardon my glove!!

That **heavy** speeding ball is going to tear your head off!

No . . . ! No . . . ! Come on! It's all part of the **game**! Nothing personal!

Oh, **good**! For a minute, I thought you were mad at me

Moonface!! Watch out . . . behind you!!

Thanks a **lot**!!

SPLAT!

Moonface! Talk to me! Are you **all** right . . . ?

You too . . . ?

I **can't** tell! I don't seem to know **what's** going on! Everything's so **confused**! I—I can't keep my **eyes** open!

Who **else** is this happening to . . . ?

The **audience!**

Jonathick, you'll have to sign this **release** so we can **let** Moonface die . . . !

Are you **crazy**? He's **ALIVE!**

That's **true!** But his **brain** has stopped functioning!

Well, **that** never bothered **ME!!** I'm gonna **take** care of him, Doc!

But he's only a **VEGETABLE!!**

For an animal, that's a step **UP!**

Can't you **understand**, Jonathick!? He's a **vegetable**! How long are you going to **keep** this up . . . ?!?

Until **HARVEST TIME!!**

There was **also** a Sport called **"Professional Baseball"**... in which **financially ailing Teams** would occasionally **switch** their franchises from **one** city to **another** to get **more** paying customers! Then, they started switching **more** and **more often** —every **year**—then every **week**—until the **fans** couldn't tell from **one** day to the **next** if their city had **any Team** at all!

Once upon a time, there were **two men**... **Frank Gifford** and **Howard Cosell**... who **killed** a Sport called **"Professional Football"** by **confusing** the fans! After Gifford would tell them how **wonderful** everything was, Cosell would tell them how **stupid** they were for **enjoying** it!

But what **really** killed Professional Sports once and for all was something called **"The Playoffs"**! Each Sport's **"season"** kept getting **longer** and **longer**... until, one day, they **all overlapped**, and all the Sports had to be played at **one time** in **one place**! This caused **confusion** and **terrible riots**...

I guess the **riots** were **so bad**, the authorities had to be called in to put a **stop** to them!

No... the riots were **more fun to watch** than the **Professional Sports!!** Besides, they were **FREE!** So **Sports** just **faded away!**

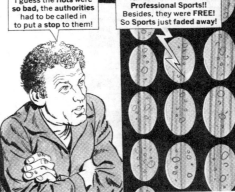

Hello... Jonathick!

My **WIFE!!** Gee... how have you **been** all these years?

Okay, I guess! You **know** that Corporation made me marry one of their **Accountants!**

What's he like?

Well, he has lots of **pencils**, he works from **nine** to **five every day**, he **brings** home **work** from the **office**, he **watches** Television all evening, **falls asleep** in his **chair** and **snores**! He's... well, he's **very different** than **you** were, Jonathick!

In what way?

He's much more **exciting!**

I came to **beg** you not to play in the **Finals**! They'll **KILL** you if you don't yield to them!

I don't know the **meaning** of the word **"yield"!**

Do you know the meaning of the word **"schmuck"**

They've changed the **rules** again! The **new** rule for this game is —**"No Time Limit"!** We play until only **one** person is left alive!

I don't care! Who do we play tonight?

I'm **not** sure! I think it's the New York City Team!

STRIKE

Yeah . . . it's the New York City Team!!

NO CONTRACT NO GAME

UNFAIR TO ROLLER BRAWL LA UNITE VOLUME 17

Okay, you guys—before I give my usual pre-game pep talk, here are your pills . . . four each!

I know one's for **power** and one's for **speed!** But what are the other two for??

Your **ears!!** They're the best plugs made for **protecting** your **eardrums** from that ridiculously loud **ORGAN MUSIC!**

Now **go out** there and **KILL!** And may the best man survive!

Hope you like your **TRIP** this **FALL!!**

SPLAT!

I surrender! I surrender!

Oh, my God, he doesn't even know the **meaning** of the word "surrender"!!

Jonathick . . . I have good news and bad news for you!

First, the bad news! All the other players . . . including your teammates and friends, are DEAD!

And the good news?

You're a cinch to win the "Most Valuable Player Award"!

CLANG

GREAT MOMENTS

ARTIST: JACK DAV

IN BAD TIMING

WRITER: PAUL PETER PORGES

Is he gone . . .?

My God! These are the worst test results I've ever seen!

. . . and so, without any further ado, here he is . . . that **great** humanitarian and upstanding citizen . . .

My **car** broke down, and I wonder if you would be **kind** enough to let me use your **phone** . . .

This article is dedicated to the proposition that all things are *not* created equal—not by today's manufacturers, anyway. But the American Consumer has an ally in his never-ending battle with poor craftsmanship, shoddy merchandise and Giant Economy Size Packages that are never more than half full...mainly, the Impartial Test Panels. Those dedicated experts who break down a product before they break down and tell us all about it in magazines like...

CONDEMNER REPORTS

OCTOBER 1969 / MANUFACTURERS HATE US SO WE GET / NO ADVERTISING / 50 CENTS

Razors and Blades
Use-Tested by a special 500-Man CR Panel

Styptic Pencils
Use-Tested by the same 500-Man CR Panel right after the Razors and Blades tests

Electric Hot Plates
Almost all models had poor insulation and none had adequate, heat-resistant handles

Burn Ointments
An unscheduled report necessitated by the tests of those % &$#@¢!! Electric Hot Plates

Mixers and Blenders
Our special 26-Man Team tests most brands

The New Long Ties
A special CR Report shows why men who use mixers and blenders should not wear them

Fire Extinguishers
None of the Fire Extinguisher Units that we tested could adequately control a fire

New Construction
CR examines new building construction as it searches for a new home after making those % &$#@¢#!! Fire Extinguisher tests

ARTIST: BOB CLARKE   WRITER: DICK DE BARTOLO   PHOTOGRAPHY: BY IRVING SCHILD

Ground Meat Contains Ground

I truly enjoyed your recent article, "Most Hot Dogs Aren't Fit For Dogs" (CONDEMNER REPORTS, July 1969). I was shocked by what you found in the hot dogs you tested. I buy hamburger meat from my butcher for 89¢ a pound, and thanks to your article, I've now started examining it. I've found what looks like bone chips, sawdust, hair, and even dirt. What can I do about it?
BROOKLYN, N.Y.   P.U.

Use a lot of ketchup and relish.

Price Puzzle

Which is actually cheaper, an 8 oz. tube of toothpaste for 59¢, a 10 oz. tube for 69¢, a 12 oz. tube for 79¢ or a full pound tube for $1.00?

Please do not send us any jokes or riddles. CR is not a humor magazine.

Executive Type Writes

In your August issue, you published the results of tests made on several portable typewriters, and our brand was one of the machines included in the report. You claimed you found a defect in our machine which you felt was a serious drawback, and therefore rated it "Unacceptable." As president of the Underglass Typewriter Company, I wish to point out that the sample you tested was obviously not typical of the machines we produce here at Underglass. I certainly hope that you will give us another chance and test a more typical example of our Model 7 Portable Typewriter—one that ten of our top engineers are building by hand especially for CR right now.
DAYTON, OHIO   CHARLES ELITE, JR.
PRESIDENT
UNDERGLASS CORP.

Mr. Elite's letter, which was obviously typed on one of his company's machines, only served to point out that the glaring defect we found in the Model 7 Portable is present in other models as well. As you can plainly see by the excerpt we found reproduced below, the "period" looks funny.

```
especially for CR
right now.
          Charles Elite, Jr.
          Pres. Underglass Corp.
```

Once Is Enough

New Toy, Not Recommended For Kids ...

Sally Suicide, the new doll that can 'take her own life 12 ways,' has earned CR's NOT-ACCEPTABLE—ICKY POO rating at press time. This new entry from Marx Bros. Toys doesn't live up to its promise, as our disappointed panel will attest: the rope Sally Suicide is supposed to hang herself with broke on the first attempt, the drugs supplied are hardly enough to induce nausea let alone suicide, and the seven story doll house that she's supposed to jump from isn't high enough for anything more than two broken legs!

If the performance of this doll could only live up to its potential, Marx Bros. would have a winner here.

Sally Suicide: "Disappointing"

Thank You, Kind Readers

CR is certainly proud of its readers who take the time to sit down and write us about differences of opinion based on their own findings. It helps us get a better picture of things to watch for when we test new products in the future. Last month we didn't think to check out the "waterproof" casing on the new Brenner Electro Toothbrush, believing in this day and age that a "waterproof" label means just that. To our surprise, many readers found out differently, and a lot of credit must be given them for interrupting their week of mourning to write us.

Brenner Electric Toothbrush: "Not waterproof"

A Note From The Checkmate Toaster Company

Gentlemen:

Thank you for your invitation to have our latest Checkmate tested by your panel of impartial judges. However, we could not get our latest model, the Mock III, out of production in time for last month's deadline, and it would be a waste to have sent you the Mock II since it is being called back.

We trust that you will include a run-down of our new model this issue. A sample of the Checkmate Mock III is enclosed.

Thank you,

William Burns
President
Checkmate Corp.

Ed. Note: As per Mr. Burns' request, a complete rundown of the Checkmate Mock III is included in this issue.

Fowoll-up

An up-dating of previous up-to-date reports

During the past few years, CR has informed its readers to be aware of the "water content" percentage listed on the labels of packaged hams.

Many meat packing houses are injecting water into the hams, raising the weight considerably. The consumer is then paying 'ham' rates for water.

The problem has been faced by town officials of two different locations.

Mayor Heinz Wipfler of Wagsville, North Carolina, is getting back at the meat packers by injecting 'ham' into the local water supply, while Mayor Eric Wessel of Chipneil, Arizona, has upped the water tax from $23 a year to $3000, making the cost of water in the area more expensive than ham, thereby discouraging the practice.

Mayor Eric Wessel

Mayor Heinz Wipfler

CR salutes both of these men with their constructive solutions to the problem.

A Change In Ratings

No one is perfect. While we come close to perfection here at CR, we too can slip once in a while. And when we do, well, you can bet your boots we'll own up to it and do what's necessary to rectify things even if it means changing a rating.

This is the case with the 1969 Corvex II which was originally listed as "NOT ACCEPTABLE — AWFUL" in the new car review 3 months ago. We now change this rating to "ACCEPTABLE— FANTASTIC".

Shown above: Staff member, pleased at test results, rates new Corvex II highly.

Our Thanks

CR wishes to thank all those who sent us congratulations on our 33rd year of publication. Special thanks go to General Motors Corporation who gave every member of our staff a beautiful new Corvex II.

Shown above: Staff member stands proudly before congratulatory gift, the Corvex II.

Work Under way

Next Month in Condemner Reports:

The Bomb

Which is most powerful, has more fallout, can be launched quicker, etc. Test panel composed of all the nuclear nations.

"Are The Funeral People Really Out To Cheat You?"

Three CR staff members posed as "Dearly Departeds" and were given a complete funeral, including burial. CR is digging up the facts for a complete report.

In Later Months:

"The Birth Control Pill —Does It Work?"

Tests still going underway due to panelists refusal to stop for a while so tabulations can be recorded. Since CR announcement for this report we have received 1,289,876 requests to participate.

1969 Calendars

Which is the handiest, easiest to read, and best buy for 1969— The full report will be ready by late November.

Sewing Machines

There are 84 models of sewing machines to choose from, and of these, 10 are the leading sellers, representing over 70% of the total sale. However, CR found that although these models are very easy to operate, they are extremely difficult to test. Instead, CR chose 10 models more difficult to operate but easier to test, and, to make things even less complicated, will review only 5 of those 10. And always with the interests and needs of *you*, the consumer, in mind.

CR's Test

While it is true that women are by far the greatest users of home sewing machines, it is the *men* who are mostly employed as professional tailors in both big and small businesses. For this reason, CR used 5 male panelists to test the 5 models chosen, but each was given typical female sewing problems: dresses, skirts, blouses, culottes, aprons, etc.

Test Results

After exhaustive tests where the male panelists had to literally "live" female wear, CR found that of the 5 machines tested, 4 operated normally, one acted strangely. This was a better percentage than the panelists of whom 3 acted normally, 2 strangely.

Shock

In any test of this sort, shock potential is always a consideration. Of the 5 machines, CR found all to be insulated against shock. However, each of the panelists were shocked at the ridiculous prices asked for the machines by their respective manufacturers, and 2 of the panelist's wives were shocked when their husbands ran off with each other.

RATINGS OF SEWING MACHINES

ACCEPTABLE — GOOD

SINGA SONGALA List price marked at $457.85, but CR shopper was able to purchase it for $29.95 at a discount store. This machine offered forward and reverse stitching only, but after being dropped by clumsy panelist, it was found that it could also sew zig-zag.

PFARFF SONGARA List priced marked at $29.95, but CR shopper purchased it for $247.95 at fancy uptown store before being fired. We found this imported imitation of the *Singa Songa* to be identical in every way except for case, motor, controls, performance and other secondary considerations.

ACCEPTABLE — NOT SO GOOD

ZOLTAN ZANDAR This was a deluxe machine with automatic button-holer, trimming device, pattern tracer, embroidery control and watermelon de-pitter. The performance of all special functions was flawless, but only when used simultaneously. For normal mending, it wasn't worth a darn. (CR rates that last gag **UNACCEPTABLE**).

ACCEPTABLE — PRETTY BAD

GIVALT 100 List price $9.00. Obviously an economy model with no chrome, no frills, and no extras. It featured only a plain, black case housing 3 needles, a spool of thread and a stereo recording of a well-operating sewing machine.

NOT ACCEPTABLE — ROTTEN

CHECKMATE MOCK III No price given. This machine would not sew forward or in reverse or at all. It had one adjustment labeled "light-dark" which might refer to the color of the material to be sewed. But then again, it might not. While there was no shock danger, the machine did heat up considerably after a few minutes and "popped up" the material inserted for sewing.

SCOTCH WHISKEY

In response to the unusual amount of inquiries (from CR panelists), we herewith disclose our findings from a recent test conducted on CR's tax deductible testing yacht, *Shnopps II*. It was the first test scoring 100% attendance of the CR panel, many bringing secretaries with them to take notes. The yacht was anchored 3 miles off the New Jersey shore to avoid Coast Guard restrictions as well as suspicious wives. A case each of the 8 generally accepted "top" scotches, 6 "second rung" brands, and 3 "swill" labels were employed along with a case of the 3 leading anti-freezes.

THE TEST

Testing started precisely at 9 AM like any normal work day. When panelist could not make the distinction between scotch and the anti-freeze, he was excused from further testing.

Results were pouring in as fast as scotch pouring out. By 11 AM more than 45% of the scotches had been tested and more than 33% of the panel were in love with their secretaries.

By 3 PM 70% of the scotch was drunk as were 80% of the panel, and the owner of a small runabout had performed 34 marriages as a qualified sea captain. (CR tests Divorces in Sept. Issue.)

By 5 PM all 20 cases of scotch and anti-freeze had been consumed, and many things were said to the boss that wouldn't have been under normal conditions. (CR tests New Jobs, P. 51)

RATINGS OF SCOTCH WHISKEYS

TEST RESULTS The top 5 choices, as recorded by the panel, are as follows:

ACCEPTABLE – ZOWIE

JOHNNY WALKUP Xsellent flavour . . . colorful animalz

PRESSEDTONE SSmmooooooothhh . . . handy cans stead of bopples

SIT CHIVAS Vary lite . . . plescent . . . I love you . . . marry me . . . doll

ACCEPTABLE – YESH INDEED

BAT 69 Nishe flavour . . . nishe shmell . . . nishe girl? Too bad . . .

HAIG ROAD Oky, not grate, but oky . . . know what I mean . . . It's oky, but not grate . . . no need to get mad, bushter . . . sho it's not oky . . . you right, I wrong . . . who carsh anyhow? Ish free . . .

STRETCH SOCKS
for men

Stretch socks can help stretch your budget. They are not only longer wearing, but because some models have a great deal of stretchability, you can put both feet into one sock, thus making a pair last even longer.

CR's test

In CR's rather grueling tests, the socks were soaked for one week in a solution of milk and butter to determine their stain resistance.

Then, as a 'mud' substitute, a mixture of flour and eggs in thick, gooey consistency was poured into the testing vat.

Finally, to simulate the effect of hot machine drying or high temperature summer wear, the socks were then placed in an oven pre-heated to 400 degrees and left for 30 minutes.

Test Results

None of the socks tested held up under CR's rugged test conditions stated above, but several pair not only smelled tempting, but tasted delicious! (Recipe available on request.)

As for our less exciting and more mundane tests of actual *wearing*, CR found only two models worth our highly coveted rating, the *left* sock of the Outerwoven 898 and the *right* sock of the Ban-Lard 989. CR suggests you buy a pair of both and throw out the right and left sock respectively.

RATINGS

ACCEPTABLE—EXCELLENT

OUTERWOVEN 898. As stated above (Test Results), the left sock of this pair was superior to any sock tested, including the right one from the same manufacturer. When purchasing, explain to salesman that you dance as if you had "two left feet" and see if he won't sell you the socks accordingly.

BAN-LARD The "two left feet" ploy will obviously not work on the superior *right* sock of this manufacturer. CR suggests you buy BOTH brands, break up the pairs as stipulated, and giving the worthless matchings to friends.

ACCEPTABLE—POOR

JERKY THOROBRED These stretch socks contained far too much stretch; one panelist pulled it up so high he didn't have to wear pants.

NOT ACCEPTABLE—ECCH

BURLYTON These socks were not color fast. The colored ones came out white after only 3 washings. The white ones came out clear after only one washing.

MANLY These socks had a severe tendency to shrink. This could be circumvented by washing while wearing, but this may prove difficult for those using automatic washers. One panelist approved of their long wear without washing, but we didn't want to get close to him for further comment.

HAND-HUGGERS This brand of socks was the worst tested. They did not stretch at all. However, they were very warm because they were made of leather and were fur lined with individual places for each toe. CR strongly advised against summer wear.

JERKY THOROBRED: No pants needed

BURLYTON: Before washing   After washing

HAND HUGGERS: Not recommended for summer wear

Magazines

Because of the increasing number of magazines available and the decreasing amount of time average consumers can allot to reading periodicals, CR has decided to rate magazines so as to weed out the extraneous from the superfluous.

RATINGS

Top choices, as recorded by panel, are as follows:

COMEDY MAGAZINES—ACCEPTABLE

TIME This weekly shows how to be very funny at everyone else's expense. Cute phrases are used to condemn books, blast plays, pan movies, wreck lives, undermine governments, etc.

SERIOUS MAGAZINES—ACCEPTABLE

MAD This hard-hitting, never-crack-a-smile periodical will appeal to those who like their reading matter straight and to the point with no humor, frivolity or satire to interfere with the somber content.

EDUCATIONAL MAGAZINES—ACCEPTABLE

READER'S DIGEST This very informative monthly enabled our test reader to give herself a heart transplant; find God; hum her headaches away; and learn to live with and love a sadist—just in the first 10 pages alone!

SPECIAL MAGAZINES—UNACCEPTABLE

CONDEMNER'S REPORT An un-biased panel of readers who had never encountered this periodical before, thought the magazine to be a "comedy" entry at first reading due to the ridiculous procedure of purchasing new products only to wreck them with insane testing devices. Several were offended by the magazine's policy of advising people on how to spend their "hard-earned money". All told, CR has no choice but to award an **UNACCEPTABLE** rating to *Condemner's Report*.

LATE ONE AFTERNOON
AT THE WARSAW DIKE

WHAT'S TH

ARTIST: BOB CLA

STORY...?

TER: DON EDWING

MAD'S "CUSTOMIZ

BEGINNER'S TRAINING SKATEBOARD

WINTER SKATEBOARD

GLASS BOTTOM SKATEBOARD

ORTHOPEDIC SKATEBOARD WITH BUILT-IN ARCH SUPPORTS

SISSY'S SKATEBOARD

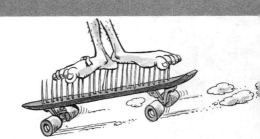

MASOCHIST'S SKATEBOARD

LATIN-AMERICAN SKATEBOARD

PIMP'S SKATEBOARD

:D" SKATEBOARDS

ARTIST: BOB JONES   WRITER: PAUL PETER PORGES

AMPHIBIOUS SKATEBOARD

OFF-ROAD SKATEBOARD

VERY FAT PERSON'S SKATEBOARD

WEIGHT-WATCHER'S SKATEBOARD

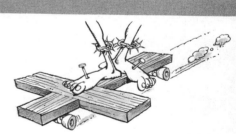

BACK-PACKER'S SKATEBOARD

RELIGIOUS FANATIC'S SKATEBOARD

WESTERN SKATEBOARD

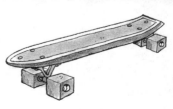

POLISH SKATEBOARD

YOU DON'T GIVE
OTHER PEOPLE

ARTIST: BOB JONES

. . . you wear T-shirts that don't have idiotic slogans or pictures on them.

. . . you're a Producer and you make a movie that takes place *after* 1947.

. . . you buy a fantastically reveali swim suit . . . and actually *swim* in

. . . you take a trip to Hollywood and you don't stop once to take pictures in front of Lucille Ball's house (or ring her bell and ask for an autographed picture for your Aunt).

. . . you give your new baby a good old-fashioned ethnic name like Moe or Izzy or Pasquale, instead of today's usual crop like Lance or Ian or Craig or Charlemagne.

. . . you show up at the ridiculous hour of 8:30 P.M., even though the party invitation clearly states you are *expected* at 8:30 P.M.

. . . you date a Stewardess . . . and admit to y friends the next day that you didn't make c

A %#*&!★? WHAT THINK WHEN...

WRITER: LARRY SIEGEL   IDEA BY: MARC BILGREY

... you own a car without a bumper sticker.

... you hire a *White* player for your Pro Basketball Team.

. you buy yourself a pet *dog* ...stead of a pet ocelot, or pet ...onkey, or pet snake or pet rock.

... you have crooked teeth, and you refuse to have braces put on them.

... you have a freshly-paved sidewalk in front of your house with no initials scratched in it.

... you hobble around on a broken leg in a cast with no funny messages by your friends written all over it.

... you admit to the Newsdealer you buy MAD for yourself ... and not for some fictitious 12-year-old idiot nephew.

It's ROMANCE when you're beguiled by an introduction to a MAD article like this one. It's LOVE when you have the blind faith to read on in the vain hope you're going to run into something funny. And it

MAD'S "ROMANCE-LOV

ARTIST: PAUL COKER

It's ROMANCE ...

... when you think her hyena laugh is cute.

It's LOVE ...

... when you accept that her hyena laugh is part of her personality.

It's a RELATIONSHIP ..

... when you realize there's more to life than just having laughs.

It's ROMANCE ...

... when you take him to meet your friends.

It's LOVE ...

... when you take him to meet your family.

It's a RELATIONSHIP ...

... when you take him to meet your analyst.

It's ROMANCE ...

... when you get excited watching his favorite football team on TV.

It's LOVE ...

... when you become as excited a fan as he is.

It's a RELATIONSHIP ...

... when you realize that's the high point of your excitement together.

RELATIONSHIP" BOOK

WRITER: FRANK JACOBS

It's ROMANCE...

... when you lie to him about your age.

It's LOVE...

... when you lie to him about your age, and he knows you're lying.

It's a RELATIONSHIP...

... when you tell him your real age, and he wishes you were still lying.

It's ROMANCE...

... when you plan your week-end around her.

It's LOVE...

... when you plan your lifetime around her.

It's a RELATIONSHIP...

... when you plan your income tax return around her.

It's ROMANCE...

... when he loves the way you dress.

It's LOVE...

... when he helps you pick out clothes at the store.

It's a RELATIONSHIP...

... when he asks you if sometimes he can wear them.

It's ROMANCE . . .

... when you surprise him with a birthday gift.

It's LOVE . . .

... when you don't mind that he doesn't like it.

It's a RELATIONSHIP . . .

... when he asks you to return it.

It's ROMANCE . . .

... when it makes no difference where you spend your vacation.

It's LOVE . . .

... when you want to go camping and she wants to go sailing . . . and you give in and go sailing.

It's a RELATIONSHIP . . .

...when you want to go camping, a she wants to go sailing . . . and y go camping . . . and she goes saili

It's ROMANCE . . .

... when she thinks you're the greatest lover in the world.

It's LOVE . . .

... when she accepts the fact that even the greatest lover in the world can't perform occasionally.

It's a RELATIONSHIP . .

... when you spend a lot of time reminiscing.

It's ROMANCE . . .

... when you spend a lot of time talking about love.

It's LOVE . . .

... when you spend a lot of time talking about a relationship.

It's a RELATIONSHIP . .

... when you spend a lot o time talking about your weigh

AROUND NOON ON A MOVIE SET

Most young people look forward to the time when they'll be grown up and their parents w
stop showering them with the same old trite words of caution, instruction and advice t
they've heard almost every day of their lives. Well, forget it! Chances are that when y
reach forty, Mom and Dad will still be counseling you to drive slower, dress warmer, a

KIDS' FRESH NE
PARENTS' TIRE

Or "What To Tell Your Parents When They Tell Yo

And **don't** smash up my **new car** trying to **drag race** it someplace!

I **promise,** Pop! In fact, I **already** have plans to smash it up trying to **back it out of the driveway** without opening the **garage doors** first!

Don't let me catch you diving off that **high board!!**

Gee, it'll be **hard** to restrain myself, considering the fact that I can **barely swim** . . . and I would **drown** for sure!

ARTIST: PAUL COKER

Don't fill up on a lot of **junk food** at the game . . . and make yourself **sick!**

Gosh, Mom! What's the fun of taking the **greatest chick in school** to **Homecoming,** and having **seats** on the **50-yard line,** if I can't end a perfect day by **throwing up?!**

All right! Here's ten bucks so you can **go** to that party with your friends! But I'd better not smell any **liquor** on your breath when you get home!

Okay, Pop! But since yo feel so **strongly** about i maybe you'd better ch in **another quarter** . . for some **breath mints**

op hanging out with the wrong crowd. However, there is a way to escape those well-meant arental clichés you've heard a thousand times. The trick is to make your folks realize at their words of "wisdom" are unnecessary, meaningless and downright silly. And to put our point across so you won't get clobbered, MAD furnishes you with tactful examples of

COMEBACKS TO OLD COMMENTS

To Do Something You Weren't Going To Do Anyway"

TER: TOM KOCH

And don't you **dare** walk in here with **wet feet** and track up my **clean floor** when you come home!

Okay, Mom! But the radio says this **rain** is supposed to **last through the week-end!** So I guess I won't see you until sometime next **Monday** . . . when my **shoes dry off!**

Shame on you! There are a lot of **hungry children** in **Asia** who would be **happy** to have those vegetables!

Really? I never dreamed there was a **shortage** of slimy, overcooked broccoli anywhere in the world!!

The **next** time you slam that door when you come in, I'll **scream!!**

Gee, Mom . . . I sure wish you **wouldn't do that!** The **noise** might **bother the neighbors!**

I really think you'd better **break up** with Milford, Dear! After all, **we don't know** anything about his **family!**

Well, **they** must have found out something about **ours** . . . because **they've** given him orders to **break up** with me!

Now, you keep **far away** from that **playground bully** who made you get **dirt** all over your **new shirt** yesterday!

Please, can I let him beat me to a pulp **again** if I promise to **take my shirt off first,** Mom?!?

Now, you come **right home** from that **picnic** if it starts to **rain,** Dear!

Okay, Mom, but I'll sure hate giving up my share of those **soggy buns** and **wet potato chips!**

ONE FINE MORNING IN A PLAY PEN

A MAD LOOK A

ARTIST & WRITE

T SUN 'N' SURF

PETER PORGES

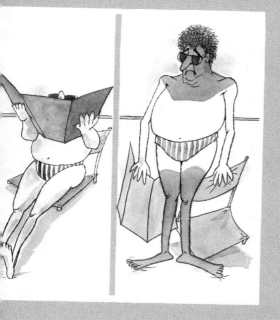

NOTE: A number of years ago, we ran a few articles entitled "MAD's Cliché Killers." Perhaps most of you were too young (or too smart) to read them, so we'll go over the premise again. But pay attention, it may be the last time!

PREMISE OF ARTICLE: Ah Have you noticed that people talk in clichés? worst part of a cliché

MAD'S CLIC

ARTIST: PAUL COKER

COMING HOME LATE

VISITING A DOCTOR'S OFFICE

at it's not really conversation, since a cliché doesn't require an answer. What are you supposed to say when those morons ask, "Hot enough for you?" Are they really looking for a response? Of course not! But now you can surprise them! Because here is some ammunition to fire right back at those insufferable cliché poppers. We call them . . .

HÉ KILLERS

SHOPPING IN A DEPARTMENT STORE

PLAYING IN LITTLE LEAGUE

GETTING ARRESTED

EARLY ONE EVENING IN THE COUNTRY

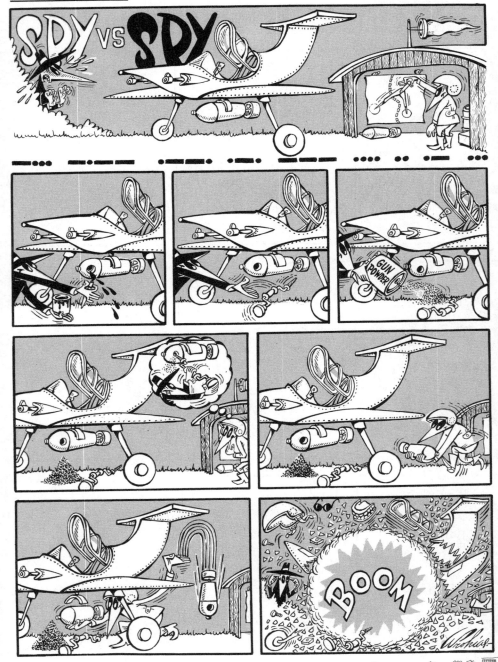

SOME MAD THINGS WE'LL NEVER UNDER- STAND

ARTIST: JACK RICKARD
WRITER: STAN HART

WE'LL NEVER UNDERSTAND WHY...

. . . the State pays $15,000 a year to feed, clothe and house a criminal . . .

while the victim's family gets nothing.

WE'LL NEVER UNDERSTAND WHY...

. . . you leave a measly quarter tip for the waiter in a luncheonette . . .

who makes as many trips as the waiter in a fancy restaurant you tip two bucks.

WE'LL NEVER UNDERSTAND WHY...

a man can get undressed in front of his wife, and not be embarrassed . . .

and he can get undressed in front of his doctor. and not be embarrassed . . .

but he'll be embarrassed when he gets undressed in front of both of them.

WE'LL NEVER UNDERSTAND WHY...

. . . no matter what city or town you're driving in when you stop for a light . . .

. . . the guy in the next car is always picking his nose.

WE'LL NEVER UNDERSTAND W

. . . the doctor's nurse will give you a specific time for an appointment . .

WE'LL NEVER UNDERSTAND WHY...

. . . you look okay in a regular mirror . . .

but you look like hell in a 3-way mirror.

WE'LL NEVER UNDERSTAND W

. . . important letters get lost . . .

WE'LL NEVER UNDERSTAND WHY...

. . . people who complain about the commercialization of everything . . .

will wear fun tee shirts with commercial messages on them.

WE'LL NEVER UNDERSTAND W

. . . someone who works hard to becom famous celebrity and be recognized .

WE'LL NEVER UNDERSTAND WHY...

but when you show up on time, there are always four or five people ahead of you.

... dog and cat lovers hate the killing of unwanted animals ...

yet let their dogs and cats run free to make all those unwanted animals.

WE'LL NEVER UNDERSTAND WHY...

le junk mail never does.

... you want your best friend to succeed ...

... but when he does, you feel depressed.

WE'LL NEVER UNDERSTAND WHY...

plains bitterly, when she finally es it, that she has no privacy.

... the U.S. Government permits the sale of arms to other countries ...

then sends emissaries all over the world to try and stop the fighting.

MAD ISSUES 201-300
"SNATCHED GLORY AND BRUISED KNUCKLES"

A MAD LOOK AT SOME UNFINI

ARTIST: BOB CLARK

Billy, your Mother and I feel it's time we rap . . .

. . . you in the **head** to knock some **sense** into your thick skull!!

Elizabeth! You certainly are **looking well** . . .

. . . **over thirty!**

Last night, Jeanie and I went all **the way** . . .

. . . to **Kazzy's** for a **pizza**, but they were **closed!!**

Listen, I could drink **three quarts of Vodka**, and it wouldn't affect me any more than drinking **three quarts of soda pop** . . .

. . . **would affect a chronic diabetic!**

Folks, this **next** song was made famous by **Mr. Frank Sinatra**, who happens to be a very very dear friend . . .

. . . of **Mr. Dean Martin!**

I'm **sorry** I nodded off, there, Professor! You see . . . I was up half the night . . . **studying** . . .

. . . the effects of **alcohol** on **shapely co-eds!**

HED SENTENCES

WRITER: JOHN CALDWELL

In case you've **never seen** this TV show before, pay **close attention** to the **opening narration,** or the show won't make any sense. Come to think of it, even if you **do** pay attention, it **still** won't make any sense!!

Dr. David Bummer, mild-mannered scientist, searching for a way to tap into the **reserve of strength** all humans have . . .

Then, a sudden accidental overdose of gamma radiation .

and suddenly a **strange metamorphosis** took place . . .

And now, whenever mild-mannered David Bummer gets **angry** .

The creature is **constantly hounded** by a **nosey reporter** . . .

The creature is wanted for a **murder** he **didn't commit,** an David is **believed dead** when he orders his **own funeral.** An he **must** let everybody **believe** he's dead until he learns t **control** the **rotten terrible temper** that dwells within him

"I'd appreciate a ride, Miss . . ."

"I'm sorry . . . but I don't pick up hitchhikers!"

"That's **unpatriotic!** Hitchhiking is an old American Tradition . . . like **baseball, hot dogs, apple pie** and **rape!** Besides, it happens to be **extremely essential** to all "Hero-On-The-Run" shows like this!"

SAN FRANCISCO OR BULK

"Okay, get in! Why should I think there's something **wrong** . . . just because you're walking around in the **snow** with **no shirt?**"

"**My shirt?** Oh—I was **washing** it when this **guy** came up and offered me **fifty bucks** for it! Then he tore it in **half,** and washed half in **my** detergent, and half in **Brand-X!**"

"**Here's** something you can **slip on!** It belongs to my **Stepmother!**"

"**Why are you going to** Frisco?"

"They have a **Lab** with a new-type **Gamma Radiation Machine** . . . and **besides**—where else can I go dressed like this?"

"Why the interest in **Gamma Radiation** research? Are you a **scientist?**"

"No, I'm more like a **bum!** I go from place to place meddling in people's affairs and doing **odd jobs** like butlering, plumbing and stevedoring! Gamma Radiation is my—**hobby!**"

"It's **amazing!** I guess **Gamma Ray Research IS** an unusual hobby!"

"No, I mean that you manage to find a **job** every week despite the **high rate of unemployment!**"

"And I do even hav[e] **Social Se**[cur]ity card, reference[s]! And I g[o] interview[s] a torn s[hirt]"

"**Why are you going so fast?!?**"

"There's **something wrong** with the **brakes!!**"

"**Women drivers** make me so **ANGRY!**"

"ARRRGGHHH!"

"Oh, my God!!"

"Big deal! If the male chauvinists in charge of **TV** would let **ME** bust out of **MY** dress, I'd get the biggest ratings in history!!"

"This is place, here!"

"No! you bloomin' idi[ot] We want the **ELEPHAN**[T] Graveyard . . . not t[he] Automobile's Gravey[ard]"

And if anything happens to **YOU** ... who gets the money?

The **Undertaker**, the **Florist**, the **Government** ... and my **Stepmother**!

We can **eliminate** the **Undertaker** and the **Florist**! And the job was **too professional** to be pulled off by the **Government**! That leaves your **Stepmother**!

You're **wrong**! My **Stepmother** loves me! She gave me my **car**! It's the **same** model she gave **Daddy**!

I'm probably being **silly** ... but let's **check** the car out!

Well, David?! **WAS** it an accident?

I ... I'm **not sure**! This bra[ke] cable was **CUT**! Either som[e]one deliberately tried t[o] **kill** you, or it's a **typical** Detroit manufacturing def[ect]

WE SELL PARTS

That's **strange**!! The **rope** we used to **climb** down has **disappeared**!

Not as strange as a **200-foot** hunk of **rope** just **lying** around in the **first place**!

How are we going to get **out** of here?

I've got an **idea**! Turn into that— that "**Thing**" —and **HE'LL** get us out!

Listen, I just **can't** have a **metamorphosis** any time I **feel** like it!!

Try, David!

I'm **trying**!! NNNGHHRHH!!

Try harder, you creep!!

What are you doing?

Trying to make you **ANGRY**, stupid! You know, **this** show is almost as **lousy** as "**THE MAGICIAN**"!!

Y[ou]
AS[
F[

L[
A[

ARRRGGGHHHHH !!!

With all the handsome **Super Heroes** in the world, how come **I** end up with an **overgrown**, **inarticulate** green clod in a **torn dress**!?

EXIT

You're **ALIVE**!! I mean— you're **late**!! I was **worried**!

I was in a **terrible** accident! But **David**, here, **saved** my life!

DAVID?!?

He looks **more** like his name should be "**BRUCE**"!

As a matter of fact, my name **IS** "Bruce" in the **Comic Book** version! But the **Producers** felt it wasn't a **masculine** enough name for **TV**!

And Je[
wins [
Decath[
BRUC[
the WO[R
GREAT[
ATHLE[

Do you **still** suspect my Stepmother?? She seemed grateful to you for saving my life!

Then why did she sic her dogs on me?!? You **tore** her **best** dress!!

If we could **only** find some hard evidence!

Maybe **this** will help! I found it under my Stepmother's **bed**!

BRAKE TAMPERING KIT
Results Guaranteed

You **botched** it, Sheriff! The **brat** **WASN'T KILLED**!! And I think she **suspects** something!

She's on her way to **see** you! There better not be any slip-ups **this time**!

There's a **man** with her! Waste him, too! Is he **WHAT**? No, he **ISN'T** over **7 feet tall**, and he **ISN'T green**! You better lay off the sauce till the **job's** over!

Listen, I **investigated** your Father's death, and it was an **accident**!

Besides, I been Sheriff on **lots** of **shows**, and I know **all** about strangers that go around, trying to stir up trouble in peaceful communities!

So **git** your **hands up**, Boy!

The old "Crooked-Sheriff-Who's-In-Cahoots-With-The-Wicked-Stepmother" routine! I should have **GUESSED**!!

Let me go!! What did you do with **David**?

I conked him on the **head** and I locked him in the **John**! When he comes to . . . he'll be **wanted** for **your murder**!

My **MURDER**?! You're going to **KILL ME**?!?

No . . . I'm taking you to a **Drive-In** to see "**The Rocky Horror Show**"! Of **COURSE**, I'm gonna kill you!

Oooohh! My **head**!! Where **am** I? The door's locked!! I think I'm in a **John**! Whew!

HEY! There's **NO PAPER**!! If there's one thing that gets me **steamed**, it's a **JOHN WITH NO PAPER**!

MEN

ROARR

ONE FRIDAY MORNING

Why restrict the awarding of medals to the military? After all, Civilians perform heroic acts while fighting life's daily battles as well! Let's recognize them with

THIS ISSUE'S PROPOSED
MAD MEDALS

. . . TO BE PRESENTED TO DESERVING CORPORATE EXECUTIVES

THE BLACK LUNG MEDAL

Awarded to Corporate Executives for outstanding service to stockholders in protecting their annual dividends by effectively avoiding and delaying the installation of those costly, but much-needed "anti-pollution devices."

THE NO-FRILLS PRODUCT AWARD

Presented to Corporation Executives who display noteworthy ingenuity in cutting costs of manufacturing their products by reducing the quality of workmanship in them . . . thus avoiding having to raise prices to consumers.

THE HANDOUT OF FRIENDSHIP MEDAL

For service above and beyond the call of any corporate duty—by brilliantly disguising campaign contributions and cash gifts to legislators in order to influence votes favorable to the company in any matters that may come up.

THE FRAMMIS AND GRIBBISH AWARD

For brilliant achievement, consisting of introducing colorful made-up words into Warranties and Guarantees, thus affording the consumer an interesting language experience, even if he does not actually understand the meanings.

THE DISTINGUISHED FLYING MEDAL

Awarded to any Corporate Officer who courageously makes use of the Company Jet to fly to a major sporting event, and then writes it off as a business trip . . . so that every taxpayer helps pay for it, not just the stockholders.

ARTIST & WRITER: AL JAFFEE

Since the dawn of time, men have been trying to get rid of their unwanted face hair. The only purpose the fuzz seemed to serve was to house insects, obscure vision, and keep track of food eaten by gathering samples of it. When the use of tools was discovered, one of their first applications was the removal of that bothersome beaver. Though crude at first, shaving instruments evolved through the ages until a major breakthrough was made: the invention of the standard safety razor. But this little marvel was so good, it almost ruined the shaving industry. It never broke down, it never needed replacing and it was handed down from father to son. The business looked dead until some genius decided to make razors the way other successful products are made: gimmicky and lousy! First they fooled around with the blades: Blades were made with chromium, platinum, tungsten and teflon, to name a few. Then they started fooling around with the razors themselves: Injector systems, double-bladed heads, swivel heads, etc. Just when you thought they couldn't possibly come up with one more "innovation," another popped up. So now, there's a new, flashier model every few months that makes the old one seem obsolete. And, cleverly, the new blade head won't fit the old handles. So where will it all end? It won't! MAD now projects some future products we're sure to see as we're hurtled deeper and deeper out into

THE SPACE AGE
RAZOR RACE

TRAC I
a very close shave

TRAC II
a truly close shave

TRAC III
a terrifyingly close shave

ARTIST & WRITER: AL JAFFEE   IDEA BY: JOHN WICK

THE QUICK-FREEZE RAZOR

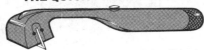

The Quick-Freeze Razor will be a simple but efficient instrument. A replaceable freon cartridge directs a blast of frigid air at beard. As whiskers freeze solid and brittle, an ice scraper follows and easily snaps them cleanly off.

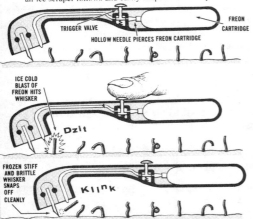

FREON CARTRIDGE

TRIGGER VALVE

HOLLOW NEEDLE PIERCES FREON CARTRIDGE

ICE COLD BLAST OF FREON HITS WHISKER

Dzit

FROZEN STIFF AND BRITTLE WHISKER SNAPS OFF CLEANLY

Kliпk

THE LASER RAZOR

SWITCH

POWER SOURCE

LASER BEAM

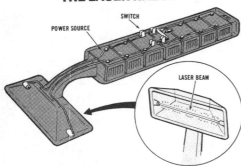

The efficiency of the laser beam is familiar to anyone who has ever seen one pierce an army tank or melt a concrete wall or open a sardine can without a key. By applying the laser beam principle to a shaving implement . . . even the mightiest and toughest beard will easily fall.

Al Jaffee

LASER BEAM RAZOR SLICES WHISKERS WITH EASE, PRECISION AND COMFORT

THE FLAME-THROWER RAZOR

TRIPLE SWITCH

FLAME PORTS

BUTANE CAPSULE

FREON CAPSULE

FREON PORTS

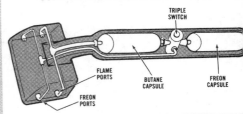

Depressing the trigger switch causes three things to happen simultaneously: (1) It releases butane gas. (2) It ignites the gas, which shoots out flames to sear off whiskers. And (3) Ice cold freon gas is then released which neutralizes the pain of your scorched and burning face.

FRONT VIEW OF FLAME-THROWER RAZOR ON SEARCH-AND-DESTROY MISSION OVER A TOUGH BEARD

THE MICROWAVE RAZOR

POWER SOURCE

ON-OFF SWITCH

CONVERTER

MICROWAVE EMITTER

When the Microwave Razor is drawn across whiskers, a high-frequency electromagnetic ray instantly withers hairs reduces them to ash. Ash is easily brushed from f

THE NEUTRON RAZOR

NEUTRON RADIATION RELEASE MECHANISM

FUSION SWITCH

MINI-CYCLOTRON

URANIUM 235 SUP

U235

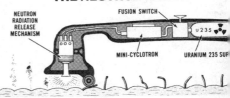

The ultimate shaver of the space age, it will be inspired by that wonderful new military weapon, the neutron bomb —whose claim to glory is that it destroys people without harming buildings. This unique razor will be capable of generating neutron radiation. As it passes over beard, it blasts each hair with miniscule radiation, and—like the great neutron bomb—kills whiskers but doesn't harm face.

THE TRAC LXXVI RAZOR

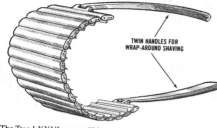

TWIN HANDLES FOR
WRAP-AROUND SHAVING

The Trac LXXVI razor will have seventy-six cutting edges on a flexible head that will wrap around an entire face and shave it close and clean in two or three effortless moves.

EACH TRAC LXXVI BLADE ENGAGES
ITS OWN SEPARATE WHISKER HAIR

THE MULTIBLADE RAZOR

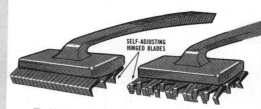

SELF-ADJUSTING
HINGED BLADES

The Multiblade Razor will be created especially for people with special skin problems. Anyone who's ever shaved with an ordinary razor and lopped off pimples, boils and other parts of their uneven face will welcome it. Dozens of tiny hinged blades adjust themselves to user's scraggy, bumpy face.

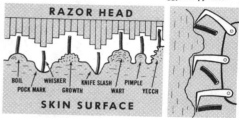

RAZOR HEAD

BOIL   WHISKER   KNIFE SLASH   PIMPLE
POCK MARK   GROWTH   WART   YECCH

SKIN SURFACE

FRONT AND SIDE VIEWS OF UNEVEN SKIN SURFACES SHOWING
HOW SELF-ADJUSTING BLADES HANDLE THESE TOUGH PROBLEMS

THE SIMPLE PLUCKER-I RAZOR

The Simple Plucker-I Razor is activated by rollers attached to a crankshaft. As rollers move across face, the crankshaft causes pluckers to go up and down, making plucking movements. When plucker encounters hair, it is firmly gripped and plucked. User may notice slight twinges of pain at first, but it all happens so fast, he will hardly notice it after a while.

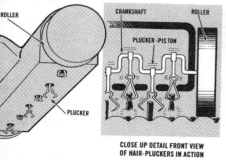

ROLLER

CRANKSHAFT   ROLLER

PLUCKER-PISTON

PLUCKER

CLOSE UP DETAIL FRONT VIEW
OF HAIR-PLUCKERS IN ACTION

THE PERMANENT PLUCKER-II RAZOR

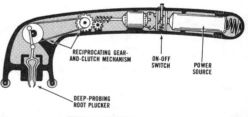

RECIPROCATING GEAR-
AND-CLUTCH MECHANISM

ON-OFF
SWITCH

POWER
SOURCE

DEEP-PROBING
ROOT PLUCKER

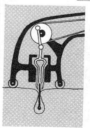 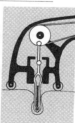 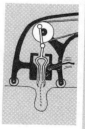

As razor head is drawn over beard, plucker moves rapidly up and down until it comes to a whisker hole. When this happens, plucker goes down to whisker root and yanks it out, completely eliminating the need to ever shave again.

ONE NIGHT IN THE MIAMI BUS TERMINAL

MAD SALUTES ONE OF OUR UNSUNG HOUSEHOLD PETS:

ARTIST:
PAUL COKER

THE TURTLE

WRITER:
PAUL PETER PORGES

EXCITING TRICKS TURTLES CAN DO...

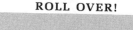

SIT!

ROLL OVER!

PLAY DEAD!

JUMP!

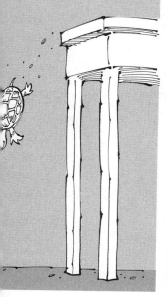

BEG!

FETCH!

STAY!

HIDE!

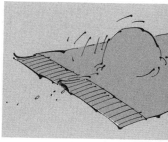

TRUMPET MUTES

SINK STOPPERS

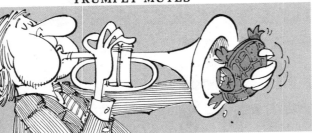

HOCKEY PUCKS

DECORATIVE COASTERS

NON-SLIP SKULL CAPS

DOOR STOPS

TURTLES ARE ECONOMICAL TO OWN BECAUS

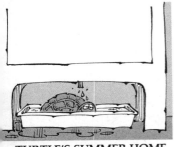

TURTLE'S SUMMER HOME

TURTLE'S WINTER HOME

TURTLE FEEDER

...SE BECAUSE THEY'RE VERY USEFUL AS

MUD SCRAPERS
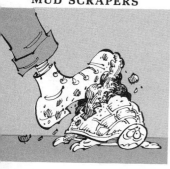

BENT NAIL REMOVERS

MATCH STRIKERS

BABY SITTERS

PRACTICE GOLF TEES

FLOATING SOAP DISHES

...EY DON'T NEED EXPENSIVE ACCESSORIES

...RTLE DRINKING FOUNTAIN   TURTLE EXERCISER   TURTLE SWIMMING POOL

TURTLES MAKE GREAT PETS BECAUSE

They don't make any noise if
you accidentally step on them!

They don't run away . . . and if they do,
they're so slow, they don't get very far!

They don't dig holes in
your neighbors' lawns!

They don't beg for food when you eat!

They don't choke on hairballs

They don't need to be spayed!

They don't need to be walked
outdoors in rotten weather!

They don't jump in your lap, or rub
against your leg in a horny fashion.

They don't have to sleep in bed
with you during a thunderstorm!

ONE SUNDAY EVENING

One of the most popular patriotic songs of all times is "America The Beautiful." Unfortunately, the words are simple and generalized, and have all but lost their meaning in these troublesome times. What we need is a new "America The Beauti

MAD'S UP-DATED REL

AMERICA
THE BEAUTIFUL

☆ ☆

O beautiful for _____①_____ ,

For _____②_____ ;

For _____③_____ ,

_____④_____ ;

America! America! God shed His grace on thee;

_____⑤_____

_____⑥_____ .

$1.50 A GALLON GAS · NUKES · CRIME · DISCO ★

ul" that has lyrics appropriate and relevant to the world we live in today. So
ere's your opportunity to re-write this great hymn. Just fill in the numbered
lanks with your choice from the corresponding numbered lists, and you'll have

ANT, DO-IT-YOURSELF

WRITER: FRANK JACOBS

spacious skies
smog-filled skies
greasy fries
Nixon's lies
flabby thighs
loud hi-fi's
Christmas ties
rents that rise

amber waves of grain
tons of rotting grain
films that dull our brain
good taste down the drain
spending that's insane
snorting bad cocaine
cars we can't maintain
Tarzan chasing Jane

purple mountain majesties
belching smoke from Factories
nu-clea-r catastrophes
modern-art monstrosities
situation comedies
money-grubbing charities
over-sized monopolies
unemployment miseries

above the fruited plain
which Carter can't explain
we need like flat champagne
and shows like "Super Train"
afflicting us with pain
and Stassen's last campaign
from Oregon to Maine
and debts that still remain

and crown thy good with brotherhood
we'll bravely guard our Visa Card
as prices rise, we'll improvise
we'll do our thing at Burger King
we'll get our kicks from porno flicks
we'll cel-e-brate the Welfare State
with joy we'll bless the I.R.S.
the end is near, but we'll stay here

from sea to shining sea
while wasting en-er-gy
for Donny and Marie
in-to e-ter-nit-y
and pray for NBC
and sing this song off-key
and play the lot-ter-y
and live in bank-rupt-cy

BERG'S-EYE VIEW DEPT.

THE LIGHTER SIDE OF... *COI*

It's **almost** like the **old** days!! We're in a **PRICE WAR** with the gas station across the street!

Are you **kidding**?! At a time of **gas** shortages...??

That makes the competition even **fiercer!**

So who's winning!

Right now, **WE** are!!

OUR prices are **HIGHER**!!

PETITION

ARTIST & WRITER:
DAVE BERG

I've got a **classic rivalry** going on in my home! The **little one** and the **big one** are **BOTH** constantly competing for my **attention!**

The **big one** is the **worst!** He's **jealous** of the little one! He pulls **all sorts** of tricks to beat him out! He even throws **temper** tantrums!

I'm going **out of my MIND!!**

How many children do you **have** in your family?

Just THOSE TWO!!

Panel 1 — "My Father can lick **your** Father!" / "Oh, **yeah?!** I'll make you a **bet**, wise guy!!"

Panel 2 — "Hey, Dad! **Bernard** says **his** Father can beat the **hell** out of you!" / "He **DID**, did he?!? Well, we'll **SEE** about that!"

Panel 3 — "Hey, Kaputnik! Your **kid** says **you** can **wipe up the floor** with me! **Put up your dukes!!**" / "Oh, **yeah?!** I'll make you a **bet**, wise guy!"

Panel 4 — "I'll bet you **my** kid is a bigger liar than **your** kid!"

Panel 1 — "Oy! My **dentures** are killing me!" / "You think **YOU'VE** got troubles? My **arthritis** is so bad, it's agony to **move** around!"

Panel 2 — "My **feet** hurt if I walk just a **couple of blocks!**" / "Is that so?! What do **YOU** know about hurt?! I know about **hurt!!** My **back** is so painful, it's a **miracle** I'm **STILL ALIVE!!**"

Panel 3 — "I can't stand that woman! All she ever **does** is complain about her **ailments!**" / "So do **YOU . . . !!**"

Panel 4 — "Yeah, but **HERS** are **always BETTER** than mine!!!"

Panel 1 — "My **Son** is a Law Student in an **Ivy League** College! It's costing me a **FORTUNE!**"

Panel 2 — "Big Deal!! My **Son** is a **MEDICAL Student** in an Ivy League College! It's costing **ME** a fortune!"

Panel 3 — "Hah!! You think **THAT'S** something!! My **Son** is a **School DROP-OUT!** He's got a nine-to-five job with a **Petroleum Company!**" / "So . . . what's to **brag** about?!"

Panel 4 — "He's **MAKING** a fortune!!"

I went to apply for a job today, and **hundreds of others** showed up! We had to fill out a **questionnaire** and submit a **resume**! When I saw what the others were putting down, I knew I was **under-qualified**!

So I **lied like hell**! I filled **pages and pages** with things I never really did! It was a **magnificent** piece of **fiction**!

So did you **get the job**?

Nope!

How come . . . ? ?

I was **OVER**-qualified! !

You **play** so **FEROCIOUSLY**!

You bet! I'm out for **blood**!

I can remember being taught, "It **matters NOT** if you **WIN or LOSE**, but **HOW** you play the game!"

That's **sissy talk**! Vince Lombardi said, "**Winning** isn't everything . . . it's the **ONLY** thing! !"

THAT'S why I show my opponent **NO MERCY**! I'm out to **MURDER THE BUM**! !

Playing **SOLITAIRE** . . . ?

It's **not fair**! ! Mommy loves **YOU** more than she loves **ME**! !

I wish it was **true**, but it **ain't**!

Mommy, **don't** you love **FREDDY** more than you love **ME**! ?

How can you **SAY** that? ! ?

My children are like **fingers** on my **hand**! If I bang my thumb, it hurts as much as if I bang my **pinky**! And I feel the **same** way about the **two of you**!

You **BOTH** give me a pain

ONE AFTERNOON ON A REMOTE JUNGLE ISLAND

Believe it or not, there are still millions of people in America who do not own a single Cabbage Patch Doll or product, like Cabbage Patch earmuffs, Cabbage Patch bedspreads or Cabbage Patch radios. It's not because these people haven't heard of them or don't have the money. It's because they can't stand the ugly

CABBAGE PATCH PRODUCTS FOR PEOPL

**CABBAGE PATCH
DART BOARDS**

**CABBAGE PATCH
TOILET PAPER**

**CABBAGE PATCH
TACKLING DUMMIES**

ttle buggers! We at MAD feel that this huge potential market for Cabbage Patch products can be tapped if new products are developed that appeal to people that re nauseated at the very sight of them! With that in mind, some of the geniuses t MAD put their wallets to the grindstone and came up with the following...

WHO HATE CABBAGE PATCH PRODUCTS

ARTIST: GEORGE WOODBRIDGE   WRITERS: JOE RAIOLA & CHARLIE KADAU

CABBAGE PATCH DUST MOPS

CABBAGE PATCH COTTON SWABS

CABBAGE PATCH PUNCHING BAG

CABBAGE PATCH ASHTRAYS

DEVICE, MAN, COMETH DEPT.

In a recent issue, we noted that everywhere we shop today, we see products with the words "NEW—IMPROVED" printed all over them. But after we buy these products and start using them, we find the only thing "new" and "improved" is the higher price.

MORE "NEW-IMPRO
REALLY ARE NEV

ARTIST & WRITER: AL JAFF

NEW—IMPROVED PEANUT BUTTER (AND OTHER STICKY STUFF) JAR

Scraping out the last remaining amounts of peanut butter (or other sticky substances like cream, paste, etc.) from a jar can often be a back-breaking, time-consuming affair.

New—Improved peanut butter (. . . and other sticky stuff) jar has double lids, top and bottom. When user gets down to bottom, he merely turns the jar over, unscrews the other lid and easily removes the contents.

STIKKY PEANUT BUTTER

NEW—IMPROVED TUBE DISPENSER

SPEERT

Rolling tubes up to squeeze out the last drops of toothpaste, vaseline, hair cream, etc., can be frustrating. No matter how hard you try, you always miss getting it all. Or else the tube bursts, oozing stuff all over your hands.

CRUST TOOTHPASTE

New—Improved tube dispenser has built-in key at its base for neat, easy, perfect rolling up to get every last drop. Holes in key are handy for hanging tube on bathroom hook.

NEW—IMPROVED BEVERAGE CAN

There are many types of beverage cans on the market, each with a different tab or other method of opening. But in one respect they are all the same. They each soak the customer.

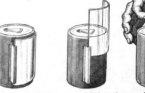

New—Improved beverage can has the usual spraying problem but it also has the solution: a spray shield attachment—which is conveniently out of the way when not in use, but slides into place to protect the user when tab is removed.

NEW—IMPROVED BOXED TISSUES

Nothing is wasted in greater amounts than disposable tissues. Nothing except the money you spend on those tissues.

KLEENKIT

New—Improved boxed tissues are dispensed to fit your need. No longer is a full-sized tissue used for a mere sniffle as well as a full-blown runny nose. Paper cutter controls size.

ich is new and improved for the manufacturer, but how about us consumers? MAD
nks it's about time there really were products that are new and improved. And so
ve gone back to the old drawing board again this issue, and we've come up with

D" PRODUCTS THAT
AND IMPROVED

A: BILLY DOHERTY

$2.00

Glitch
CEREAL
NEW-IMPROVED
A MOVING EXPERIENCE

NEW—IMPROVED OLIVE JAR

Regular olive jars are long and thin, and after a while,
olives are out of reach of even the longest finger. Even
forks are useless when skittery olives are way at bottom.

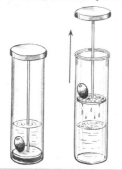

lew—Improved olive
ar has a plastic
etriever inside it,
ade up of a rod and
erforated disc at-
ached to the jar's
d. When lid is un-
crewed and raised,
od and disc bring
ives up. Perfora-
ons in disc allow
quid to run down
to jar while drip-
ee olives—even
e last one—can
e easily removed.

NEW—IMPROVED DIGITAL WATCH

ost digital watches, especially the LED (light emitting
ode) types, cannot be read in bright sunlight. This is
e drawback that annoys many owners and is hurting sales.

ew—Improved digital watch has telescoping viewing tube
at lifts easily for daylight use and completely elim-
ates the annoying problem of reading watch in bright light.

NEW—IMPROVED PAPERBACK BOOK

Anyone who has lost his place in a paperback book knows
how frustrating it can be. And bookmarks always fall out.

New—Improved paperback book has bookmark as part of back
cover. It is folded inside for protection against handling
in stores, but easily folds out to be placed anywhere in
the book. Losing bookmark or your place is now impossible.

NEW—IMPROVED MULTI-PACKS

MULTI-
PAK
PHOTO
FILM
$59⁹⁸

X110 X110 X110 X110
X110 X110 X110 X110
NOT GOOD AFTER JULY 1

Anyone who's been forced to buy several multi-packed items
when all he needed was one knows how infuriating it can be.

CIGARETS
3¢ EACH

NUTS &
BOLTS
20¢ EA.

TENNIS
BALLS
$1²⁵ EA.

WATERMELON
$3 EACH

EGG
1

New—Improved multi-packaging lets you take as many items
as you actually need . . . and that's all you have to pay for.

NEW—IMPROVED TELEPHONE

The standard telephone is difficult to hold between your shoulder and your ear when both your hands are occupied.

New—Improved telephone has concealed "Head-Hook" © that can be pulled out and adjusted to fit any shape of head.

NEW—IMPROVED BUTTON

Regular buttons have a habit of popping off at the most inconvenient times. Finding needle and thread, especially correct color thread, is usually difficult or impossible.

New—Improved button has snap-off/snap-on outer ring. A slight thumb pressure snaps off ring, and hidden needle and thread is revealed. After sewing, ring snaps back on.

NEW—IMPROVED PICTURE FRAME

Under the best of circumstances, hanging a picture is a pain in the part you sit on. Not only is it blind guess-work as to where it will wind up, but trying to get the wire onto the hook behind it is enough to drive you nuts.

New—Improved picture frame has hollow channel in one side of frame for wire to pass through. Picture wire is easily placed over hook, and by pulling wire through channel, the picture is hoisted to exact position desired. Wire is then fastened to tie-down post, and excess wire can be cut off.

NEW—IMPROVED BATTERIES

Regular batteries go dead without warning, mostly at the most critical times. Often they even go quietly dead when not in use, corroding the insides of valuable equipment.

New—Improved battery contains a tiny micro alarm system. Just before battery goes dead, last bit of remaining power turns on buzzer to alert owner, thereby avoiding problems.

NEW—IMPROVED TWIST-OFF CAP

Anyone who has ever broken nails or torn fingers trying to open a twist-off cap knows what sheer agony it can be.

New—Improved twist-off cap comes with its own handy easy-to-use twist-off wrench. In addition to convenience, user has better control and, by opening cap slowly, is able to release pressure so carbonated soda doesn't spray all over.

NEW—IMPROVED TENNIS RACQUET

Regular tennis racquets have handles that always seem to be in the way when being carried or packed for traveling.

New—Improved tennis racquet has collapsible telescoping handle that folds away for convenient carrying or packing.

ONE MORNING ON A STREET CORNER

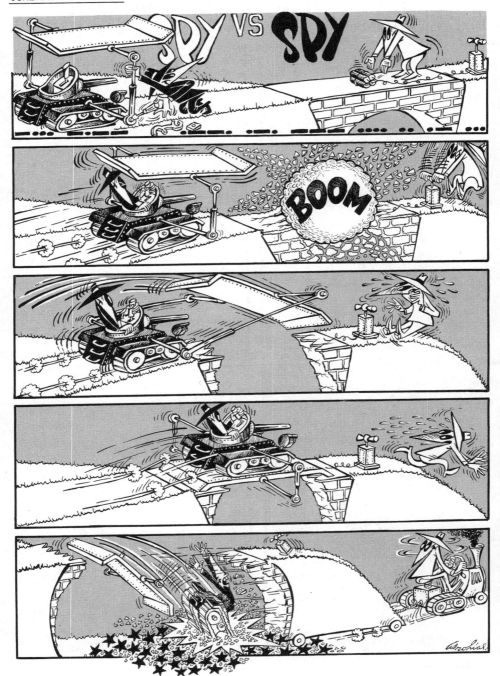

MAD'S INGENIOUS PLAN FOR A MORE EFFICIENT GOVERNMENT

ARTIST: JACK DAVIS   WRITER: BARRY LIEBMANN

Candidates will not be allowed to receive campaign contributions from individuals or large corporations. However, they will be allowed to finance their campaigns by driving a cab or panhandling on the street.

Outside interests in large corporations, real estate ventures or the stock market will be forbidden to all politicians. However, they will be allowed to moonlight as garbage men, soda jerkers, gas station attendants or something equally suitable.

The President of the United States will receive a minimum wage ($2.65 an hour) and, at the end of his term, will be "tipped" by the American Public. Tips will not be allowed to exceed $5 per person (since that's too small to be considered a bribe).

The salaries of the President, his Cabinet members, and all members of Congress will not be raised in accordance with the rising cost of living, since it's their job to keep it down in the first place.

In order to prove their dedication to their job, all politicians will be forced to take a "vow of poverty" before entering office.

In order to speed up the Congress, a limit of 5,000 words will be placed on every speech, and a fine of $10 per additional word will be imposed on any Congressman who goes over this reasonable limit.

Because Congressmen have a tendency to fall asleep while on the job, a Surprise Quiz will be given at the end of each daily session of Congress, and the results published.

A fine of $50 (per word) will be charged to all candidates who use five-syllable words where a two-syllable word (or less) would do just as well.

Government agencies will no longer be allowed to spend tax dollars (for any reason whatsoever) without first having to ask permission from each and every taxpayer.

Any politician claiming to be "one of the common people" will be required to live among the "common people" in a slum neighborhood while serving his full term of office.

Expense allowances for Congressmen will not exceed $149.50 per week. (If they can't manage THEIR budget, why should they be allowed to manage OURS?)

After the election, all candidates (winners OR losers) will personally have to eat all their posters, handbills, and stickers that haven't been removed by mid-December.

olitical candidates will be obliged to draw up a contract explaining utline form) what they plan to do if elected. And at the end of their s, they will be paid a flat fee for every promise that wasn't broken.

To avoid further hanky-panky on Capital Hill, all new Secretaries will be chosen by a Committee of Congressional Wives.

Congressmen, Governors, Mayors and Supreme Court Judges will not be given bodyguards or Secret Servicemen since it's their job to keep the streets safe to begin with.

When they retire, all politicians will receive the same type of pension that is given to the average school teacher, coal miner, auto worker, clerk, etc.

The latest hit movie making the rounds is about a creature from another planet. It's supposed to be an original film, but it's a lot like an old movie called "The Thing," and a little like "The Exorcist," with a touch of "Star Wars," and a hint of "The Creature From The Black Lagoon," with a slight echo of "Lost in Space." As a matter of fact, it reminds us of so many movies, instead of "Alien," it should be called . . .

ALIAS

Good morning, Mother . . . ! !

Good morning, Son! Did you **brush** your teeth? Did you **take** a bath? Are you wearing **clean underwear** in case you have a **space accident?**

I think we made a **bad mistake**—nicknaming the computer **"Mother!"** The darn machine is **carrying the role too far! !**

Calling **Antarctica Control** . . . Calling **Antarctica Control** . . . This is Space Tug **"Noisy Roamer"** . . . Do you **read? ?** **Come in, Antarctica!**

Save your **breath!** We're **nowhere near home!** When certain conditions arise, Mother **changes our course!** Those conditions have **arisen!**

I bet we're supposed to **stay** out here in **space** until the **price** of the **oil ore** we're carrying **doubles!** The oil companies make us **do** that every few years or so!

MOTHER, THE DISCO COMPUTER BY LITE LAB

ARTIST: MORT DRUCKER   WRITER: DICK DE BARTOLO

Mother has intercepted transmissions of **unknown origin!** She's already diverted our space tug to **investigate!** We'll probably be settling down into a **hostile environment** where they'll be speaking a **mysterious language!**

Oh, **boy** . . . We're going to **Washington, D.C. . . . !**

Ready for **"Undocking"** . . . !

Set all gauges to **450°** . . . ! Turn microwave to **"latch!"** Activate **teflon pans** . . . ! Grease **cookie sheets,** and—

I hate to **interrupt** during the **countdown,** Dripley . . . but I believe you're reading the ship's **"Cookbook"** not the ship's **"Manual!"** !

Too late! Hang on! ! I already pushed **"GRATE & CHOP!"**

GRATE CHOP

What WAS that ugly hideous thing?!

All I know is . . . it wasn't MINE!! It didn't have my eyes, or my nose, or my beard . . . or ANYTHING!!

I . . . I can't stop sobbing!

Don't be jealous, Lambaste!

Someday, you'll have a baby of your OWN!!

Whatever it is . . . it killed Pain! And now it's loose in the ship . . . and I'm SCARED!

Oh, don't be such a baby! Now, get some sleep, and we'll look for it in the morning! Good night, everybody!

And don't anybody get up to go to the bathroom without the other five!

Good night, Dull!

Good night, Bark!

Good night, Drip!

Good night, Frett!

I've heard of "Burials at Sea" . . . but this is my first "Burial at Space" . . .

I know that the FIRST thing that flew out was PAIN . . . but what was the OTHER thing?

His tombstone! The Captain wanted it to be a "proper burial!"!

Okay, here's a weapon for each of you! It's a portable Cattle Prod! It's insulated here . . .

. . . and here . . .

. . . and here . . .

BUT NOT HERE!!

And this is a special "Tracking Device"! If you get within ten feet of the monster, micro-changes in air density sets it off!

I don't need that! I've got my OWN Scientific Device! If I get within ten feet of the monster, I pee in my pants!

I don't mind when Jokes—the cat—eats left-overs . . . but THIS is ridiculous!

Wait a minute! I think I see the cat in the ventilating system! Or IS it the cat?!

Let me try and remember! Was our cat eight feet tall . . . and hideously ugly?

GORE!!

Frett is dead!

Did the thing get him . . .??

Well, sort of! He WET himself to death!

DICK DePARTMENT

OOH! AAH! GOLLY! GEE! BARF! WURP!

OOH! AAH! GOLLY! GEE! BARF! WURP!

Look at all these **grossly over-priced prizes!** From Boilhill—a **queen-sized** bed with a **king-sized price,** $2033! And soft, comfortable pillows **worth** about **five bucks** each, but they're yours for **only $200 a pair!** And this **veneer** over **plywood end table! Looks** like a $4000 antique, but its **actual cost** is $200! However, **YOUR** actual cost is **$4000!** Yes, **every time** this program is broadcast across the country...

YOU COULDN'T AFFORD IT!

$75,000

$1000

$3000

200

ARTISTS: WILL ELDER AND HARVEY KURTZMAN WRITER: DICK DeBARTOL

Our first contestant, Anne, will **spin the wheel.** The amount of money the wheel lands on is **multiplied** by the number of times the letter she picks is found in the puzzle. However, if we feel you're winning **too much** money, our computer will credit you with a **lower amount.** And remember, the **object** of the game is for the people at home to figure out the puzzle **before** a contestant does! That way they feel **superior** and will continue to tune in **eleven** times each week for their **"ego fix"!**

Okay, Anne, the wheel landed on **$150.** Pick a letter. And remember the puzzle is a **famous saying.** Maybe not famous to **you** or the **audience,** but **certainly** famous to **us!**

I'd like an **"N,"** Pat.

Yes, there is an **"N"!** Spin again!

WE'LL MAKE A FORTUNE

Hi, I'm **Pat Somejerk**, host of **We'll Make A Fortune!** This is the show that **costs little** to produce, takes **little intelligence** to play, has **little** for me or my lovely co-host **Vanilla Wipe to do,** but has so many **plugs** for our sponsors' **products** that **We'll Make A Fortune!** Since our game is nothing more than a **rip-off** of the old kid's game **"Hangman,"** everyone already knows how to play, so let's get right to it!

...ke an **"L."**

There are **two** "L's" at **$300** each. That's an additional **$400!**

Two at **$300** is **$600!**

Your job is to **solve** the **puzzle, not** do the **arithmetic!**

Pok!

Do you have a guess?

No, **that's** at the portion of the show when you **pick the prizes.** What do you think the **puzzle** says?

Yeah, **I guess I'm being screwed!**

There are **no** "L's" in **"I Have No Idea!"** Spin again!

I have no idea.

SEEDED KEEP OFF

ATLANTIC CITY

ONE DAY IN THE CITY

ARTIST: DON MARTIN   WRITER: DON EDWING

RAVIN' MANIAC DEPT.

Many years ago, Edgar Allan Poe concocted a celebrated poem about a lonely creature who, for mysterious reasons, came out of nowhere to appear suddenly at weird hours. Poe called this creature "The Raven," probably the strangest bird in all of literature. Today, there's another creature who, for equally mysterious reasons, also comes out of nowhere to appear suddenly at weird hours. Meet this strangest of modern birds, as MAD presents . . .

THE

ARTIST: JACK DA

Once upon a morning dreary,
half awake and eyesight bleary,
While I fetched the "Daily Herald"
lying there outside my door,
As I stood there, stretching, yawning,
Wond'ring what the day was spawning,
Came a figure through the dawning,
fiercely running as to war;
"Who is this," I asked myself, "who
runs as if he's off to war?"
"Just a loony, nothing more."

I could see his Pro-Keds clearly,
and his perspiration nearly
Soaked right through the cotton sweatshirt
and the running shorts he wore;
Shorter breaths he now was taking,
And from grunts that he was making,
I felt sure he must be aching
from the labors of his chore;
"Does your body ache," I asked, "each
time that you perform this chore?"
Quoth the Jogger, "Ev'ry pore!"

JOGGER

WRITER: FRANK JACOBS

WITH APOLOGIES TO EDGAR ALLAN POE

Striding down the street, he ran there,
  trotting past each parked sedan there,
Till the air was filled with gasps that
  I had not heard heretofore;
    Soon I knew as he came closer,
    He was not a loony, no sir,
    Or some early-rising grocer
      racing toward some distant store;
"You're a Jogger," I exclaimed, "and
  not some grocer with a store!"
    Quoth the Jogger, "To the core!"

Round the block he now was veering,
  then quite soon was reappearing,
Battered, scarred and bleeding in a
  state most people would deplore;
    Ev'ry garment he was wearing
    Now was either ripped or tearing;
    Furthermore, his legs were bearing
      signs of toothmarks by the score;
"What on earth," I asked, "has caused these
  signs of toothmarks by the score?"
    Quoth the Jogger, "Dogs galore!"

Suddenly, it started raining,
  and I thought he'd be complaining
of conditions unforeseen that
    Mother Nature had in store;
    Drenched with rain, he soon was dripping,
    And sometimes he lost his gripping
    Causing him to wind up slipping
      on the pavement bruised and sore;
"Give it up," I pleaded, as he
  lay there gasping, bruised and sore;
    Quoth the Jogger, "Let it pour!"

On and on, he did continue,
  straining ev'ry bone and sinew,
Round the block and back again
    until each passing was a bore;
    "Hey," I asked him, "aren't you done now?
    "Surely this can't be much fun now;
    "Fifteen miles or more you've run now
      since I've been here, keeping score:
'Isn't that enough?" I uttered,
  as I stood there, keeping score;
    Quoth the Jogger, "Just one more!"

Then it was that I did see there
  just how old he seemed to be there;
Ancient was his weathered face with
    wrinkles I could not ignore;
    Years of running so insanely
    Made him look much older, plainly,
    Than his age, which I felt mainly
      must be fifty-five or more;
"What's your age?" I asked, expecting
  he'd say fifty-five or more;
    Quoth the Jogger, "Twenty-four!"

ONE AFTERNOON DOWNTOWN ON MAIN STREET

What's happening in Nursery Rhyme Land? The same as what's happening in the entire U.S.A. There's no gas, no heating oil, and Tom, Tom the Piper's Son is running . . . just to keep warm! Yes, that's the way it is in Nursery Rhyme Land, and that's the way we write ridiculous introductions to ridiculous articles such as this, namely:

MAD'S ENERGY CRISIS MOTHER GOOSE

ARTIST: PAUL COKER
WRITER: FRANK JACOBS

Little Miss Muffet

Little Miss Muffet
Turns blue on her tuffet
Because it has dropped below freezing;
Little Jack Horner
Curls up in his corner;
For weeks he's been coughing and sneezing;
Old Mother Hubbard
Has ripped up her cupboard
And burned it, which isn't surprising;
There's simply no way
That these poor folks can pay
As their fuel costs are steadily rising.

Hickory, Dickory, Dock

Hickory, dickory, dock!
There isn't a car on the block;
    The pumps are closed down
    Ev'rywhere in the town
Till next Monday at seven o'clock.

Hickory, dickory, day!
The sky isn't smoggy or gray;
    The air's fresh and clear;
    We can breathe without fear;
Could it be life is better this way?

The Car-Makers Say

The car-makers say
That their models today
Guzzle gas in amounts most excessive
   Rich Arabs conclude
   That their prices of crude
Must be lowered because they're repressive;
   Big oil-men state
   That their profits of late
Are so great that they're clearly a crime;
   If any poor sap
   Really falls for this crap,
He'll believe any nursery rhyme!

Peter, Peter, Pumpkin Eater

Peter, Peter, pumpkin eater,
Bought a new electric heater,
Plugged it in his pumpkin shell,
Hoped that it would warm him well.

Peter used it just one night,
Blew out fuses left and right,
Said, "Some changes are required;"
Paid to have his shell re-wired.

Peter's heater worked, but then
Late that night conked out again;
In the dark, there was no doubt
That the city was blacked out.

Peter's shell is now for sale;
He's moved to Fort Lauderdale,
Shacked up, if the tale is true,
With the Woman in the Shoe.

As I Was Going To St. Ives

As I was going to St. Ives,
I saw four people taking drives,
And every car ran out of gas
And blocked six vans that tried to pass;
And every van was likewise stuck
And blocked eight buses and a truck,
And each of them blocked nine MG's,
And they, in turn, blocked ten Capris.

How many drivers got screaming mad and went berserk,
resulting in fist-fights, pummelling, 15 serious
injuries, and one homicide on the road to St. Ives?

Freddie Siphons Gas Tanks

Freddie siphons gasoline;
   Mike hits tanker trucks;
Charlie bootlegs heating oil;
   All are in the bucks.

Freddie, Mike and Charlie
   May come off as slobs;
Still, in this economy,
   It's nice that they've found jobs.

Jack Be Nimble

Jack be nimble, Jack be quick,
Jack jump into the oil slick;
Jack fill bucket, Jack not stop,
Jack now icky and smeared with glop;
Jack not caring, Jack not pay,
Jack now heating his house this way.

Little Boy Blue

Little Boy Blue,
    You knuckle-head!
Your sheep's glowing purple;
    Your cow just dropped dead!

Little Boy Blue,
    When will you see
That Three Mile Island
    Is no place to be?

Harry Has a Row of Pumps

Harry has a row of pumps
And sells us gasoline;
    He's most polite,
    And day and night
He keeps his restrooms clean.

Harry hands out trading stamps
And highway maps and such;
    He checks the air
    In ev'ry spare
And says, "Thanks very much."

Harry isn't run by greed;
His profit isn't large;
    Most folks declare
    He's very fair
And doesn't over-charge.

Harry seems a super guy
Who treats the people great;
    Alas, alack,
    This poem dates back
To nineteen sixty-eight.

Exxon, Mobil, Gulf and Shell

Exxon, Mobil, Gulf and Shell
Tell us they've less gas to sell;
Claim they're victims of a squeeze,
Caused by Arabs overseas;
Hope that we will understand
Why there's panic through the land;
With a story sad to tell
Are Exxon, Mobil, Gulf and Shell.

Exxon, Mobil, Gulf and Shell—
We have heard the tale you tell;
Seen the tankers off the shore;
Seen your storage tanks galore;
Seen gas prices swiftly rise;
Seen your profits reach the skies;
Won't you please go straight to hell
Dear Exxon, Mobil, Gulf and Shell?

ONE DAY ON A DESERT ISLAND

ANOTHER DAY ON A DESERT ISLAND

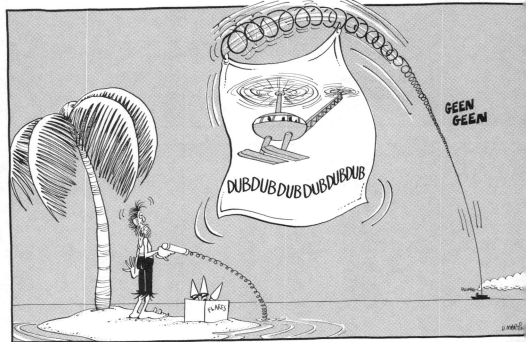

THE LAST DAY ON A DESERT ISLAND

Every day there seems to be another newspaper story dealing with the energy crisis. And every day we get more confused trying to figure out what's happen... and how we're supposed to deal with it. Well, the...

MAD'S ALL-INCLUSI

ENERGY CRISIS NEWSPAPER STORY

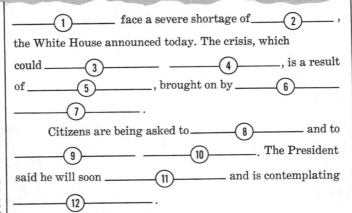

P) — The
at an an-
he final
showing
dicated,

ational
ation's
r infla-
ated at
will be

ent's re-
nal prod-
easured
vas 8.7
e same
wth of
so was
ort.

.N.P. in
was at-
tment,
adjust-
higher-
accord-

_____ ① _____ face a severe shortage of _____ ② _____ ,

the White House announced today. The crisis, which

could _____ ③ _____ _____ ④ _____ , is a result

of _____ ⑤ _____ , brought on by _____ ⑥ _____

_____ ⑦ _____ .

Citizens are being asked to _____ ⑧ _____ and to

_____ ⑨ _____ _____ ⑩ _____ . The President

said he will soon _____ ⑪ _____ and is contemplating

_____ ⑫ _____ .

WAS...
United...
nual ra...
quarte...
than e...
the Gov...
The...
prod...
good...
tion...
1.4 pe...
made ne...
The...
vised re...
uct sho...
by the...
perce...
as init...
2.3 per...
uncha...
Busi...
Th...
the f...
tribu...
which...
ment fo...
than or...
ing to...

WRITER: FRANK JACOBS

7.

in the Middle East
in Iran
in Congress
in the War of 1812
on Three Mile Island
in Studio 54
on the street where you live
in "Airport '79"
in Jerry Brown's camper
on the yellow brick road
at the Indy 500
on public television

8.

use mass transit
phone Prince Faud
die early
build their own reactors
read the 23rd Psalm
travel by ricksha
sleep with their clothes on
reincarnate as sparrows
avoid sex
free their slaves
tie up their children
buy Ethiopian

9.

drive
fill up
bathe
run naked
breathe
evacuate
get stoned
walk their clones
phone Grandma
crawl on all fours
wander lonely as a cloud
conceive

o need to wade through long articles any more, because
4AD is now, once and for all, wrapping up the entire

energy mess. Simply fill in the numbered blanks from
the corresponding numbered lists, and you'll have . . .

E DO-IT-YOURSELF

1.

Motorists
Home-owners
Balloonists
Geminis
Mouth-breathers
Whigs
Gay doormen
Sinus sufferers
All states but Georgia
Unwed furriers
Dwarfs
Ted and Linda Feingold

2.

gasoline
heating oil
cocaine
warm Dr. Pepper
leadership
energized gravel
see-through dickeys
non-stick bubblegum
calcium
effective deodorants
soy sauce
good news

3.

close down
bankrupt
put the screws to
take the fun out of
clean up
blow the lid off
end diplomatic relations with
unionize
give the Mafia control of
bring back vaudeville to
stop those whispers about
inspire a TV series about

4.

service stations
the West Coast
the Alaskan Pipeline
scenic lookouts
Krypton
Warren Beatty's fun room
Middle Earth
six stamp clubs in Wichita
Boys Town
Al's Pizzeria
Monday Night Football
The King Tut Exhibition

5.

reduced imports
Arab greed
gas-guzzling Mopeds
the Susan B. Anthony dollar
powerful trolls
careful planning
"Tip" O'Neill's biorhythms
the Scarsdale Diet
Miss Piggy's nose-job
the Great Depression
rolling double sixes
man's inhumanity to man

6.

anti-American feeling
lack of refineries
sloppy drilling
longer coffee breaks
smelly truckers
a Darth Vader look-alike
an obscene phone-call
a savage game of "Go Fish"
the sky falling
the ghost of Howard Hughes
enraged shepherds
Werner Erhard showing up

10.

only when necessary
in groups of five
during reruns of "Benson"
at 55 miles an hour
when Mars squares Saturn
with a trained squirrel
only on Arbor Day
with Howard Baker
during "60 Minutes"
uring months having an "R"
at reduced temperatures
when it's Miller Time

11.

address the nation
set up guidelines
tear up his Exxon card
close Utah
resort to groveling
burn whale blubber
back Teddy Kennedy
convert to buffalo chips
become a Moslem
be nicer to Mondale's niece
admit he is a droid
have his teeth bronzed

12.

gas rationing
resigning
his navel
the return of the horse
suicide
unleashing Billy
traveling by Greyhound
renting out Camp David
pardoning Schlesinger
out-of-body travel
a roller-disco in the Oval Office
living under an assumed name

DON MARTIN LOOKS AT SP[

DER-MAN

KLOMP

ZIT ZIT ZIZIZIZ ZZZZZ

THUD

Raid
KILLS SPIDERS

N'T TRAP

ROACH PILL

ROACH-PILL

, slow
w! It's
tting
mpy!!

Relax!
We're
almost
there!

BUNKY

ACE
WINDOW
CLEANERS

WHIR
IR

WHIR
WHIR

WET PAINT

THUD

One of the newest and fastest-rising sports here in the United States is also one of the oldest and most popular sports in just about every other country in the world. We're referring, of course, to Soccer. Those of you who are familiar with Soccer might as well skip this article . . . because there is nothing in it you don't know! Those of you who are unfamiliar with Soccer might as well skip it, too . . . because there is nothing in it you'll *want* to know! Which leaves us and the Printer to enjoy . . .

THE MAD SOCCER PRIMER

ARTIST: JACK DAVIS
WRITER: LARRY SIEGEL

Chapter One

See the men in the funny short pants.
What are they doing?
They are playing a game called Soccer.
It is the most popular game in the world.
What is the foremost rule of Soccer?
That you may kick the ball . . .
Or hit it with your head . . .
But you may never touch it with your hands.
What was potentially the greatest Soccer Team
In sports history?
Probably the 1979 New York Mets.

Chapter Two

What is the primary idea of Soccer?
To get the ball into your opponent's goal.
How will these men move the ball
Down the very, very large Soccer Field?
Perhaps by dribbling it with their feet.
How else will they move the ball?
Perhaps by passing it with kicks.
When do you think one team will get the ball
Close enough to take a shot at the other goal?
Perhaps by next Thursday.

Chapter Three

Soccer is considered to be
The fastest-growing sport in the United States.
Here we see two typical American Soccer Teams in action.
There are eleven men on a side in Soccer.
How can we tell that these 22 players
Make up two typical American Soccer Teams?
Because on the field, this is what we see . . .
(And suppose, instead of saying it,
We sing it . . .)

Six Germans running,
Five Ar-gen-tines.
Four Spanish Backs,
Three French men,
Two Turkish Wings,
And a pair o-of Polish Goal-ies!
How come there are no Canadians playing American Soccer
Because they are busy in Chicago and Boston and Detroit
Playing American Hockey!

Chapter Four

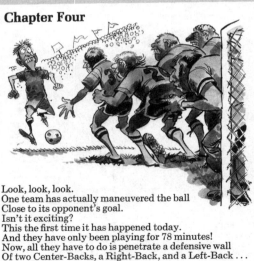

Look, look, look.
One team has actually maneuvered the ball
Close to its opponent's goal.
Isn't it exciting?
This the first time it has happened today.
And they have only been playing for 78 minutes!
Now, all they have to do is penetrate a defensive wall
Of two Center-Backs, a Right-Back, and a Left-Back . . .
Not to mention the Goalie . . .
And they might get a shot at the goal.
What are the chances of scoring in Soccer?
About the same as Truman Capote's chances of scoring
At the office Christmas Party of Cosmopolitan Magazine.

Chapter Five

As we have said before,
In Soccer, you may kick the ball
Or hit it with your head . . .
But no one must ever touch it with his hands.
Except the Goalie!
The Goalie follows his own set of rules.
He can kick the ball, and head the ball,
And punch the ball, and sit on the ball,
And catch the ball, and throw the ball.
He can do anything he wants at all times!
He even wears a different-colored jersey
Than his team-mates.
The Goalie is a very important and powerful person.
What will this Goalie do when he retires from Soccer?
Either become the Dictator of a South American count
Or Chairman of OPEC.

Chapter Six

See the crowd watching an American Soccer game.
A Soccer crowd is a lot like the United Nations.
Why is that?
Because it is comprised of people
Of all different nationalities?
Partly . . .
But also because they make a lot of noise
And they usually accomplish nothing.
South Americans are fascinated
By the teamwork in Soccer.
Europeans are fascinated
By its finesse.
Asians are fascinated
By its competitive spirit.
Why are Americans fascinated by Soccer?
Because they want to see for themselves
If it's true that Soccer
Is the only sport ever created
That is more boring than Baseball.

Chapter Seven

See the angry Soccer fans.
They take the game very seriously
And they have very short tempers.
Look, look, look.
The stands have gone berserk.
The Italian fans are beating up on the British fans.
The Brazilian fans are belting the Portuguese fans.
The Indonesian fans are pounding the Egyptian fans.
Isn't this dreadful? !
Isn't it inexcusable? !
It sure is! !
Don't they realize that
Because of this terrible racket they're making,
They just woke up the American fans? !

Chapter Eight

Soccer is a very strenuous game.
Play very rarely stops.
The only one who calls time is the Referee.
And only if there is serious injury on the field.
Look at the player
Lying motionless in a crumpled heap.
He was killed by angry fans
Who are rooting for the other team.
Why doesn't the Referee call "time"?
Because, compared to what Soccer fans
Usually do to rival players,
Death is not considered a serious injury.

Chapter Nine

Soccer is a very democratic sport.
Almost anybody can play it.
Weight and height are unimportant.
See that 14-year-old boy?
He is only 4-feet, 11 inches tall.
He doesn't have to grow up to be 7 feet tall
So he can look like Bill Walton
And play Professional Basketball.
Instead, he can grow up to be only 5 feet 8 inches tall
And look like Pelé
And play Professional Soccer.
But supposing he doesn't grow up at all! ?
That's okay, too.
He can always look like Paul Williams
And write songs.
Come to think of it,
Who needs Soccer? ! ?

Recently, there was a horror film that made the rounds which had as its advertising slogan, "FOR GOD'S SAKE, GET OUT!" Well, not until millions of moviegoers had paid their admissions fees did they realize that it was a warning to the audience—to GET OUT OF THE THEATER before this "horror" unfolded on the screen! But the warning had come too late to save both their money, and them from suffering through

THE CALAMITYVILLE HORROR

ARTIST: MORT DRUCKER   WRITER: DICK DE BARTOLO

What do you mean, it was a burglar?!? The door was broken OUT... from the INSIDE! A burglar breaks IN! Not OUT!

Maybe it was his first job, and he was confused! What IS strange, though, is that everything happens in this house at exactly 3:15 on your bedroom clock!

That's not so strange! Our bedroom clock is broken! It ALWAYS says 3:15!

Your business partner's new house gives me the creeps! Let's go inside!

But I thought you said it gives you the creeps!

It DOES!! I love having the creeps!

Hi! Come on in—and make yourselves at home!

Thanks! I'll just go down the cellar!

The cellar?!

Yeah! That's where I'm at home!!

This ALL is here the demons go back and forth night!

Hey! What are you going to do!?

I'm gonna put in a revolving door! Maybe then those demons will make less noise, and let us get some sleep at night!

Gored, let's rent an apartment!

I don't want to live in an apartment!

Not for us, dummy! For the GHOSTS! I want to move to where there's sunshine and blue sky!

Where? Florida?

No, across the street!!

Good Lord... the windows are breaking... and the wallpaper is oozing puss... and the stairs are bleeding...!!

We shouldn't have taken a MORTGAGE on this place! We should have taken a MAJOR MEDICAL POLICY on it! Let's get out of here... for good!

'mon, Nipper, we're all aving! Hey, Nipper... NOW I'm covered with ack gook, but it's ME!

Schmuck, I know it's you!! Why do you think I'm biting you?!

I'd rather stay here with the GHOSTS! They're a lot saner than OUR family is!

The Klutzs left their house and never went back for their personal belongings. They didn't have to! With the million bucks they've made from the book ... and a few million more from the movie ... why would they want any of that old junk, anyway?!

RE-BY-FEATURE
ERTISING

ARTIST: BOB CLARKE   **WRITER: DICK DEBARTOLO**

ᴴᴱᴿᴱ ᵗ ᴵˢ! THE ACME CALENDAR

ITE IN A DATE WITH MADONNA OR SPRINGSTEEN! WRITE IN A TRIP TO EUROPE!
VRITE IN A DATE FOR AN EXPENSIVE DINNER!

THE CHAIRMAN OF GENERAL MOTORS couldn't run his business effectively unless he knew what day it was. Why not give yourself the very same advantage?

EVERY MONTH OF THE YEAR INCLUDED! Three for the winter, three for the spring, three for the summer and yes, even three for the fall!

DAYS OF THE WEEK are sensibly arranged in the way you've come to know by heart—Sunday, Monday, Tuesday, Wednesday, Thursday, Friday and Saturday too!

SAY GOOD-BYE TO SILLY POEMS! Know for yourself which months have 30 days and which have 31. All this hard work has been done for you!

NO MORE CONFUSION! Get the day, week and month right every time with consecutively numbered dates!

FILL IN AS MANY DATES AS YOU WANT! Be a social whirl and fill in all 365 days with something to do. Or just be a homebody and fill in one or two a month. This calendar lets you decide how to run your life!

IT'S HERE! THE ULTIMATE SANITARY DRINKING DEVICE...
SANI-STRAW!

NOW YOU CAN SIP ANYTHING
from tap water in a plastic cup to
champagne in a glass slipper!

**THE PRESIDENT OF THE U.S.A.,
THE POPE AND EVEN KINGS**
of foreign countries have savored
beverages from one of these
handy devices!

SPECIAL ROUNDED EDGE will
never catch on your mouth! Whether
you have large pouty lips or pencil thin
lips, Sani-straw molds itself to your
personal contours!

LIGHTWEIGHT PLASTIC, the
very kind important switches and
buttons found on 747's and fighter
planes are often made from, is used for
strength and durability.

CUSTOMIZED CARRYING CASE
included with each purchase, every
one fitted like the finest glove.

ONE SIZE FITS ALL!

THE COCKAMAMIE CONGO COOKOUT

ARTIST AND WRITER: DUCK EDWING

LAST WEEK IN A FREENSVILLE DINER

ARE YOU HAPPY NOW . . .

. . . that you finally got your kid to take up the violin . . . and he loves it so much, he won't stop playing it?

ARE YOU HAPPY NOW . . .

. . . that you got your boyfriend to see a shrink about his problem . . . and the solution is that he should dump you?

ARE YOU HAPPY NOW . . .

. . . that you finally got your Boss to give you a big job with "more responsibility" . . . and you can't handle it

ARE YOU HAPPY NOW . . .

. . . that you nagged your daughter into ditching the goon she was dating . . . and she's going with an even bigger schmuck?

BACKFIRE-CRACKERS DEPT.

ARE
HAPPY

ARTIST: PAUL COKE

ARE YOU HAPPY NOW . . .

. . . that the Superstar your team paid half a million, to win the pennant, has finally united the team—against him?

ARE YOU HAPPY NOW . . .

. . . that you got your agnostic kid to "take a look at religion" . . . and he's become a fanatic in some weird cult?

ARE YOU HAPPY NOW . . .

. . . that you've worked hard and finally amassed all the money you'll ever need . . . and you're too old to enjoy

ARE YOU HAPPY NOW . . .

. . . that you succeeded in losing those 40 pounds . . . and replacing your entire wardrobe is gonna cost you four grand?

ARE YOU HAPPY NOW . . .

. . . that the political party you hate has been voted out . . . and the winner you supported is doubling your taxes?

ARE YOU HAPPY NOW . . .

. . . that you finally made a small profit on that stock you held for years . . . and inflation has wiped out the gain?

YOU NOW...?

WRITER: FRANK JACOBS

ARE YOU HAPPY NOW . . .

. . . that you've finally turned 18, and you're allowed to see those "X-Rated" movies . . . and you find them a big bore?

ARE YOU HAPPY NOW . . .

. . . that you've managed to keep all our New Year's resolutions . . . and fe for you has become a total bore?

ARE YOU HAPPY NOW . . .

. . . that you persuaded your Wife to join a "Swinging Couples" group . . . and she loves it . . . and you don't?

ARE YOU HAPPY NOW . . .

. . . that you finally got the nerve to move out of your parents' house . . . and your roommate is even more of a nag?

Everybody loves television programs about Cops and Robbers ... but there
a popular TV program on the air that has us worried! It's about Cops th
ARE Robbers! Well, maybe not exactly ... but it does show people in char

THE DOPES OF

HERE WE GO WITH ANOTHER STORY ABOUT THEM DOPE BOYS OF HAPHAZZARD COUNTY! TONIGHT
EPISODE SHOULD GO DOWN ABOUT AS SMOOTH AS A JUG OF BLACK STRAP MOLASSES ... AND HA
THE SAME EFFECT: MAINLY, IT'S GONNA MAKE YOU SICK TO YOUR STOMACH! IN CASE YOU'
NOT FAMILIAR WITH THE FOLKS OF HAPHAZZARD COUNTY, YOU'RE LUCKIER THAN A PIG THA
OWNED BY A KOSHER FARMER! BUT, FOR THE SAKE OF THE STORY, LET ME INTRODUCE THEM .

THAT'S BOSS SLOB! HE
OWNS THE TOWN! HE'S
DECEITFUL, DISHONEST,
A CROOK, A CHEAT AND
A CON ARTIST! HE'S
ALSO A POLITICIAN ...
BUT THAT'S REDUNDANT!

THE FELLOW TALKING TO BOSS
SLOB IS SHERIFF BOSCO G.
GOLDRAIN! THE SHERIFF IS A
BUMBLING IDIOT LAW OFFICER!
F'RINSTANCE, SLOB TOLD HIM
TO POLISH UP HIS GUN ... AN'
THAT'S JUST WHAT HE'S DOING!

THE OTHER GUY'S THE SHERIF
ASSISTANT, ANUS! HE ASSIS
THE SHERIFF IN BEING A TOT
SCREW-UP! BUT HE'S SMART
THAN THE STUPID SHERIFF! H
NOT DUMB ENOUGH TO BE USI
SHOE POLISH TO SHINE HIS GL

ARTIST: ANGELO TO

tealing, and citizens breaking all kinds of laws and getting away with it! After all, television should really entertain us! It shouldn't force us to ace what we see all around us in everyday life! Yep, we're talking about

HAPHAZZARD

"KE THE EXOTIC DANCER SAID WHEN SHE TOOK OFF THE FIRST FLIMSY LAYER OF CLOTHES . . . FOLKS, YOU AIN'T SEEN NUTHIN' YET!" NOW LET'S MEET THE MEMBERS OF THE DOPE FAMILY!

HAT'S LOVEABLE LD UNCLE JAZZY! E'S SO OLD AND OVEABLE THAT, OMETIMES, YOU EALLY WANT TO UST SQUEEZE HIM . . TIGHT AROUND IS NECK, WITH OUR BARE HANDS!

THAT'S DIZZY DOPE! SHE'S NOT A GOOD-ENOUGH ACTRESS TO APPEAR IN FEATURE-LENGTH MOVIES, SO THEY PUT HER IN SHORTS . . . SHORTS THAT ARE CUT RIGHT UP TO THE NETWORK CENSOR'S LIMITS!

AND STANDING IN FRONT OF THAT TREE IS ME! WELL, YOU DON'T SEE ME IN THE REAL TV VERSION, EITHER! I'M WHAT YOU CALL THE NARRATOR!

NOW IT'S TIME TO MEET THE DOPE BOYS, BOO AND PUKE! AS USUAL, THEY'RE DRIVING THEIR SOUPED-UP CAR DOWN SOME DESERTED RURAL HIGHWAY FASTER THAN A GREASED RATTLE-SNAKE GOING DOWNHILL ON AN ICY ROAD WITH AN 80-MILE WIND AT ITS BACK!

know, Dizzy, you're a g girl, now! It's about e I talked to you about e birds and the bees!

That's really GREAT, Uncle Jazzy! I'm just so sick and tired of hearing the boys talk to me about SEX!!

We're really movin, Puke! I'm doin' 60 miles an hour . . . !

Ahhh, 60 miles an hour ain't so fast!

Inside a Church . . . on a Sunday?

HOOOOOOBOY!! You're right!! That IS fast!!

Not so LOUD, Puke! We don't want to disturb the folks while they're praying . . . !!

ER: DICK DE BARTOLO

g on, Bob! I'm doing ne of our fantastic ying leaps! Up this mp, and over the top f that railroad train!

Pretty good, huh? We didn't hit a THING!!

Oh, yes, we DID!!

Boo, we missed the top of that train by a country mile!

I know that! What we DID do was scrape the bottom of an airplane!!

Alfred E. Neuman for President

SOUTHERN

Here comes the Sheriff! He tried the same leap!!

Did he make it?

HE did . . .! But his Police Car didn't!!

OF COURSE, THE CHIEF OF THE STATE POLICE, HAVING BEEN TIPPED OFF ABOUT THE MOONSHINE, WAS CLOSE ON THE DOPE'S TAILPIPE! BUT THE BOYS HAD A PLAN TO DIVERT THE CHIEF'S CAR TILL THEY COULD DUMP THE "SHINE!" THEY USED ONE OF THE CLEVER "FAKE SIGNS" SO POPULAR IN THIS SERIES . . .

PARADE ROUTE

Well, **that'll** slow down the **Chief** of the **State Police!** But I see **Anus** and **Bosco** are following us in **two new Police Cars,** so we'll have to do some **fancy driving!**

How's that, Boo? I just drove for a whole mile on **two** wheels!!

Big deal!! I drove **40** miles on two wheels yesterday!

Yeah . . . but **YOU** were on your **MOTOR-CYCLE!!**

Hey, Boo! It just **dawned** on me! We're running from the **Chief** of **Police** of this **State** . . . but **WHAT STATE** is **Haphazzard County** supposed to be **IN?**

I **don't** know, Puke! And even if I **DID** know, I wouldn't be allowed to tell! If we claimed that **ANY** of the **50 States** would **TOLERATE** these wild goings-on, they'd **sue** our **britches** off!!

Hey, Boo! You know what we **haven't done** yet . . . ? We haven't done our famous and absolutely unbelievable **"Shoot-The-Flaming-Arrow-Out-The-Window-At-110-Mile-An-Hour-And-Hit-The-Target-Perfectly"** trick!

Hey, Boo! That was perfect!

Perfect except for one little thing!!

What's that?

I think **one** of us should have stayed at the wheel . . . !!

CRASH!

ONE AFTERNOON IN THE SOUTH SEAS

A MAD GUIDE TO...

THE DOUBLI

When you're a kid, and you insist on having things done your way, you're . . .

A SPOILED BRAT

When you're older, and you insist on having things done your way, you're . . .

A PERFECTIONIST

When you're 18, and you chase ev girl in sight, you're a young man

SOWING HIS WILD OATS

When you're in school, and you only do well in some subjects and the rest you just aren't interested in, you're . . .

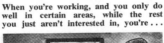

AN UNDER-ACHIEVER

When you're working, and you only do well in certain areas, while the rest you just aren't interested in, you're . . .

A SPECIALIST

When you're young, and you're alw criticizing people and pointing their faults, everyone says you're

A SMART-ALEC

When you're young, and dress and act like everyone else your age, you're . . .

ONE OF THE CROWD

When you're older, and dress and act like everyone else your age, you're . . .

A CONFORMIST

When you're young, and you ma couple of dumb mistakes, you're

IRRESPONSIBLE

STANDARDS OF AGE

ARTIST: BOB JONES   WRITER: BARRY LIEBMANN

When you're 65, and you still chase every girl in sight, you're just . . .

A DIRTY OLD MAN

When you're young, and you speak up and demand your rights, you're . . .

A PUSHY LITTLE KID

When you're older, and you speak up and demand your rights, you're . . .

A SELF-ASSERTIVE PERSON

When you're older, and you're always criticizing people and pointing out their faults, everyone says you're . . .

TELLING IT LIKE IT IS

When you're a high school student and you like to read comic books, and you love to watch trashy movies, you're . . .

A TASTELESS ILLITERATE

When you're a grown-up, and you still like to read comic books and you still love to watch trashy movies, you're . . .

A NOSTALGIA BUFF

When you're older, and you make a couple of dumb mistakes, you're . . .

JUST BEING HUMAN

When you're young, and you lie, cheat and steal, your parents brand you as . . .

INCORRIGIBLE

When you're older, and you still lie, cheat and steal, you're known as . . .

AN AGGRESSIVE BUSINESSMAN

Are you a doormat for the whole world to step on? Do friends walk awa
while you're talking? Are you credited with inventing the yawn? Are yo
introduced to people as "Mr. What's's-Name"? Then you need help. And w
don't mean the kind of help that everyone else has offered you in th

MAD IMAGE

HIGH-CLASS BOOK COVERS

Carrying highly-intellectual books onto buses, trains and planes will make people admire and respect you. However, such books are almost impossible to read. But these book jackets slip easily over those trashy books you love and understand...and other passengers will look with awe at how absorbed you are in reading such classy literature.

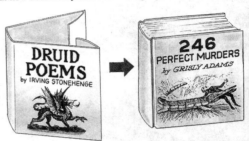

V.I.P. BUSINESS CARDS

You can make yourself into anything you want with business cards, and the people you give them to will shower you with ego-gratifying attention. Later, if they chance to call you at "your office," they'll find out the truth, but so what?! By then, you'll be working your card trick on someone else.

THE "FANTASTIC STUDENT" PLOY

If you want a really effective image booster, merely take
a course in a school subject that you're already thorough
ly expert in, without letting on that you are. The respec
and admiration you get will make you feel just marvelous

ast . . . like suggesting that you become "educated," or "talented," or more interesting." We know that's impossible for you. But there is a ractical way to make you appear terrific without changing that simple-iinded clod you've always been. Just try these sure-fire guaranteed . . .

-BUILDERS

ARTIST & WRITER: AL JAFFEE

THE "TOUGH CROSSWORD PUZZLE" GAMBIT

When sitting next to someone while traveling, tear *The New York Times* puzzle out and start filling it in very quickly with a pen. To your neighbor's astonishment, you will have it lone in less than three minutes. Then, mutter something ike, "I wish they'd come up with a real challenge for a change!" and angrily crumple it into a ball and discard it. Your fellow passenger will be unbelievably impressed, and never know you filled the puzzle in with absolute nonsense.

WRONG-WAY TWIST-OFF JAR TOPS

These jars and jar tops have left-handed threads. That is, they open the opposite way from normal. When you're going to a party, bring along one or two of these —filled with nuts or candy. Soon, some pretty young thing will try to open one and fail. Next, she'll ask some jock to try, and to everyone's amazement, he too will fall down exhausted with the unopened jar. Then, to everyone's astonishment, you open the jar effortlessly.

THE RIGGED TV GAME

Millions of TV-owners now own "Pong"-type TV games. Unfortunately, some jocks are hard to beat at these games because they do nothing but hang around bars, practicing on coin-operated ones. With this electronic cheater transmitter, you improve your image and win every time.

VIEW OF CHEATER TRANSMITTER IN POCKET.
BUTTON IS PRESSED. OPPONENT'S SIGNAL IS
LLY REVERSED, WHICH DRIVES HIM INSANE

MOBILE CAR TELEPHONE

Here's an easy way to look and feel important. Any old used telephone instrument, placed in your car, will do the trick. Merely lift receiver, and hold important-sounding business conversations while people are watching. And if you want to impress them more, a hook-up to car's cigarette lighter can make phone ring when you touch a secret switch.

FANTASTIC DISPLAY OF STRENGTH

When you offer this spring-stretcher to a jock, he cannot budge it. But when you take it, you stretch it out a mile. Secret lies in middle rubber tube, which contains a steel cable that you can release by pushing a button in handle. When stretcher is relaxed once more, cable automatically locks into position. Thus, when you hand stretcher back to the jock, he goes crazy again with shame and frustration.

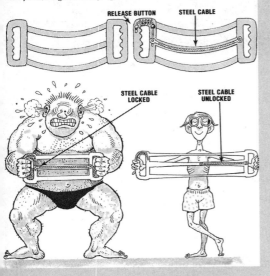

HERO AWARDS

A sure-fire way to improve your image is to be a hero. But how many of us ever get the chance to be one? And even if we got that chance, how many of us would have the courage to act? Well, with a simple, high-sounding citation, all these problems are solved, and so you become a hero instantly.

THE SPEED-READING EXHIBITION

Before boarding a bus, train or plane, read a copy of *Time* or other popular magazine thoroughly. Then, when you're on board and sitting next to a stranger, ask the Stewardess for a copy of that same magazine. Next, pretend to read it by running your finger down each page at the rate of one a second. Then, hand the magazine over to your neighbor, and recommend several articles in detail. To his (or her) utter amazement, your facts will be correct, and he will believe that you can actually read faster than is humanly possible.

FRAMED NEWSPAPER STORIES

People will believe anything they see in print, and almost any printer can produce a facsimile newspaper story for you at a nominal charge. Framed and placed in den or office, a news story about you can add immeasurably to your prestige, and no one will ever question its authenticity.

STATUS TRASH

A terrific image-builder is to let your neighbors know that you can afford the best of everything. One sure-fire way of letting those nosey creeps know is by the kind of trash you put out. By collecting an assortment of impressive cartons, and placing them outside your home on trash pick-up days, you will elevate yourself to top dog in your neighborhood.

EXOTIC LUGGAGE LABELS

A well-traveled person is always envied and admired. So no matter where you go, even if it's just to visit your Aunt May for a weekend, if you carry a heavily-labeled suitcase, people will look at you with envy and admiration.

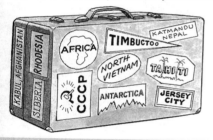

WELL-WORN SAFARI JACKET

A Safari Jacket is always associated with macho adventure. To heighten the effect, jacket should look beat up, as if wearer has been through hell in the jungles of Africa. And wearing an eyepatch will add immeasurably to your image.

PHONY "FOIL" BEER CAN

Have you ever watched some gorilla crush an empty beer can while girls look on in awe and admiration? Well...now you can show him up! After drinking from "real" can, switch it with phony "foil" can, neatly crumple phony into tiny ball and calmly toss it away. Your resultant image is fantastic.

If you could read people's minds, you'd probably be surprised to find out that what you think other folks are thinking is really not what they're thinking at all. Which is exactly what this article is all about ...namely, samples of...

THOUGH
FOR ASSORTED RE

IN A HOSPITAL OPERATING ROOM

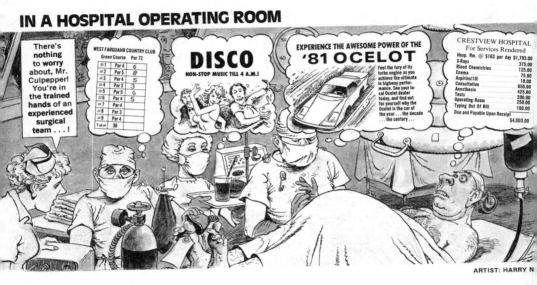

ARTIST: HARRY N

IN A COURTROOM

T PATTERNS

-LIFE EVERY-DAY SITUATIONS

IN AN ADVERTISING AGENCY

Although we've **lost** our **biggest account**, there's **no cause for alarm!** This Agency will **always** provide for its **employees**, because I believe that **faithful service** should be re- warded, in **bad times** as well as **good** . . .!

POTRZEBIE NATIONAL BANK

Sir:

Your request for a second mortgage on your house has been received. Our mortgage officer is presently review- ing your financial statement and, if satisfactory, will

GONIFF & SCHEISTER
Attorneys-At-Law

Dear Sir:

We have been instructed by our client to remind you that you are presently six months behind in your ali- mony payments, and we will soon be compelled to take legal action, including a

PETITION FOR PERSONAL BANKRUPTCY

RITER: FRANK JACOBS

AS THE EARTH MOVES
Serial

ladys and Carl plot to disinherit ark from the will as Dona suffers other nervous breakdown over er ill-fated affair with George while arcia and John contract an un- own disease while on their trip to as Vegas. Meanwhile, Arnold loses

```
                NORTH
                ♠ 74
                ♡ Q7543
                ♢ 983
                ♣ AQ6
    WEST                    EAST
    ♠ QJ952                 ♠ K1083
    ♡ J82                   ♡ 1096
    ♢ J2                    ♢ Q1075
    ♣ 953                   ♣ K8
                SOUTH (D)
                ♠ A6
                ♡ AK
                ♢ AK64
                ♣ J10742
```

MEN

La Grubonze

ENTRÉES

Roast Prime Rib Of Beef
Breast Of Spring Chicken
In White Wine Sauce
Succulent Spare Ribs
Roast Long Island Duckling
With Orange Sause
Filet Of Dover Sole
Alaskan King Crab Legs

A CURE FOR BALDNESS

Our revolutionary new method of hair trans- plants can give you a full, thick head of hair in only a few short months. Why be

IN BUSINESS

IN A SUBURBAN NEIGHBORHOOD

IN ROMANCE

IN SPORTS

IN CHURCH

Out in Lake Havasu City, Arizona, the London Bridge—formerly of London England—has been re-erected and now serves as a tourist attraction. In Long Beach, California, one of the world's great ocean liners, the Queen Mary, has been permanently moored, also for the benefit of tourists. And recently, a real estate firm in Missouri attempted to purchase England'

THE MAD SALE OF EX PROPERTIES, LANDMA

ARTIST: SERGIO ARAGON

THE WASHINGTON MONUMENT

DRESS UP any metropolitan area with this distinctive 555-foot high marble obelisk. Since 1885, it has dominated the Washington, D.C. skyline as a towering testimonial to both George Washington and to the ideals of honesty, integrity and selflessness which he embodied. The deterioration and ultimate disappearance of these qualities among contemporary lawmakers, however, had rendered the monument obsolete. Thus, today, it merely serves as a painful conscience-goader for American politicians.

PRICED TO SELL AT ONLY . . $17,750,000

ALCATRAZ

MAXIMUM SECURITY ATTRACTION, ANYONE? Once the "Pearl of the U.S. Penal System", Alcatraz no longer houses convicted criminals, since most felons today either go scot-free or prefer accommodations nearer their literary agents while they work on their autobiographies, etc. This "Slammer Supreme" is a one-of-a-kind property and an ideal stop for tourists in high crime areas. Included are dining facilities, cell blocks, exercise grounds, solitary confinement sections—**plus**—the world famous "big cage"...once occupied by the Birdman of Alcatraz himself.

YOURS FOR A SONG AT ONLY $7,500,000

THE WHITE HOUSE

RONALD REAGAN SLEPT HERE! But not for long, after he learned that heating and cooling costs alone for this historic barn of a home was increasing the National Debt. by 1.5% annually. So the cost-conscious Chief Executive, who set examples of frugality by first selling the Presidential Yacht, and later hiring out the Presidential Honor Band to play at weddings and bar mitzvahs on weekends, has decided that the upkeep at this Pennsylvania Ave. address is more than the U.S. can afford. The First Family has re-located in a modest but comfortable motel in Alexandria, Virginia, and the famous White House will be delivered safely to any location in the nation of your choice.

PRICE? NO WHITE-WASH HERE AT ONLY $4,250,000

istoric Victoria Station so it could be moved to Kansas City and turned nto a shopping mall. Considering our country's current balance of trade payments deficit, maybe we should take a lesson from the English and pick up some badly-needed foreign bucks by following suit and unloading some f our less-than-essential national landmarks and properties. Here, then, is

PENDABLE AMERICAN
RKS AND MONUMENTS

WRITER: DENNIS SNEE

THE SAINT LOUIS ARCH

THE CITY FATHERS of St. Louis, Missouri, hated putting this impressive landmark on the market, but after their unsuccessful court battle over trademark infringement with McDonald's Hamburger Corp., they were forced to. So why not turn St. Louis's loss into your city's gain with this bargain buy? You aren't likely to find another architectural attraction like this at any price. "You deserve a break today," and at this low, low price you're getting one!

GOLDEN OPPORTUNITY AT . $3,250,000

THE ASTRODOME

IT'LL NEVER RAIN ON YOUR PARADE—or sporting event, either —once you take delivery on this spectacular climate-controlled arena. Texans don't like being topped...and since New Orleans one-upped them by building a bigger "dome" the powers that be in Houston have elected to let their Astrodome go, and concentrate on their next "super" achievement...enclosing Texas! But in the meantime, you can close in on this unbeatable Texas-size bargain.

YOURS TODAY FOR A PALTRY............................$15,500,000

THE BOARDWALK

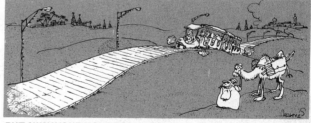

PUT AWAY YOUR MONOPOLY MONEY AND LET'S TALK DOLLARS on this famous 7-mile stretch of Atlantic City ocean-front walkway. Always synonymous with successful restaurants, stores, boutiques and other tourist diversions, why not let this famous Boardwalk do the same for your slumping business district? With the advent of legalized gambling in Atlantic City, a new breed of visitors are finding the old wooden Boardwalk ill-suited for their needs. Syndicate "Helpers" constantly require fresh cement in which to dispose of undesirable elements, and "Doorway Debutantes" find it difficult to walk a "street" in which they can catch their heels in gaps between the boards. Therefore, a new, all-concrete sidewalk will replace the famous old Boardwalk just as soon as we can find a buyer for it at our absurdly low, low asking price.

YOURS NOW FOR A BREEZY $1,350,000

THE FRANTIC FOG-FILLED FOLLY

ARTIST AND WRITER: DUCK EDWING

Ever wonder what became of the tens of thousands
of screaming rock fanatics who were part of...

woodstock 1969

Well, for one thing, they're a lot older! For another, they're now
part of that large group of Americans called **"Yuppies"** (**Y**oung **U**rban
Professionals)! What's it like when **flower children** and **protesters**
turn into **high-tech, tie-wearing, church-going, money-making
achievers?** Let's hear from the **Yuppies themselves** as Mad presents...

woodstock
revisited

ARTIST: SERGIO ARAGONES   WRITER: FRANK JACOBS

we were the world!

We were the voices!
We were the ones... who **burned the flag**
    and **led a rev-o-lu-tion;**
"Filthy punks," **they called us;**
It suited us just fine;
**But now... we're suited by Bill Blass
And Calvin Klein.**

Once our hair was **long,** and **blowin'** free and **wild;**
Now we **pay thir-ty bucks** to have it **set** and **styled;**
Hell, hell, hell—**once** we used to **march...go stormin'**
    down the street
Now **"The...Establishment's"** real **neat!**
Yeah! Yeah! Yeah! Yeah!

we were the world!

We were the spirit!
We were the ones... who **screamed for "Peace"**
    and **hollered, "Screw the System!"**
All the dreams **we fought for—**
They never came about,
Be-cause... some-where **along the line
We all sold out.**

There was a **time**…that we **barely can recall**
When we **flipped out** at that **great Wood-stock Fair**;
    Though you're **sure** to **won-der**
    When you look at us today,
If…**we**…**were**…**real-ly**…**ev-er**…there.

Those days are **gone**…and we've **found a brand-new cause**;
Now it's **big bucks** that we **groove, yes-sir-ee!**
    With our **wives** we're **talk-in'**
    Stocks and bonds and pension plans—
What's…**more**—**we**…**dig**…**the**…**G**…**O**…**P**

we were the world!

We were the children!
We were the ones…who **told off cops**
    and **crooked pol-i-ti-cians**;
But those **kicks**…**we**…**got**…**then**
Are nothin' like the thrill
We get…from braggin' **what we paid**
For our Seville.

Once we'd **turn on**, and get **mellow** from the **high**,
But the **glow** is **for-got-ten** and gone;
Today…we **turn on**…whatever's on **TV**;
Ain't no grass—**ex-cept**…what's…on…our…**lawn**.

THE DEMONIC DETECTOR DISASTER

ARTIST & WRITER: DUCK EDWING

EARLY ONE MORNING IN A HOTEL ROOM

All along U.S. highways, there are roadside plaques and historical mar[...] that provide information to tourists about local phenomenon. Most moto[...]

ROADSIDE

...THAT WE N
AROUND TO

ARTIST: JACK RICKARD   WRITER: FRANK JA[...]

RATTLER HILL

THIS HILL GETS ITS NAME FROM THE LARGE NUMBER OF RATTLESNAKES THAT ARE FOUND HERE. SINCE 1930, AN AVERAGE OF 92 PEOPLE A YEAR HAVE BEEN FATALLY BITTEN...

SAN DURANGO FAULT

YOU ARE STANDING AT THE MOST SEVERE STRESS POINT OF THE SAN DURANGO FAULT, SITE OF NUMEROUS EARTHQUAKES. OCCURRING WITH NO WARNING, QUAKES HERE OPEN UP HUGE CREVICES, WHICH SWALLOW...

PAWADAKA RIVER

THE WATERS OF THE PAWADAKA, JUST BEYOND THIS MARKER, HAVE BEEN KNOWN TO RISE IN A MATTER OF SECONDS AND FLOOD THE IMMEDIATE AREA, WASHING AWAY HOUSES, TREES, LIVESTOCK, AUTOMOBILES AND...

WEMBLEY'S GRAVE

IN 1872, OTTO WEMBLEY WAS HUNG AT THIS SITE BY VIGILANTES. JUST BEFORE HE DIED, HE VOWED THAT ANYONE SETTING FOOT NEAR HIS GRAVE WOULD BE CURSED AND SUFFER THE TORMENTS OF HORRIBLE...

BARNETT'S CURVE

NAMED FOR HORACE BARNETT, THE FIRST MOTORIST TO CRASH HERE, BARNETT'S CURVE HAS BEEN THE SITE OF MORE THAN 500 AUTO ACCIDENTS, WITH TERRIFIED DRIVERS SKIDDING OUT OF CONTROL AND RAMMING...

PLAQUES

ER WAITED ISH READING

Y: W. G. WILL

WHITE GRASS PARK

THE REMARKABLE WHITE COLOR OF THE GRASS HERE IS DUE TO THE THOUSANDS OF BIRDS ROOSTING IN THE TREES OVERHEAD. DAY AND NIGHT, THEIR DROPPINGS...

GUSTY POINT

THIS LEDGE LOOKS DOWN ON GUSTY CANYON, SO NAMED BECAUSE OF THE POWERFUL UPDRAFT, WHICH HAS BEEN KNOWN TO SUCK UP ANY OBJECT OR PERSON UNLUCKY ENOUGH TO...

TEETERING ROCK

ALTHOUGH THIS 400-TON BOULDER IS CONSIDERED A WONDER OF NATURE, SCIENTISTS BELIEVE IT WILL SOON TOPPLE, AS THE SLIGHTEST SOUND OR VIBRATION WOULD BE ENOUGH TO...

GIANT FOOTPRINT

AT THIS SITE IN 1958 WAS DIS-COVERED THE FIRST MAMMOTH FOOTPRINT OF THE DETESTABLE SLEETMAN. THE DISCOVERY MAY HELP EXPLAIN THE 27 UNSOLVED STRANGLINGS THAT HAVE OCCURRED HERE, BAFFLING AUTHORITIES...

PLOTKIN'S PEAK

THIS MARKER AT THE FOOT OF PLOTKIN'S PEAK IS THE 11TH PLACED HERE SINCE 1975. THE PREVIOUS ONES WERE ALL BURIED BY AVALANCHES, SWEEPING DOWN SUDDENLY FROM THE MOUNTAIN...

A SWORDED TALE DEPT.

One of the best known of the famous legends is the story of King Arthur and the Knights Of The Round Table. Someday, someone is going to make a comprehendible, exciting movie based on this theme. Until that happens, we will just have to be satisfied with—

DON MARTIN'S
VERSION OF A MOVIE OF E

ARTIST: DON MAR

FERR

ECCHCALIBER

R: LARRY SIEGEL

Ardor . . . your **first duty** as **King** will be to Knight this man for **bravery** in battle!

Can't they get someone else? I can't seem to get the **hang** of this "**King**" business!

You must **try, Sire!**

Oh, very well! Here goes . . .

I dub thee . . . Sir—

OOOOPS!

Sir OOOPS?!? I—I **think** you have that **wrong!** His name is **Sir Fingbum—**

Yecch! I—ulp I see what you **mean!**

Practice, Sire! You must **practice!**

SKUTCH

Look, Mervyn . . .! There is the beautiful **Lady Grin'nleer!** I must take her for my **Bride!** What **magic** do you have that could **make her fall madly in love** with me?

Let me think! **Ahh!** Suppose I change you into a frog, Sire! **Then,** when she **kisses** you, you will be transformed into a **handsome Prince,** and—

A handsome **PRINCE?!** You **idiot!** I'm **ALREADY** a handsome **KING!**

Lady Grin'nleer . . . I have **loved** you since I **first saw** you, and I **want** you to **marry** me! Before you give me your **answer,** remember this! The **new Constitution of Medieval England** decrees that **anyone** who **disobeys** the **King** shall be **tossed** into a **fiery abyss** where he—**or she**—shall be **devoured** by **snakes** and **dragons** . . . and what remains of her **entrails** thrown to **wild dogs!**

Can I **think** about it?

Why not? It's a **free country!**

See? I didn't **need** your magic, Mervyn! I simply told her that if she **didn't marry** me, she'd be **eaten** by **snakes** and **dragons** . . . and she said "**yes**" happily!

I suppose when it comes to **affairs of the heart, SWEET TALK** will **do** it every time!

Sire, I have **always wanted** to serve a **good King** who is **vulnerable,** who **truly needs** his Subject's help! And . . . **frankly** . . . you're the most **helpless** man I've **ever** met!

Good! I will dub you **Sir Lungealot,** and you will join my **Royal Court!** You are **gallant, noble, kind** . . . and you have a **fine head** on your shoulders!!

Not for long if **YOU** Knight me!

SPY vs SPY

Many years ago, in Charles Dickens' "A Christmas Carol," Scrooge was visited by ghosts who frightened him into examining his life and changing his ways. Well, this year at Christmas time, we feel it's appropriate for another colorful character to reflect back on his deeds and see whether he is truly behaving in the spirit all his TV fans have come to expect of him. So join us now as we visit:

"STARCHIE BONKER'S PLACE"
OR
A CHRISTMAS CAROL O'CONNER

ARTIST: MORT DRUCKER   WRITER: ARNIE KOGEN

I—I can't believe it! He's buying Japanese oys . . . and wishing e a Happy hanukah!!

Is that Starchie Bonker— or has Grandpa Walton moved to Queens?!?

Since **Gorier** and **Mite** left an' **Edict** died an' the **format** changed, ol' **Starch** ain't the same!

He's become a regular **Marie Osmond** in **overalls** . . .!!

That's not Starchie . . . the racist we all knew and loved!!

That's not the same Starchie who told me that I was **LUCKY** . . . because at least "Blind was better than Black!"

He's giving **bigotry** a **bad name**— especially now—at **Christmas** time!!

Harried, give me a **scotch!!**

Doin' some **Christmas celebrating**, Vernica . . . ??

No, I wanna **drown my sorrows** and **forget** what a **brilliant career move** I made . . . joining a **hit series** four years after it's **peaked!**

ey, that was quite Christmas dinner ere . . . turkey an' tuffin' an' mince ! You know what gonna do **now??**

t out a **belch?!?**

Nahh, I don't do them **bodily sounds** any more! What **I AM** gonna do is go over there an' sit in my **favorite easy chair** . . .

Ooops! I keep **forgettin'!** They **donated** my **chair** to the **Smithsonian Institute** in **Washington!**

That was a **great meal** you cooked up, Mrs. Campy! Can I level with you about somethin'??

I know . . . You're going to tell me that "**we Black 'Mammys'** really know how to **cook** . . . especially **pancakes** and **fried chicken!**"

. . . if you don't have to walk five miles in the rain in the town's local parade.

. . . if they don't make you kiss those weird relatives that you only see on Thanksgiving.

. . . that the Pilgrims decide go with turkey, and not buff

. . . if there are no left-overs.

ANOTHER TURKEY DEPT.

GIVE T

. . . if you don't get stuck sitting next to your Grandmother who drools.

. . . if your spoiled-rotten little Cousins don't destroy everything of value you own.

. . . if no one pinches your cheeks and tells you how big you're gett

GIVE THANKS FOR ON THANKSGIVING

. if you don't get stuck sitting the little kiddies' table again.

. . . if your Uncle, who smokes those 10" smelly cigars, can't make it this year.

. . . if that bitter old family feud doesn't erupt at the dinner table again this year.

HANKS

ARTIST: SERGIO ARAGONES   WRITER: JOHN FICARRA

. . . if you own a dishwasher.

. if your widowed Aunt doesn't start ing over her husband who died in '61.

. . . if you remembered to stock up on stomach remedies the day before.

. . . if nothing you've eaten today is found to cause cancer in rats tomorrow.

MAD VISITS A LOC

GUN CLUB PICNIC

ARTIST: JACK DAVIS   WRITER: LARRY SIEGEL

Isn't this an exciting event?

Call me a **dreamer**, but I **still miss** those **good old fashioned** picnics where they used to have **Father and Son BASEBALL GAMES!**

That's a **nice catch** dear, but we'd have a lot **MORE to eat** if you used a **fishing pole** instead!

Last one in is **Teddy Kennedy!**

I **thought** it's supposed to be, "Last one in is a **rotten egg!**"

What do **YOU** call a guy who wants us to register our guns?!? An **OMELET?!?**

I told Ernie he needs to wear **glasses** when he goes hunting, but he thinks he's **too macho** to get a pair!

I love these **three-legged races** at our **picnics!** What's the **next event?**

A **ONE-legged race** between **six club members** who thought they were cleaning **unloaded guns!**

We **really should clean up** all this **garbage!**

Don't worry about it! In **five years** or so, it'll **break down** and help the **plants** grow!

Willie just **cannot stand ANTS** at a picnic!

I **know!** But **Black Flag** isn't **NEARLY** as **messy!**

Shut that thing off! I **don't** want you **watching** all that **violence!** Get your **B-B-gun** and go shoot some **birds!**

LATE ONE AFTERNOON ON AN INTERSTATE HIGHWAY

ISN'T IT SU

ARTIST: PAUL CO

. . . that doctors are allowed to park their cars anywhere they like so that they can make emergency house calls

. . . even though there isn't a doctor alive who makes emergency house calls.

...that the clergymen who piously nounce gambling because they fee evil to receive money that's "tai

. . . that the people who scream the loudest about crime in the streets

. . . will then encourage it by happily buying color television sets and other goodies that they know are "hot."

. . . that your electric company seriously ask you to conserve e

. . . that film directors constantly complain that they don't have enough "creative control" over their films

. . . yet when they are given creative control, they turn out turkeys like "Heaven's Gate," "1941," "Cruising," "The Shining" and "At Long Last Love."

. . . that your guidance counselo advise you to stay in school be graduates earn far more money an much better jobs than non-grad

SPICIOUS...

WRITER: BARRY LIEBMANN

. . . will eagerly sanctify it when the proceeds go to a church or synagogue.

. . . that your nosey landlord always questions you for hours when you want to bring a guest into your apartment

. . . but never bothers to question the three strange men who are moving out your furniture at two in the morning.

. . . and then, a month later, justify request for a rate increase because you're not using enough electricity.

. . . that celebrities are always up in arms about the type of malicious gossip that's printed in many fan mags

. . . yet they think nothing of writing gossipy "memoirs" that are even more malicious and spiteful than the mags.

. . . even though he makes less money than an A & P stock boy, gets laid off every time there's a budget cut and he's a COLLEGE GRADUATE!

. . . that parents who are so concerned about starving children in other countries when they're trying to get their own kids to finish eating their supper

. . . aren't quite so concerned when asked for a donation to some charity for starving children in other countries.

LITTLE-KNOWN AND RARELY DIAGNOSED MAD

"THE AIRPORT MAZE NECK CRICKS AND CORONARY PALPITATIONS"

"THE 'WHAT-THE-HELL-DO-I-NEED A-REDCAP-FOR?' MUSCLE STRAIN"

"THE PRE-FLIGHT OMENS AND APPREHENSIONS SUDDEN HIGH FEVER"

"THE 'FLIGHT-DELAYED-FOR-THE FIFTH-TIME' BODY COLLAPSE"

"THE 'HOW-THE-HECK-DOES-THAT-THING-GET-OFF-THE-GROUND!?' SHAKES"

ARTIST AND WRITER: DON EDWING

AILMENTS

CONTRACTED AT...
AIRPORTS

"HE AIRPORT TERMINAL WALKING MARATHON LEG CRAMP AND ARM STRETCH"

"THE 'HOW-COME-EVERYBODY-BUT ME-GOT-THEIR-LUGGAGE?' BLUES"

"THE NERVE-RACKING STOMACH-TURNING SECURITY BELL-RINGING JITTERS"

"THE DIRTY LAUNDRY CUSTOMS PROBE RESPIRATION FAILURE"

E LOG-JAMMED LUGGAGE DISPENSER ANXIETY ATTACK AND WRIST WRENCH"

There currently exists around the country specialized clusters of fervent fans who have formed clubs to pay tribute to their favorite cult heroes. We're talking about clubs like "The W.C. Fields Society", "The Baker Street Irregulars" (Sherlock Holmes fans), and "The Sons Of The Desert" (Laurel and Hardy addicts). These groups hold meetings, watch films, discuss trivia, collect memorabilia and engage in unique rituals saluting their idols (The Sons Of The Desert have an annual pie throwing fight). Although the above mentioned clubs are the best known and have flourished for years, we've recently heard about some _other_ little sub-culture groups popping up around the country. Each have their own tradition, requirements and rituals and each pays tribute, in their own special way, to other popular culture and media heroes. Who knows...you may find yourself wanting to join one of these......

LITTLE KNOWN CELEBRITY CULT GROUPS

ARTIST: ANGELO TORRES

WRITER: ARNIE KOGEN

THE SECOND BANANA JOLLYS
(Cult Followers Of Ed McMahon)

ENTRY REQUIREMENTS: Must be jolly, laugh heartily and be a good listener. Must be second in charge or an assistant with no chance of advancement to the top spot and _be able to live with this._

SECRET PASSWORD: Heeeeeeeeere's (Fill in your name)...

HANDSHAKE: Fraudulently firm, warm and jolly.

ACTIVITIES: The first member to arrive at a meeting immediately goes and sits on the couch. As each new member enters, he gets up and moves one over. Then, one person gets up to tell about his day. The others laugh heartily at this, whether the stuff is funny or not. During the speech they interject with cries of "_How_ hot was it?", "_How_ cold was it?", "_How_ crowded was the bus?" At the end of the evening six-packs of Bud are served. As the cans are shpritzed open, members laugh heartily at this.

CAUSE FOR DISMISSAL: Failure to laugh hearty.

THE RENEE RICHARDS IRREGULARS
(Cult Followers Of Dr. Renee Richards)

ENTRY REQUIREMENTS: Must have either had a sex change operation, or are contemplating one, or, on at least one occasion, have been arrested for "propositioning yourself" in public.

SECRET PASSWORD: "Knock Knock" "Who are you?" "If I knew who I was would I be _here?_"

HANDSHAKE: Not quite limp-wristed yet not quite firm.

ACTIVITIES: The "Irregulars" have an annual country club bash in tribute to their idol and celebrating their new identities. The session opens with members singing "Hey, Look Me Over," followed by: A tennis tournament (mixed doubles), Self-help lectures ("I'm Okay, You're Okay, But The Guy In The Homburg Hat and Calico Dress Could Be In Trouble."), Medical films (Dr. Renee Richards "before" and "after"—there are no films of "during"), and climaxing with a gala dance. Prizes are awarded to members who continue to dance backwards without ever slipping back to their "former" selves and trying to lead.

CAUSE FOR DISMISSAL: Looking too much like a real woman.

THE NOT-SO-NUTTY PROFESSORS
(Cult Followers Of Jerry Lewis)

ENTRY REQUIREMENTS: Must wear a pair of socks once and *only* once. Must be able to, in the space of a minute, go from being a nine-year-old clown to a grim, sullen, pompous adult. Must have I.Q. of 180 and an ego slightly bigger. Must wear a strange hairdo from no known period in our history.

SECRET PASSWORD: Mellman-Klevman-Lendl

HANDSHAKE: Handshake has been replaced with the French Legion Of Honor Kiss on both cheeks. (*Anything* French is worshipped in this club.)

ACTIVITIES: Members meet once a year at telethon time. In tribute to Jerry they stay up 24 hours without sleep. During this marathon they review in English and French) Jerry's classic films. They applaud his development from the early 1960 films when he played a busboy and a Japanese General with buck teeth all the way to his current films where he plays a busboy and a Japanese General with buck teeth. Members then go into a verbal rampage about the state of the film industry, using four-letter words while decrying the lack of decent "family" pictures".

CAUSE FOR DISMISSAL: Failure to recognize French movie audiences and critics as the only knowledgeable people in the world.

THE HELLO LARRY LEGIONNAIRES
(Cult Followers Of McLean Stevenson)

ENTRY REQUIREMENTS: Must have the personality of a shoe store clerk on uppers. Must worship and enshrine mediocrity, cheeseburgers, trailer parks, Ken Berry, Disney World, penny loafers, Sears lumber department and Robert Young commercials. Must not like or quite understand fettucini, New York Times editorials, Nureyev or Trini Lopez.

SECRET PASSWORD: Hi, how are ya? Really?... Well that's just great!

HANDSHAKE: Anything but a soul handshake.

ACTIVITIES: Members meet twice each year—on the first week of the new television season when McLean usually has a series—and four weeks later when the series is cancelled. The club flag (with the symbol "white bread over a pack of 'no doze' ") is raised and saluted. This is followed by a debate as to whether it was a right or wrong career move for McLean to quit M*A*S*H after only a few seasons. The same people then debate whether it was right or wrong for the Titanic to steer directly into the iceberg. The "Hello Larry Relief Fund" was established in June 1980. Underprivileged nations who don't have anaesthesia or medical supplies are sent the pilot film of "Hello Larry." Surgeons report that most patients fall into a deep sleep during McLean's first entrance.

THE I-DON'T-GET-NO-RESPECT SOCIETY
(Cult Followers Of Rodney Dangerfield)

ENTRY REQUIREMENTS: Must wear a tie. Must shrug and turn your head a lot, making it look like there's a coat hanger still in your jacket. Must look like you slept in your clothes. Must have had, on at least one occasion, the Surgeon General of the United States offer you a cigarette.

SECRET PASSWORD: I tell ya, my wife doesn't respect me. On Halloween she sends the kids out dressed like me!

HANDSHAKE: Sweaty.

ACTIVITIES: Club chapters are presently located in Jersey City, Three Mile Island, Mt. Saint Helen, an abandoned Chrysler factory, and Appalachia. Members meet on the 13th of every month and regale each other with stories about how they get no respect and have been mistreated. Veteran members ignore the person talking to them, causing them further despair and lack of confidence. Most chapters have a men's boutique that specializes in selling cheap blue suits and ill-fitting dress shirts. Meetings usually end when the manager announces, "You people will have to leave, we want to start the Happy Hour'."

CAUSE FOR DISMISSAL: Getting even the slightest hint of respect from a person or thing on the face of the earth.

THE ANNIE HALL MISFITS
(Cult Followers Of Woody Allen)

ENTRY REQUIREMENTS: Must be despondent. Must be in therapy. Must have hangups about sex, death, religion and having your pants altered without your knowledge.

SECRET PASSWORD: My grandmother was raped by Cossacks.

HANDSHAKE: Manic-depressive. Either totally ignoring the person you're supposed to be shaking hands with, or, using a novelty store joy buzzer.

ACTIVITIES: Meetings open with everyone chanting, "My one regret in life is that I am not someone else." This is followed by a hot lunch. After this, Woody's films are analyzed. His early funny films are compared to his later serious ones; his color films versus his black and white; Louise Lasser versus Diane Keaton and, mainly, what fears you experienced while sitting in the movie theatre. Field trips are taken to Brooklyn where members meet Woody's ex-teachers, the first haberdasher to sell him corduroy pants and the first bully to break his glasses. (This led to one of Woody's earliest lines, "The bigger they are, the greater the beating they're likely to give you.") Members then take subway rides home where they are mugged and sprayed with graffiti by cult followers of Charles Bronson.

CAUSE FOR DISMISSAL: Having a good time.

moters these days. Their items range from nking mugs to bedspreads, from notebooks knapsacks! And they're not finished with

us yet! MAD feels that it's only a matter of time before these money-hungry promoters will be offering us the following assortment of...

ISING WE'RE ALMOST SURE TO SEE...AND HATE!

RUG PRODUCTS...

After Chomping Down That Big Meal...
PAC-MAN
Antacid Tablets
For **GAS**

OME PRODUCTS...

PUT A **SMURF** IN YOUR **TANK**

...AND SEE YOUR TOILET FLUSH BLUE...LIKE ME!

PUBLICATIONS...

BUGS BUNNY PRESENTS
THE HOLY BIBLE

N'YEHHH... WHAT'S UP, GOD ?

ND, FINALLY, R GOING UT IN STYLE...

OUT OF THE FRYING PAN AND INTO THE IRE DEPT.

WE WON'T MISS TH

WE WON'T MISS THOSE
ELEVATOR OPERATORS...OR WILL WE?!?

WE WON'T MISS THOSE
BANK TELL

WE WON'T MISS THOSE
GYM INSTRUCTORS...OR WILL WE?!?

WE WON'T MISS THOSE
SALESLA

EM...OR WILL WE?!?

WRITER AND ARTIST: PAUL PETER PORGES

...OR WILL WE?!?

CASH-O-MATIC

YOUR CODE NUMBER IS INCORRECT—

YOUR CARD IS BEING DESTROYED—

CRUNCH

WE WON'T MISS THOSE
SWITCHBOARD OPERATORS ...OR WILL WE?!?

Three-nine-four-eight...! **Hold on,** please! Three-nine-four-eight...! **Hold**, please! Hi, Ethel, I'm **back!**

Hi! This is frax snt wmpleveep! We're sorry beer rotzaph home bite oww, but fiff goo leep nyor maim and number at the beep, veeble vetz glack to you—grrrrrrr snig blaxxxxxxx vort **BEEP!**

OR WILL WE?!?

Thank you for calling **The Catalogue Shopper!** Our "Return-For-Credit" Department is located in **Santa Bacokta, Honduras!** This is a recording...

WE WON'T MISS THOSE
SHOE SHINE BOYS ...OR WILL WE?!?

Your **shoes** are **done!** So are my **socks!**

WE WON'T MISS THOSE HEADWAITERS...OR WILL WE?!?

WE WON'T MISS THOSE TOLL COLLECTORS...OR WILL WE?!?

WE WON'T MISS THOSE GAS STATION ATTENDANTS...OR WILL WE?!?

ONE NOT SO FINE AFTERNOON DOWNTOWN

A MAD LOOK AT AN

OCCUP-ANT

FLAMBOY-ANT

INF-ANT

IMPORT-ANT

CORRESPOND-ANT

CLAIRVOY-ANT

VAGR-ANT

TEN-ANTS

ARTIST AND WRITER: BILL JOHNSON

TS
GONG SHOW

IGNOR-ANT

PEAS-ANTS

CONTEST-ANT

DETERR-ANT

RELUCT-ANT

INFORM-ANT

INCUMB-ANT

MILIT-ANT

DISSID-ANT

FLIPP-ANT

TRIUMPH-ANT

Some time ago, a promising young film star rose to new heights portraying a brilliant Italian-American college graduate who takes over a huge criminal empire. Now, more than ten years later, this same film star sinks to new lows portraying a sick, amoral Cuban junkie who takes over another huge criminal empire. In real life, this would be called "degeneracy." In Hollywood, this is called "progress." Anyway, here's our version of—

SCAR

ARTIST: JACK D

RED FACE

WRITER: LARRY SIEGEL

ONE FINE DAY CROSSTOWN

While today's literary market has been flooded with "How-To" books, we at MA find that there's a shortage of books that explain "How-Not-To" do things. V

THE MAD "D

CHAPTER I: WHAT NO

ARTIST: PAUL CO

At the wake, DON'T use the dearly departed's forehead as a resting place for your drink.

DON'T try to cheer up the wife of the deceased by showing her sna shots of her husband having a great time on a recent business tr

If you're employed at "Disneyland," DON'T go to the funeral service direct from work.

DON'T wear your "Walkman" if you're one of the pallbearers.

DON'T use stilts in order to g better view of the burial ceremo

think there's just as much value in knowing what *not* to do as there is in knowing what *to* do. And so, with this in mind, the Editors of MAD proudly present:

ON'T" BOOK
O DO AT A FUNERAL

RITERS: JOE RAIOLA AND CHARLIE KADAU

hen you send your condolences to the grieving family, DON'T use the "Belly-Gram" message service.

DON'T arrive at the cemetery services in a hot air balloon.

DON'T play with your frisbee during the cemetery services.

DON'T slip the organist $5.00 and tell him that the deceased's favorite song was "Girls Just Want To Have Fun."

At the reception following the funeral, DON'T entertain the guests with a hand puppet of the deceased.

LOOK FOR CHAPTER II OF "THE MAD 'DON'T' BOOK" IN AN UPCOMING ISSUE OF THIS IDIOTIC MAGAZINE

SIMPLE GAMES
FOR THE SCHO

TWO-COLOR RUBIK CUBES

FOUR-WALL DARTS

SINGLE SOCK COLLECTING

TOENAIL SPLATTER PAINTING

MOSQUITO SPOTTING

AND PASTIMES
OL DROP-OUT

WRITER AND ARTIST: PAUL PETER PORGES

BASIC WORD PROCESSING

STYROFOAM PACKAGING RESTORING

BEAN BAG PING PONG

SLAM-DUNK SNACKING

ONE-CARD MONTE

LAST YEAR AT THE FREENSVILLE MARATHON

How can anyone **stand** to read the **"Airline Information Cards"** that are always in the seat pocket in front of them? The information is either **stupid**, or **useless**! Like what kind of **idiot** needs **twenty pictures** to explain how to buckle their **seat belt**?

Even **worse** are the **"Emergency Instructions"**! Like, what kind of **moron** is actually going to **believe** he can paddle across the **Atlantic** on a **seat cushion**?! And in **February**, no less! What we **really** need is **practical** information! Like how to get the **Airlines** to adopt the **suggestions** made in this **MAD** article:

USEFUL AND PRACTICAL INFLIGHT INFORMATION WE'D LIKE TO SEE

Chapter 11
Airlines
F A T B E L L Y
S U P E R J E T
S E R V I C E

UN-KINKING YOUR NECK AFTER A THREE-HOUR MOVIE IN AN IMPOSSIBLE SEAT

CIRCUMVENTING THE FOOD OR LIQUOR CART WHEN YOU ARE ON AN EMERGENCY TRIP TO THE TOILET

CONTROLLING BODILY FUNCTIONS WHEN COMMANDED TO RETURN TO SEAT JUST AS YOU ENTER TOILET

BALANCING YOUR FOOD TRAY WHEN YOUR NEIGHBOR HAS TO MAKE A HASTY EXIT TO USE THE TOILET

PROPER SIDE BENDS (WHILE WEARING SEAT BELTS) WHEN FELLOW PASSENGER IS USING A BARF BAG

LEG MANEUVERS AND EXERCISES TO RESTORE CIRCULATION WHEN JAMMED IN TIGHTLY-PACKED SEATS

WATCHING THE MOVIE WITHOUT BEING BLINDED WHEN UNCOOPERATIVE PASSENGER WON'T PULL SHADE

AVOIDING THE SMOKE WHEN YOUR "NO SMOKING" SEAT IS DIRECTLY BEHIND THE "SMOKING" SECTION

EARPHONES

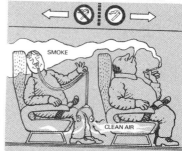

SMOKE

CLEAN AIR

RETRIEVING ITEMS FROM OVERHEAD STORAGE COMPARTMENT WHEN AISLE IS JAMMED AFTER LANDING

@Jaffee

ONE FINE DAY IN CHICAGO, ILLINOIS

Hey, Diddle Diddle
You're fat in the middle;
Your body has never looked worse;
Whatever you're needing,
You won't get it reading
This half-baked collection of verse—

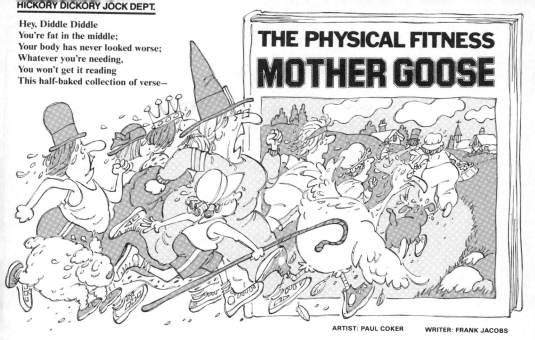

THE PHYSICAL FITNESS
MOTHER GOOSE

ARTIST: PAUL COKER   WRITER: FRANK JACOBS

Solomon Grundy

Solomon Grundy
Did push-ups on Monday,
Went jogging on Tuesday,
Played handball on Wednesday,
Swam rivers on Thursday,
Rode horses on Friday,
Climbed mountains on Saturday,
Pumped iron on Sunday;
Won't somebody please, for the sake of
everyone who gets near him, come up
with an effective deodorant for Solomon Grundy?

Humpty Dumpty

Humpty Dumpty was a fat blob;
Humpty's friends all called him a slob;
But then he was told of a wonderful diet,
Which prompted fat Humpty to say, "I shall try it."

Humpty Dumpty strove for success;
Humpty Dumpty soon consumed less;
Today, after months of just yogurt for dinner,
He's still the same slob—but at least he is thinner.

Jack Sprat

Jack Sprat
Will eat no fat;
He's heard that it will harm him;
He'll never touch
Fresh fruit and such;
The sprays they use alarm him.

Jack eats
No fish or meats;
He fears contamination;
From foods impure
He's now secure—
He's also near starvation.

Little Jack Horner

Little Jack Horner
While rounding a corner
Is met by a mugger, who states:
"Hand over your cash
"Or your head I will smash,
"Which is not the most happy of fates."

Little Jack Horner
Takes off from the corner
In hopes of outracing disaster;
But though he's in shape,
He won't make his escape,
'Cause the *mugger's* a runner—but faster.

Five Health Fanatics

Five health fanatics,
Sweating from each pore;
One passed out at racquetball—
Now there's only four.

Four health fanatics,
Filled with energy;
One fell off a vaulting horse—
Now there's only three.

Three health fanatics,
Puffing till they're blue;
One collapsed while lifting weights
Now there's only two.

Two health fanatics,
On a ten-mile run;
One was clobbered by a bus—
Now there's only one.

One health fanatic,
Swimming after lunch;
Ulp! Looks like he swam too soon
That wraps up the bunch.

The Old Woman in the Shoe

There was an old woman who lived in a shoe,
Which gave off a foot-smell, as shoes often do;
She said with a gasp as her breathing grew weaker,
"I'm lucky, at least, that it isn't a sneaker."

Wee Willie Winkie

Wee Willie Winkie
Plays all sports with zest—
Basketball and football,
Skiing and the rest;
If you think that Willie's
Keeping fit, we're sorry;
Willie only plays these sports
At home on his Atari.

Taffy Owns a Health Club

Taffy owns a health club;
Taffy staffs it well;
He's now discovered to his joy
How exercise can sell.

Taffy pulls in people;
Taffy pitches Health;
And now 3,000 memberships
Have brought him instant wealth.

Taffy weighs 280;
Taffy's five feet wide;
Which may explain why Taffy
Never shows his face inside.

Jack and Jill

Jack and Jill
Run up the hill
In sixty seconds flat;
They jog and swim
And keep in trim
Without an ounce of fat.

Jack and Jill
Derive no thrill
From staying up past nine;
They've sworn off booze
And both refuse
A glass of beer or wine.

Jack and Jill
Are never ill;
They're careful what they eat;
Small wonder they're
The dullest pair
You'll ever want to meet.

Sing a Song of Fitness

Sing a song of fitness,
A body full of pain;
Jogging 20 miles,
Through a driving rain.

Muscle pulls and jock-itch,
Dislocated bones,
Heart attacks and hamstrings,
Bruises, sprains and moans.

Someday in the future,
When the craze is done,
Ask yourself the question—
Wasn't fitness fun?

ONE EVENING IN THE LIVING ROOM

One of the top priorities of many teenagers today is to get their own apartment and escape forever from the agony of parental supervision and nagging. But like most dreams, this one requires considerable expertise and knowledge to make it come true. So when and if that moment arrives for you, pay close attention to—

MAD TIPS ON MOVING OUT...
AND MAKING IT ON YOUR OWN

ARTIST: GEORGE WOODBRIDGE   WRITER: LARRY SIEGEL

THE VERY IMPORTANT PRELIMINARY STEP

Keep in mind that, at the beginning, your parents will automatically be against your moving out. So how you conduct yourself at this stage may determine the whole direction of your life.

THE WRONG WAY TO BRING UP THE SUBJECT
...Grabbing The Bull By The Horns

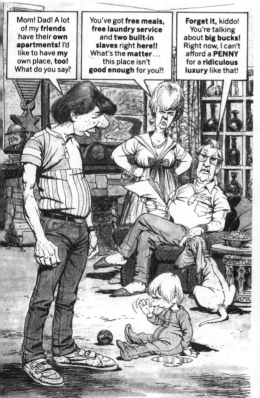

Mom! Dad! A lot of my **friends** have their **own apartments!** I'd like to have **my** own place, **too!** What do you say?

You've got **free meals, free laundry service** and **two built-in slaves** right here!! What's the **matter**... this place isn't **good enough** for you?!

Forget it, kiddo! You're talking about **big bucks!** Right now, I can't afford a **PENNY** for a **ridiculous luxury** like that!

THE RIGHT WAY TO BRING UP THE SUBJECT
...Throwing The Bull, Horns And All

How do you like my **stupid friend, Lance!?** He moved into his **OWN APARTMENT!** Boy, I wouldn't leave **MY** terrific parents in a **million years!!**

You're a **good boy,** Son, but... *heh-heh*... isn't saying you're not leaving us in a **million years** a bit of an **exaggeration?!?**

Sure it is, Mom...! Make that **28 YEARS,** when I **get married!!**

You're planning to get married when you're **46?!** *Uh*—maybe Lance **ISN'T** so dumb! I could sell our **car,** take your sister out of **college,** borrow—

SELECTING THE PROPER ROOMMATE

Now that you have the go-ahead, it is important to find someone to share your apartment. But remember that, just as in a marriage, familiarity breeds contempt, and the only real purpose a roommate serves is to split the expenses. The less you have to do with each other, the better!

TWO DESIRABLE ROOMMATES TO LOOK FOR

Medical Students or Law Students

So long, Roomie! I'm off to the **library** to study for **19 exams!!**

Good luck, fella! I'll have **breakfast** waiting for you when you **come back in April!**

Night Watchmen Or Graveyard Shift Workers

Okay...the bed is **all yours!** I'll be back from **work** at **eight** in the morning...right after **you** leave for **class!**

You're a **terrific roommate**, a **wonderful peson**, and I'll **cherish** our close friendship as long as I **live**, Marty!

My name is **Bob!**

Whatever!

SOME ROOMMATES TO AVOID

Jocks And Body-Builders

Hey, Man...you mind getting **lost** for around **four hours?!** I'd kinda like to spend a romantic evening **alone** with the **one I love**...and with **you** around, **TWO's a CROWD!**

24-Hour-A-Day Headset Freaks

Hey, Roommate! Have you heard our **apartment is on fire?!?**

Didn't **Jefferson Starship** record that in **1976**, on the **Grunt** label?!

Members Of The Opposite Sex

Ciao, Sweetie! I'm your **new roommate!** Where do I put my **horsies**...and how do you feel about **long engagements??**

CHOOSING A GIRL AS A ROOMMATE

Nowadays, it's not uncommon for young men and women to room together on a friendly basis, and you might do well to consider that possibility. But first, let's put things into their proper perspective by examining the changing male and female roommate trends over the past decades.

MALE AND FEMALE ROOMMATES OF THE PAST

In the 1940's, unmarried people never shared an apartment together. In fact, according to all the movies of that era, husbands and wifes never even shared the same bed together!

But in the 1950's things loosened up a bit and young people at least thought about sharing an apartment together for an hour or so. But parental reactions were usually ridiculous.

Darling, the **Doctor** was here yesterday...and **guess what?!**

You mean...?? You mean...??

Right!! Our **night table** is **pregnant!**

Mr. Gorman...I'd like to invite your **daughter** over to my **apartment** tonight to watch **Milton Berle** on **television!**

You **DO**, by God, and **you'll MARRY her!!**

MALE AND FEMALE ROOMMATES TODAY

Beginning in the '70's and carrying through to the present time, it has become fashionable for young men and women to share an apartment with no physical involvement between them whatsoever.

If you can accept this roommate as someone who'll help clean your apartment...and nothing MORE than that...

If you can accept this roommate as someone who'll help shop for groceries...and nothing MORE than that...

If you can accept this roommate as someone who'll help cook all your meals...and nothing MORE than that...

If you can do all that without climbing the walls and going off the deep end and being carried out like this

...then you're obviously very mature, very sexually liberated, very much in control of your life...and completely dead from the ankles up!

FINDING THE RIGHT APARTMENT

Now that you've chosen your roommate, whoever he or she may be, it's time to select the apartment you'll be most happy in. When you have a choice, be sure that you make the correct one!

THE WRONG APARTMENT FOR YOU

This apartment may look beautiful, but you'll be asking for trouble living near a construction site. You'll be constantly bothered by workmen asking you to turn down the volume on your stereo...because they can't hear themselves excavating.

THE RIGHT APARTMENT FOR YOU

This apartment is perfect. It's not near a construction site, it's close to shopping, and most important, it should remind you of your room at home—just after you straightened it up.

LIVING WITHIN YOUR MEANS

When you are on your own, you must make every penny count. Here are two tips on economizing:

To save money, you may find that you will have to slightly alter your eating habits from the way they were at home...

Don't ever be too proud to buy anything second hand. Just remember that such economizing can sometimes backfire on you!

IMPROVING YOUR SOCIAL LIFE

The two main reasons why you moved out and took an apartment was to escape your parents prying eyes, and to have fun. So let's examine your new-found social-life freedom in two areas:

PARTIES

Throw parties as often as you like. It is perfectly okay to have your guests help defray the costs with food and booze.

Just don't over-do this sort of thing. If you try to get too cute and expect too much...it could lead to total disaster!

MAKING OUT

Of even greater importance in your social life, of course, is now having the privacy to make out in your own apartment...

If your roommate is a guy, you will usually have no problem.

If your roommate is a girl, you could have a slight problem.

THOSE ALL-IMPORTANT VISITS HOME

And finally, from time to time (for whatever reason, be it guilt or love), you will want to return home and visit your parents. When you do, there are only two major things to remember

Never Return Home Empty-Handed

Never Go Back To Your Apartment Empty-Handed

ONE FINE THURSDAY IN SEATTLE

WRITER: LARRY SIEGEL   ARTIST: SAM VIVIANO

Everyone loves those "Indiana Jones" movies, but they take so darn long to make,
easy to get bored while waiting for the next one. Not any more! Now, whenever you
the urge to experience a pulse-pounding new "Indiana Jones" adventure, merely star

MAD'S DO-I
"INDIANA JO

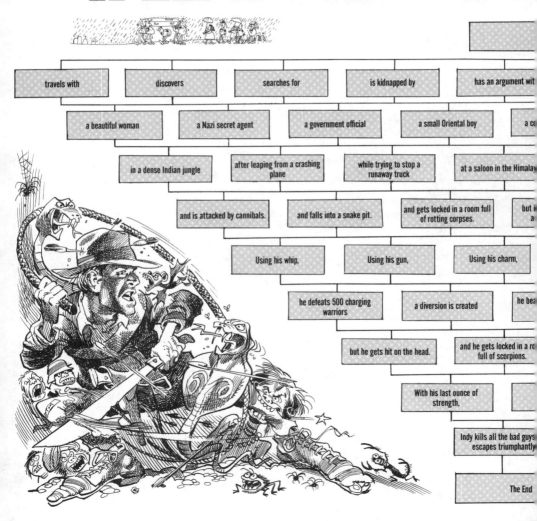

travels with	discovers	searches for	is kidnapped by	has an argument wit

a beautiful woman	a Nazi secret agent	a government official	a small Oriental boy	a c

in a dense Indian jungle	after leaping from a crashing plane	while trying to stop a runaway truck	at a saloon in the Himala

and is attacked by cannibals.	and falls into a snake pit.	and gets locked in a room full of rotting corpses.	but i a

Using his whip,	Using his gun,	Using his charm,

he defeats 500 charging warriors	a diversion is created	he bea

but he gets hit on the head.	and he gets locked in a ro full of scorpions.

With his last ounce of strength,

Indy kills all the bad guys escapes triumphantly

The End

top of the accompanying chart and work your way down, pulling one exciting story ~ment from each row. By the time you reach the bottom, you'll have the plot summary a brand new, thrilling sequel that even Steven Spielberg himself would be proud of.

-YOURSELF
~ES" SEQUEL

ARTIST: JACK DAVIS   WRITER: CHARLIE KADAU

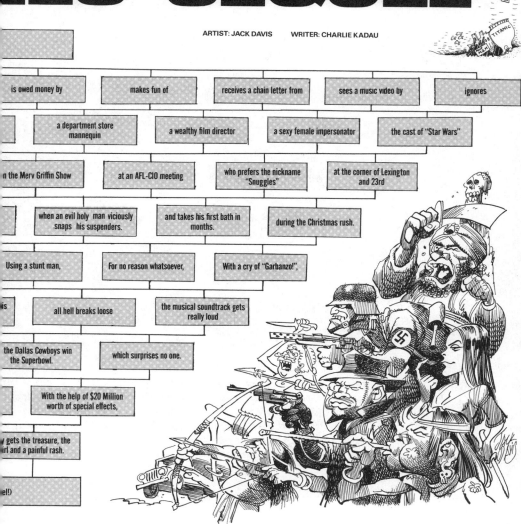

| is owed money by | makes fun of | receives a chain letter from | sees a music video by | ignores |

| | a department store mannequin | a wealthy film director | a sexy female impersonator | the cast of "Star Wars" |

| n the Merv Griffin Show | at an AFL-CIO meeting | who prefers the nickname "Snuggles" | at the corner of Lexington and 23rd |

| | when an evil holy man viciously snaps his suspenders. | and takes his first bath in months. | during the Christmas rush. |

| Using a stunt man, | For no reason whatsoever, | With a cry of "Garbanzo!", |

| is | all hell breaks loose | the musical soundtrack gets really loud |

| the Dallas Cowboys win the Superbowl. | which surprises no one. |

| With the help of $20 Million worth of special effects, |

| gets the treasure, the rl and a painful rash. |

el!)

WHERE'S THE BEAST? DEPT.

*In the wilds of the forest, where all God's creatures roam freely, animals must constant
be on the lookout for predators. Mother Nature, in her infinite wisdom, has provided f
these animals by giving them the ability to blend in with their wilderness surroundings. B
what about those unfortunate creatures who don't live in the wilderness? What about the a
imals that have to endure the hardships and hassles of city life? Well, not to worry, b
cause Mother Nature has taken care of them quite well, as you'll see by taking a look at .*

CAMOUFLAGE TRICKS OF CITY ANIMALS

ARTISTS: HARVEY KURTZMAN & WILL ELDER   WRITER: RURIK TYLER

BULLET BEETLE

Bullets in the big city are so common, no one takes notice of them. So while the Bullet Beetle's disguise saves it from predators it is often trampled to death by pedestrians.

BANG!

RADIO-FACED RACCOON

The Radio-Faced Raccoon looks like the gear of a typical city kid—a radio face and sports bag body with a clip on raccoon tail. Known to hang on to unsuspecting passersby when in danger, it is a nasty surprise for people who think they have found a free radio.

GRAFFITI LIZARD

The Graffiti Lizard is practically invisible when standing next to a wall. But it is a fairly stupid animal, and doesn't move when the owner of the wall comes out to scrub it clean, or to repaint it.

ANTENNAE BUG

The Antennae Bug lives a symbiotic life with the Radio-Faced Raccoon, living off the Raccoon's food scraps. It can also live on top of T.V.'s, buildings and certain visiting martians.

NEWSPAPER PIGEON

Taking advantage of high winds that send newspapers flying, these birds can soar undetected. They are a treat for winos who start out looking for something to use as a blanket and wind up with a meal.

WALKING WINDOW CRACK

The Walking Window Crack is a thin white insect. It's disguise works so well, it is virtually invisible to its predators. It's only worry is being drowned or crushed by the squeegees of window washers who don't realize it's there.

CLOTHESPIN CRICKET

The Clothespin Cricket is a harmless insect. It is threatened only by nearsighted people who ordinarily step on clothespins thinking they are crickets.

HUBCAP TURTLE

Very slow and harmless, the Hubcap Turtle is fine until a young hubcap thief figures him for an easy score.

BEER TAB BUTTERFLY

beautiful creature, the er Tab Butterfly has no emies except oddball bag dies who use beer tabs jewelry.

CRAWLING COMB CENTIPEDE

Wonderfully disguised, the Crawling Comb Centipede only faces danger from those people who don't have any qualms about acquiring their grooming items from the gutter.

CIGARETTE WORM

The Cigarette Worm's camouflage is very effective. Its only enemies are smoking birds.

CHANGE PURSE CLAM

The Change Purse Clam is a miser's delight. Once something finds its way in, the jaws snap shut and nothing gets out again.

PADLOCK BEETLE

The Padlock Beetle has super strong mandibles that allow it to hang from anything! Yet, when lying in the gutter, it looks like a snapped lock and is left alone. It lives with constant fear of being impaled by the tools of would-be lockpickers.

XTENSION CORD NACONDA

e Extension Cord naconda is a cousin the electric eel. is usually found in display ns at big city hardware stores here it is often mistaken for e real thing, taken home d electrocuted.

RHINO CAB

This big lumbering animal roams the street with no worries. It's built better than any modern car and can walk away from a collision. It comes with its own horn.

WRITERS: SERGIO ARAGONES AND DON EDWING   ARTIST: DON MARTIN

There's been *Live-Aid, Band-Aid, Hands Across America* and other events which have raised millions of dollars for worthwhile causes. But what about those **other fund raisers** which go neglected and get completely forgotten, huh? Yeah, what about **those!** Well, **Mad** doesn't forget! Not us! **Hoo hah!** We herewith present...

FUND RAISERS
that never made it!

ARTISTS: WILL ELDER & HARVEY KURTZMAN   WRITER: DICK DEBARTOLO

LEMON-AID was to be a line of defective American-made cars stretching from the east and west coasts and meeting in Detroit. Driven by frustrated owners who received no satisfaction from indifferent auto dealers and manufacturers, LEMON-AID never had a chance—only **seven cars** were able to make it to their positions on the line!

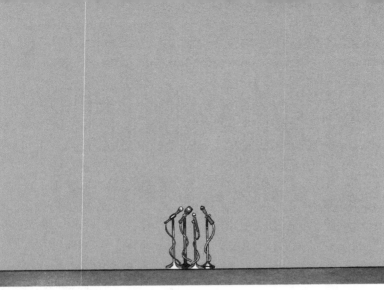

was the rock world feeble attempt t raise money for th enormous task of tr ing to keep track rock bands and pe formers who disa pear, reappear, sk from group to grou change name: change hair, etc. Th problem, of cours was that those ch sen to appear cou not be **located** ar few pledges we called in during tl 3-hour screening of bare stage!

HAMS ACROSS AMERICA was intended as the "life of t party" answer to the successful COMIC RELIEF event staged by **professio comedians.** The frustrated would–be funny folks, decked out in lampshades a

BRAND-AID

was planned to relieve the nation of the current *"Damn, I wish I'd bought the other one"* disease now reaching epidemic proportions. GE owners with second thoughts about a recent refrigerator purchase, for instance, could swap theirs with a Westinghouse buyer suffering from the same ailment. The event ended in a shambles when 7000 Sony Betamax VCR owners showed up hoping to swap for VHS equipment and found **no takers!**

NO-HANDS ACROSS AMERICA

was not in "good hands" with Allstate or any other insurance company, for that matter! This event was organized to put together all those people whose insurance premiums have doubled and tripled along with those who can't get insurance at all and to raise enough money for one huge policy covering **everybody!** This wonderful idea fell apart when it was learned that in order to be legal, the event itself had to be **insured,** and of course, no insurance company would cover it!

quipped with whoopie cushions and seltzer bottles might have had a good thing ьing, but their **inflated egos** got in the way, and some types of **ham** can never be ιred. Upstaging each other at every chance, the event ended in a **humorless riot** at collected neither laughs nor bucks for the noble cause!

**FRONT ROW CENTER
*AT THE WRESTLING MATCH***

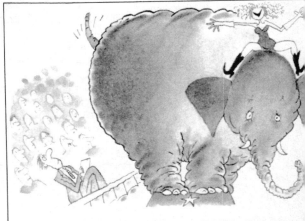

FRONT ROW CENTER *AT THE CIRCUS*

FRONT ROW CENTER *AT SEA WORLD*

FRONT ROW

Risks of ROW CENTER

ADMIT ONE
FRI., MAY 30 $100.00

ARTIST AND WRITER: PAUL PETER PORGES

FRONT ROW CENTER AT *AN NBA GAME*

FRONT ROW CENTER
AT THE SHAKESPEARE FESTIVAL

A 4TH OF JULY DISPLAY

FRONT ROW CENTER *AT THE RODEO*

Repent, you worthless sinners! Repent, you swine! You scum!

FRONT ROW CENTER **AT THE SERMON!**

FRONT ROW CENTER **AT THE INDY 500**

FRONT ROW CENTER **AT A DAVID LETTERMAN STUPID PET TRICK TAPING**

FRONT ROW CENTER **AT A HEAVYWEIGHT BOXING MATCH**

ONE DELIGHTFUL JANUARY MORNING

ARTIST: DON MARTIN   WRITER: DON EDWING

ONLY WHEN YOU

...does your student advisor have domestic problems!

...do they have management problems!

...do they start maintenance on your elevators!

ARTIST AND WRITER: PAUL PETER PORGES

...must the supermarket cashier insert a new roll of register tape!

RE IN A HURRY...

...is your breakfast piping hot!

...do they break in new help!

HERE'S HOW YOU **CANCEL** THE **CODE 40--PUNCH IN** THE **FRIES**, ADD THE **TAX**, RING CASH **DRAW #3** 'CAUSE CANDACE IS ON **#2** UNTIL SHARKY GETS BACK...

...does your rich uncle call you long distance!

...AND CHIP, **HERE'S** WHAT I WANT YOU TO DO WITH MY **TENNIS TROPHIES**...

...do you have to wait for a salesman to finish checking out his orders!

LET ME GET THIS **STRAIGHT--**IS THAT **48 GROSS** AT **$60** OR **60 GROSS** AT **$48** ? OKAY! NOW, LISTEN SWEETIE, IS THAT **MODEL #5, SIZE 6** OR **MODEL #6 SIZE 5** ?

CAT TH

UGHTS

ARTIST AND WRITER: PAUL PETER PORGES

Nothing makes the skin crawl like that tired old parting remark "Have—" (Whoops! You kn
the one we mean!) Maybe it used to generate good feeling—30 years ago—but now it gi

STEWARDESSES

SUPERMARKET CHECKERS

MORE FARE TO REPLAC

ARTIST: PAUL COKER

WAITERS

OGICAL
YELLS
E DREADED

Have a nice day!
Have a nice day!
Have a nice day!
Have a...

WRITER: MIKE SNIDER

POLICEMEN

Have a lenient traffic court judge!

See you when I have to meet another quota!

May your insurance premiums rise only **slightly!**

MECHANICS

Hope I remembered to put back **all** the parts!

May you break down in a **good** neighborhood!

Good luck getting those upholstery grease stains out!

DR.'S OFFICE RECEPTIONISTS

May the pharmacist give you the right drug!

May the lab keep all your test results straight!

Hope the **rest** of your busy day isn't wasted!

MIRTHQUAKE DEPT.

When we want to measure the power of an earthquake, we use the Richt
Scale, ranging from 1 for a mild tremor to 9 for a quake of total destru

THE MAD RICHTER SCA

ARTIST: AL JAFF

YOUR BODY

YOUR MONEY

1

Except for a hangnail and some excess ear wax, your body functions adequately for someone of your nationality.

You learn too late that your Daily Horoscope is an unreliable investment guide. The interest on your VISA Card exceeds your salary.

2

Because of a fungal disease, hair sprouts from your ribs. A shattered kneecap ends all dreams of playing professional lacrosse.

Your tax accountant begs off, saying he "doesn't want to get involved." There are no buyers for your bowling trophies.

3

With no warning, you throw up four times a day on mixed company. Your only comfortable position is crawling on all fours.

Restaurants require you to put down a cash deposit before ordering. The word "Deadbeat" is imprinted by your bank on your personal checks.

4

Back spasms rack your body, ruining your plans for Arbor Day. Having no sense of smell, you are unaware you are giving off a terrible odor.

Bleeding in an alleyway, you learn that loansharks are not good listeners. Your scheme to mortgage your children is unsuccessful.

5

You are rejected by your life-support system for not "playing the game." Your vital organs give out one by one and later will be sold, though at a substantial discount.

A bus driver refuses your IOU. You wrestle a bag-lady for territorial garbage rights.

E FOR HUMAN BEINGS

WRITER: FRANK JACOBS

YOUR PUBLIC IMAGE

Although you are not totally liked and often rub people the wrong way, your essential dullness still shines through.

There is something about you no woman can resist, and one day you hope to find it.

You are trailed by a security guard while shopping for wash-cloths at a local K-Mart. Your camper is turned away at an RV park.

Two former girl-friends send you picture sex manuals on your birthday. Your dinner date takes along a pit bull as a chaperone.

No one knows who you are at a family reunion. Your minister requests that you change religions.

Dancers at a nude bar put on clothes when you enter. You see a sex therapist, who triples his fee after your first visit.

Large dogs use your leg as a hydrant. While taking your vacation, neighbors have your house towed away.

Alone with a date, you get your first sniff of Mace. A supermarket checker washes her hands after touching your groceries.

You collapse on a downtown street and someone calls for a sanitation truck. Because of "prior commitments," your family can't make your funeral.

The manager of an X-rated theatre says you're giving the place a bad name. You scout funerals for new widows.

Sure, you already know about lung cancer, emphysema and heart disease, but what about the...

OTHER DANGERS OF

THE INVOLUNTARY BEARD AND MUSTACHE SINGE

THE HIDDEN CIGARETTE INTERNAL COMBUSTION

NO SMOKING

THE PIPE-IN-POCKET BURN-OUT

THE SPRINKLER SYSTEM SET-OFF SOAK

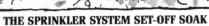

SMOKING

THE FILTER TIP LIGHT-UP FLASH

THE EXPLODING BALLOON CIGAR-STARTLE

THE STUCK BUTT LIP-STRETCH

ARTIST AND WRITER: PAUL PETER PORGES

THE DROPPED ASHES FLAME-UP

PORGES

Do you remember when your family would go on those long boring car trips! And do you remember how your Mother would try to keep you kids entertained with "Auto Bingo"... that stupid little game with the cows and stop signs, etc. Well, what we have here is a similar game for another boring activity kids have to do with their parents. Here's

SUBWAY BINGO

ARTIST: BOB CLARKE   **WRITER: RURIK TYLER**

SMELLY BUM

SPIDER GRAFFITI

BIG CRAZY GUY STARING AT YOU

"BLIND" BEGGAR

POLE TWIRLER

PICKED POCKET

TRANSVESTITE

CHAIN SNATCHING

PUKING DRUNK

Y-OLD NEWSPAPER

GUARDIAN ANGEL

BLASTING RADIO

ROLLING BOTTLE

OMEONE TAKING
UP TWO SEATS

FREE
SPACE

SOMEONE FALLING
ASLEEP ON SOMEONE

PREGNANT WOMAN
STANDING

LONG DELAY

OVER-THE-SHOULDER
NEWSPAPER READER

BLACKOUT

SEAT SQUEEZER

DOOR-HOLDER

SOMEONE STUCK
IN DOOR

DEFIANT SMOKER

DERAILMENT

...the medical researchers we're expecting to find a cure for AIDS and cancer are the same ones who have been completely stumped by the annoying common cold for 100 years!

...the "Star Wars" defense, if ever approved, would be built by the crooks who charge $600 for a hammer, and be operated by the cretins who were stupid enough to buy those hammers!

...most states have more formalized training and licensing requirements for hairdressers than they do for owners of cheap handguns!

An IRS audit, riding the subway in New York City, the threat of nuclear war, being locked in a room with Don King...

It's really

SCA

to think

...the nuclear power industry still refers to a near catastrophic melt-down which cost $1 billion to clean up as a "minor incident"!

...psychiatrists—those claiming expertise in helping others deal with their problems—have the highest suicide rate of any profession!

...the only thing standing between us and fatal food-poisoning is the Food and Drug Administration—an agency that says it's okay to have up to 14 rat droppings in a 10 ounce can of chili.

...for every one television show that gets on the air, there are a dozen others even worse that the networks turn down and we never see!

e mere thought of these things terrifies . But they're not so bad when compared *really* horrific stuff. For example...

ARTIST: PAUL COKER   **WRITER: MIKE SNIDER**

RY

that...

...the huge multi-national banks controlling the entire world's economy are totally inept at keeping your measly little savings account straight!

...tomorrow's teenagers will have to come up with music loud and tasteless enough to offend parents who grew up loving The Beastie Boys!

...every year, thousands of big, mean college football players not drafted by the NFL will hit the streets as jobless and bitter rejects!

ONE LUCKY MORNING ON FRIDAY THE 13TH

There was once a classic television show called "The Untouchables." It had powerful characters and crisp dialogue, and it entertainingly chronicled a feeling of what Chicago was like during the time of Prohibition. It became a cult favorite! Wouldn't you think Hollywood execs would leave well enough alone and keep a classic "untouchable"? Hoo-Hah! Get real! Not when there's mega-bucks to be made! They went ahead and made a feature film version of that popular series! For those who fondly remember the TV show, this new cast isn't the "Untouchables." They're more like...

ARTIST: ANGELO TORRES   WRITER: ARNIE KOGEN

Welcome to **Chicago**, 1931! It is a city of **violence** and **corruption**! It is a city run by **gangsters**! There's only **one man** who can put a **stop** to this! Unfortunately, **Superman** won't be created for another **seven years**! So, we'll have to **settle** for the **chump** here on my left!

Hi! I'm **Elliot Nice**! I'm a **clean-cut, square, ideal-istic Treasury Agent**! If J. **Edgar Hoover** and **Snow White** ever had a child. it would be me! I'm **new** in Chicago and have **a lot** to **learn**! All I know is I will try to live up to the **Treasury Agent's oath**: "An agent is **trustworthy, loyal, helpful—**"

That's the **Boy Scout** oath, **idiot**!

Oops! **Sorry**! I **told** you I had a lot to learn! Anyway, just as **well**! That Boy Scout oath is too **dirty** for us!

Hi! I make a film every **fifteen years** or so! Perhaps you remember me from **American Graffiti**! In that film, I was a **nerd** with a **Chevy**! My career has come a **long way**! Now I'm a **nerd** with a tommy gun!

I'm **Al Capon**! I'm **powerful** and **ruthless**! I'm the **King of Chicago**! I own the **Mayor**! I own the **cops**! I own the **courts**! Obviously, the only thing I **don't** own is a calorie counter!

RECYCLING T

Shampoo Neck Brace

Baby Walker

Snow Shoes

Memorial
Wreath
Support

WE LOVE YOU POPS AND MOMSIE

FIFI
1973   1985

Short Distance
Boomerang

LET SEATS

ARTIST AND WRITER: PAUL PETER PORGES

Pool Rack

Hanging Plant Holder

Life Saver

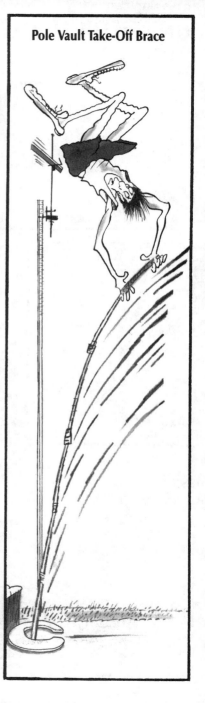

Pole Vault Take-Off Brace

ONE RIDICULOUS EVENING IN THE JUNGLE

Oh, **drat it!!** Tarzan, my **hair** is **TOO CURLY!!** What can I **do...?**

Jane need good old-fahioned **jungle FWOF** to straighten out hair...!!

A **FWOF?!?** Okay...get me a **FWOF!!** because I **can't stand** this **hair!!**

BAAEEFWOFAAEE

DOOBADOOBADOOBADOOBADOOB

FWOF

D.MARTIN...

A man-eating alien creature? Wow! A fight to the death between the alien and one last survivor of his rage? Hoo-boy! Such an original premise! It's already been done! This creature isn't a Predator, he's just like his...

PREDECESSOR

Ditch, how come you're **lifting** that **truck?**

Because is a **pick-up** truck! What **else** I supposed to do with it? Besides, I pick up **anything** that lets me **pump iron** and show off my **big belching biceps!**

Hack, why'd you bring **two dozen razors** on this **mission?**

Ditch said we should all be **prepared** for a few **close shaves!**

Does anyone know why they **picked** Ditch for this **secret mission?**

Yeah, because **Chuck Norris** and **Sylvester Stallone** have already **done** this plot!

ARTIST: JACK DAVIS   WRITER: DICK DEBARTOLO

...ve some **food!** Under the **conditions** ...rovided for the **Geneva** ...invention, we ...ave to **feed** ...e **hostages!**

I wouldn't want to **break** Geneva Convention **regulations!** Let's just **shoot them all** so we don't have to **share!**

Hey, guys, am I seeing things or is that **pick-up truck** coming right at us?

Sure **looks** that way! Maybe some idiot thinks this is a **drive-in restaurant!**

Well, you leave the **tip**— I'm getting my butt out of here!

Okay, men, zis **attack** is ofer! Vas is the **casualty count?**

We **killed** all 23 of them, **leveled** their **compound**, **destroyed** all their **weapons**, and blew up all their **ammunition!** Our side **suffered** a **scraped knee!**

A **scraped knee!** Damn! I vas hoping we'd get off **scotch free!** No vonder they sez, **"War is hell!"**

Don't worry, guys, I've got my **mini-machine gun** and **six more bullets!**

Six bullets von't stop dot ting!

The six bullets are for **us** — **one each! Suicide** will be quick and painless compared to what the **monster** will do to us!

...else is **gone!** Und I don't stand a **chance** against zat **thing** vit all his sophisticated **electronic surveillance devices!** But **vait!** It **stopped!** The monster **can't see** through a simple, light coat of **mud!**

go get your own @#$%& mud!

your at it, **creep**, get your own **plot!** You're doing "**Aliens III**"!

The **Predecessor** vants to engage in **face-to-face combat! Good!** I know I can **win** because I've **suspended** a huge **log** above his **head!** That, and **suspending** any trace of **reality** or **credibility**, vill give me the hedge I need to **destroy him!**

KAWHAM

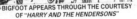

BIGFOOT APPEARS THROUGH THE COURTESY OF "HARRY AND THE HENDERSONS"

Gee, with all this **radioactive dust**, I can't find Ditch! Do you see him anywhere **down there?**

After the creature blasted himself to bits in that **nuclear explosion**, try **looking up!** Ditch has gotta be **floating around somewhere!**

How are you, Ditch? Are you **okay?**

Idiot, vot do you hexpect after a **nuclear explosion?** Of course I'm **not okay!** I **scraped** my **other knee!**

ONE MORNING ON A CORNER DOWNTOWN

ONE AFTERNOON ON A CORNER DOWNTOWN

ONE EVENING ON A CORNER DOWNTOWN

LADY GODIVA

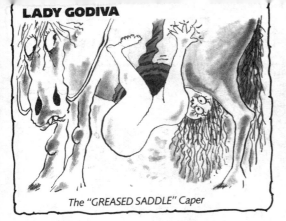

The "GREASED SADDLE" Caper

DR. JEKYLL

The "DRIBBLE GLASS" Bit

RIP VAN WINKLE

The "DRIPPING FAUCET" Routine

The Ten All
LEGENDAI
JO

DRACULA

The "BOTTOMLESS COFFIN" Zapper

ROBIN HOOD

The "PERMANENT-KNOTS-IN-THE-PANTYHOSE" Pu

NINJA

The "STRETCHED PANTS ELASTIC" Prank

ZORRO

The "RUBBERIZED SWORD" Zinger

...ime Greatest
PRACTICAL
...ES

ARTIST AND WRITER: PAUL PETER PORGES

TARZAN

The "SHREDDED VINE" Stunt

...HE FRANKENSTEIN MONSTER

The "STUPID SIGN PINNED-TO-THE-BACK" Gag

THE FUTURE KING ARTHUR

The "LOOSE-HANDLED EXCALIBUR" Schtick

WHY ARE WE ALWAY

...EXPENSIVE "DESIGNER JEANS"...*that are turned out in the same Hong Kong factory that makes cheap, ordinary jeans.*

...THE LATEST DISCOVERIES IN MEDICAL SCIENCE...*w the odds of finding a doctor who knows about the latest techniques are exce only by the odds of being able to pay for them.*

ARTIST: ANGELO TOR

...THE PENTAGON'S NEW, ULTRA-SOPHISTICATED WEAPONS...*when most of the teenage personnel who'll be handling these complicated weapons probably won't even be able to read or write.*

...A CONTEST WITH $150,000 WORTH OF PRIZES...*when can bet your life that the prizes consist of one expensive item...and $149 worth of shoddy merchandising gimmicks.*

...RUSH-HOUR RADIO REPORTS THAT TELL US WHAT HIGHWAYS AREN'T CLOGGED WITH BUMPER-TO-BUMPER TRAFFIC...*when everyone else is listening to the same reports, and the roads that used to be traffic-free will soon be just as crammed.*

...PUBLIC BROADCASTING AS AN ALTERNATIVE TO SOAP OPERAS, SITCOMS, OLD MOVIES AND ENDL ADVERTISEMENTS SEEN ON COMMERCIAL TELEVISIO...*when all we ever see on PBS are British soap operas, British sitcom British movies, and endless appeals to viewers to send in their money.*

IMPRESSED BY...?

COSTLY VCRS THAT CAN RECORD SIX HOURS OF PRO-
RAMS OVER 14 DAYS...*when nothing on TV is worth watching even
ce...much less saving for posterity.*

TER: BARRY LIEBMAN

...FOODS LABELED "ALL NATURAL"...*when the term can also be
applied to appetizing items like fungus, crabgrass and horse manure.*

THE LATEST "SAFETY DEVICES" IN OUR LOCAL
JCLEAR POWER PLANT...*when we can plainly see—just by reading
own electric bill—what kind of incompetents are working there.*

...ANY TOY ADVERTISED ON SATURDAY CARTOON SHOWS
...*when—minus the actors, props and special effects used in all the hard-sell
commercials—the average toy is about as fascinating as the box it comes in.*

NY MAN'S COLOGNE WITH A MACHO NAME THAT'S
CKAGED WITH SCENES OF THE OLD WEST AND A
UGH-LOOKING COWBOY...*when in reality, any guy caught wear-
sweet-smelling cologne in the Old West was probably strung up on sight, or
ken for a dance-hall girl.*

...A MOVIE THAT WINS "THE ACADEMY AWARD"...*even
though the Motion Picture Academy is filled with the same idiots who gave us
"Ishtar," "Shanghai Surprise," "Back to the Beach," "Blind Date," and "The
Care Bears in Wonderland."*

ONE FINE DAY IN A DEPARTMENT STORE

Everybody has seen television commercials promoting some sort of "special offer"...

...and then heard the fast-spoken voice-over disclaimer at the tail end of the commercial.

...fortunately, not all commercials have disclaimers, which is why consumers so often end up ...ped-off and disgusted. And which is why MAD, ever eager to improve the world, presents...

DISCLAIMERS
FOR TV COMMERCIALS
THAT DON'T HAVE
DISCLAIMERS

ARTIST: GEORGE WOODBRIDGE WRITER: FRANK JACOBS

I'll do **anything** when I'm close to a man who wears **Ultra-Stud Aftershave!**

Use of this product does not guarantee making out. In real life, actress in commercial is married to a CPA and is the proud mother of three. Actor is gay.

Work out at a **gym**? Not **me!** I do it at home with my **Mr. Muscle Exerciser!** Order yours now for only $119.95! Comes with a **lifetime warranty!**

Warranty does not cover parts which arrive damage Replacement parts available only from manufactur in Karachi, Pakistan, requiring payments in Paki tani rupees. ''Lifetime'' refers to lifetime of th company, which is currently filing for bankrupto

Why do I start my day with **Bran-Plus Cereal?** Because Bran-Plus gives me **twice** the **minimum** daily requirements of vitamins, minerals and fibre!

Minimum Daily Requirement is based on the nutritional needs of 100 fasting religious fanatics.

Right now you can get **Wally's Breakfast Bonanza**—two eggs, bacon, pancakes and hash browns—for only $1.99. Look for a **participating restaurant** in your area!

This offer is not available weekends or during pee breakfast hours. 93% of the franchised restaurar have chosen to not participate, so look very har

Provides temporary, occasional and minor relief only. Total, around-the-clock, odor-free breath calls for gargling thoroughly every 15 minutes and purchase of three large-size bottles daily.

Supply lasts four months if used once every two weeks. 30 day money-back guarantee begins on the day we receive order. Allow 30 days for delivery.

Unit delivered unassembled. One year warranty will elapse before you can put clock together. Add $129.50 for shipping and handling charges.

Slug also goes crazy for cole slaw, macaroni salad, pecan shells, stale Snickers bars, pancake batter, head cheese, watermelon rinds and month-old lard.

ONE MORNING ON THE WEST COAST

SCHWARZENEGGER

WITH A TIP OF THE HAT TO HANK "HIAWATHA" LONGFELLOW

ARTIST: MORT DRUCKER   WRITER: FRANK JACOBS

By the shores of the Pacific,
In the town of glitz and hustle,
Strode the mighty Schwarzenegger,
Baring chest and flexing muscle;
Biceps twitched in perfect rhythm
Through his skill with isometrics, —
Feats that Letterman, on seeing,
Sought to use as Stupid Pet tricks.

But the bulging Schwarzenegger
Set his sights on goals much higher,
As the lure of movie stardom
Pumped him up with great desire;
Soon he found himself in epics,
Slaying enemies like vermin,
Tearing dialogue to pieces
With his accent, sorta German.

Clenching jaw, he raged as "Conan,"
Who, upset by double-dealing,
Slaughters half the population
To express his depth of feeling;
Next "The Terminator" starred him
As a droid bent on aggression,
Killing victims for two hours
Without changing his expression.

As a soldier in "Commando,"
On whole armies he was feasting,
Shrugging off a hail of bullets
Like a flea-bite or a bee-sting;
Not Stallone in Panavision
Matched the fury of his scowling
When in "Predator" he thrilled us
In the art of disemboweling.

In his latest quest for glory
As "The Running Man" he bears up,
Bringing down the rule of evil
While assorted foes he tears up;
See him punch out his oppressors,
Rip apart a villain's torso,
Bludgeon killers into meatloaf
Like Chuck Norris, only more so.

Yes, the massive Schwarzenegger,
Muscles rippling, tendons straining,
Now, through fame and sky-high grosses,
As a super-star is reigning;
Let the critics crucify him
When his lines he seems to louse up!
If it's brains that wins the Oscars,
It's the beef that fills the house up!

There's a popular new board game out called "Pictionary"! A ripoff of TV's "Win, Lose or Draw" (which is a rip-off of the old parlor game "Charades"), a player has 60 seconds to draw some thing while his teammates try to gues what it is. Anyway, we got to wondering what it would be like to play "Pictionary"

PLAY PICTIONARY

John
Caldwell

Jack
Davis

Mort
Drucker

Dave
Berg

Don
Edwing

Bob
Jones

Sergio
Aragones

Bob
Clarke

Paul
Coker

with some of MAD's so-called "artists" and see how *they* stack up against a 60-second stopwatch! Okay, so it's not such a great idea! But we're stuck with it! Here's :

THE RULES: Each MAD artist was sent a sealed list of things to draw. They had five seconds to think about, and 60 seconds to draw, each item listed. No words or symbols could be used.

⁄ITH THE MAD ARTISTS

WRITER: J. PRETE

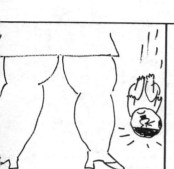

Al
Jaffee

Sam
Viviano

George
Woodbridge

Harvey
Kurtzman

Paul P.
Porges

Angelo
Torres

Jerry
Gersten

Antonio
Prohias

Richard
Williams

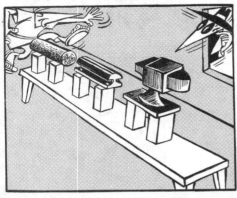

ONE DAY IN A POLICE DEPARTMENT

In the past year there has been a spate of those "body exchange," "role reversal" films. One body switches with another...A father switches brains with his teenage son; a ninety-year-old trades bodies with his grandson. Thrilling concept? Come on!!! How many people really want to see Dudley Moore switch brains with Kirk Cameron? We here at MAD were hoping for one more of these body exchange films, one where a Hollywood Studio Executive switches bodies with a movie-goer and actually has to pay six bucks, sit in a theatre with sticky floors and watch the drivel his studio produced! Of course, that didn't happen. But Hollywood *did* make yet another body exchange film and, for some unexplainable reason, it was a huge hit! In fact, at the box office this summer, it was a real...

biggie

ARTIST: MORT DRUCKER

WRITER: ARNIE KOGEN

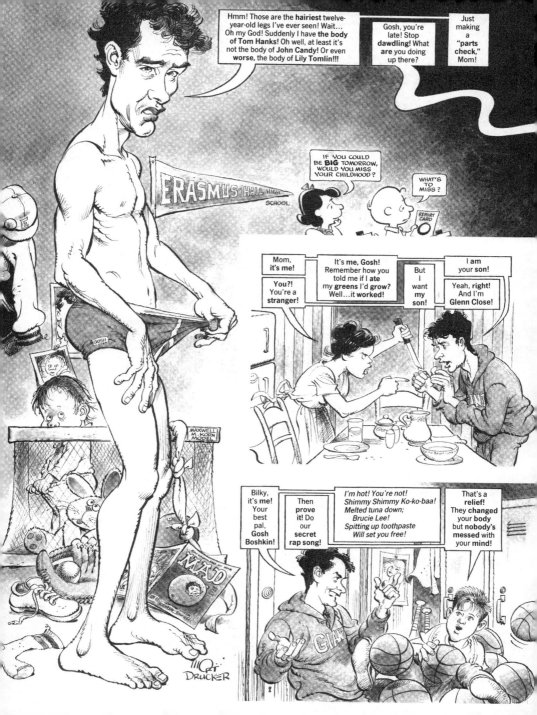

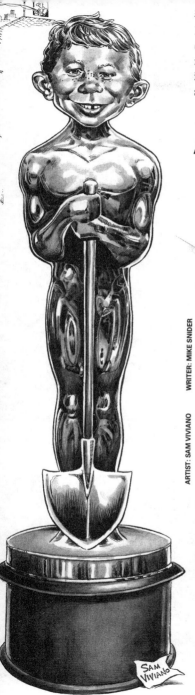

STATUES FOR LIMITATIONS DEPT.

Each year the Motion Picture Academy gives its little pal, "Oscar," to actors, writers, hairdressers and other toads. But the Academy never recognizes the most important group — the people who pay to get in! And it's high time they did, because the best entertainment's not on the screen, it's out in the audience! That's why MAD thinks there should be...

ACADEMY AWARDS

FOR MOVIE AUDIENCE MEMBERS

BEST FORCED CHUCKLE at an obscure Yiddish gag in a Mel Brooks film that has everyone else laughing — even though only 10% of them get it, won by...**JILL WASPBRED**, Snooty, VT

BEST SCREAM OF SURPRISE in a "Friday the 13th" crowd by someone who hasn't caught on that a hop in the sack means automatic death, won by...**HAROLD QWERTY**, Poiuyt, WY

BEST PSYCHOTIC CACKLING during a Rambo shoot-em-up scene, won by...**TOM PUTZKOWSKI**, Untitled, IL

BEST CASUAL EXPRESSION while paying $2.50 for a spritz of 7-Up and 16 ounces of ice, won by...**CHIC GLITZ**, Las Vegas, NV

BEST GROAN at the start of another "thrilling" car chase just like the 3,000 other car chases in film history, won by...**MAXWELL KORN**, Duke, NC

MOST RIDICULOUS "JUNGLE CAMOUFLAGE" at a Vietnam war movie, worn by a punk who's never been away from home over night, won by...**ELMER MIFSUD**, York, PA

Well, he's driving a **Chevy** in this film. That's something **new** for him!

BEST-SOUNDING ARGUMENT that Burt Reynolds isn't "skating" through the twilight of his career in dull, predictable films, won by ...**NANCY ANNE HAZEL**, Gainesville, FL

MOST ANNOYING BEHAVIOR by an idiot who thinks imitating Eddie Murphy's laugh throughout one of his films is the height of cleverness, won by...**JED FLOONMAN**, Arsenio, SD

BEST "HMMM" at the end of one of Woody Allen's newer, supposedly "deeper" movies, won by... **PAUL PETER BORGE**, Raiola, NM

BEST FAKED LAUGHTER at a *Police Academy* sequel by a person of average intelligence who doesn't want to look like a snob, won by ...**PAT PROFT**, Neal, Israel

BEST ICY STARE on a girl dragged to the latest *Porky's* sequel by a no-taste cretin she's dating for the first—and last—time, won by ...**JANE SIANCI**, Cousin, NY

BEST INDIGNANT "SHHHH!" directed at the pseudo-scientist who's explaining to his friends how the special effects were done, won by...**POINDEXTER STARLOG**, Lucas, CA

BEST GLAZED-OVER LOOK while watching another self-indulgent "turkey" by Prince, Warren Beatty or Barbra Streisand, won by... **DONATO DITONNO**, Chafeville, GA

MOST DELUDED USE of "movie critic jargon" to convince yourself that the pretentious bomb you just saw wasn't a total waste of $7.00, won by...**HANS BRICKFACE**, Sambro, MI

FROM BAD TO REVERSE DEPT.

*Attention readers! Get ready for MAD Switcheroos!! What are they you ask? Well, here'
one: What's the difference between a smiling coward and a tired ape? A smiling cowar*

MAD SWIT

ARTIST: AL JAFF

Q. What's the difference between a limping jogger and Robin Givens?

A. A limping jogger pulls
a MUSCLE ON A HIKE;

A. Robin Givens pulls
a_____.

Q. What's the difference between an angry general and the New Jersey shore?

A. An angry general is
POORLY SALUTED;

A. The New Jersey shore
is_____.

Q. What's the difference between an Irish setter and a student eating school cafeteria food?

A. An Irish setter is
RED AND FETCHES;

A. A student is___
_____.

CHEROOS

WRITER: FRANK JACOBS

Q. What's the difference between a hit-and-run stabber and a shy exhibitionist?

A. A hit-and-run stabber
SLASHES ON THE FLY;

A. A shy exhibitionist
_____.

Q. What's the difference between a so-so wide receiver and Dan Quayle on *Meet the Press*?

A. A so-so wide receiver is
BUMPED AND STUMBLES;

A. Dan Quayle on *Meet the Press* is_____.

Q. What's the difference between a drowsy night watchman and a swamp creature?

A. A drowsy night watchman
SLEEPS THROUGH THE CRIME;

A. A swamp creature_____
_____.

ONE FINE SUNDAY AFTERNOON IN THE JUNGLE

Hi, I'm Jugg Hurtz. If you don't mind, I'm going to walk you through an episode of my new sitcom. At first you may think this entire show is just a second-rate rehash of *Taxi*—you know, an average middle class guy surrounded by a group of wise-cracking semi-wierdos. But when you take a closer look, you'll see it's nothing at all like *Taxi*! Notice, there's no garage, no cabs—and some people would say no laughs! is it any wonder why they call this show

Dreary John...

ARTIST: SAM VIVIANO   WRITER: DICK DEBARTOLO

I'm L. Sleaze, head of this group of recently **divorced** people! I'm just divorced **myself**! My husband was pressed and had s-s-sexual problems of a s-s-sexual nature concerning s-s-sex. Luckily, I'm **mature** and can talk openly about such things! But rather than talk about s-s-sex, I prefer to show you some pictures!

I'm **Curt**! Women I meet say I'm just a **pushy** and **obnoxious** egomaniac! But I'm much more than that! Once I turn on the "old Curt charm" they have to **admit** I'm also a **rude chauvanistic pig**!

I'm **Raff**! My ex-wife says all I do is **complain** and **whine** and **complain** and **whine**! Not really! While I may complain a lot and whine a lot, I **NEVER** do both together!

I'm **Bate**! I'm pretty, sensitive and recently **separated**. No, not from my **husband**, from my **agent**—for hooking me up with this neurotic group of **weirdos** where I obviously **don't belong**!

I'm **John Racy**! When my wife left she split everything we owned in two and then took both halves! All I came away with is the clothes I'm wearing!

That's not entirely **true**! She also left this very, very thin **premise** for this very, very **ho-hum** sitcom!

BIRD   BEE

ONE BRIGHT MORNING AT THE BOSTON CEMETERY

WRITER: DON EDWING

A MAD LOOK AT BASIC TRAINING

ARTIST AND WRITER: SERGIO ARAGONES

ONE NOT SO FINE DAY IN THE LIFE OF ARTIE CHARNEY

WRITER: DON EDWING

THE MAD MERCHANDISE MART

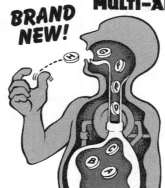

THE SIZZLING SOUTH SEAS SUPPER

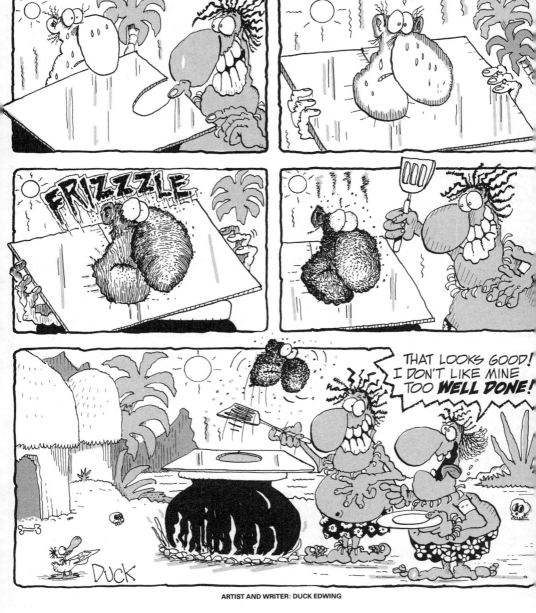

ARTIST AND WRITER: DUCK EDWING

ONE DAY IN THE COUNTRY

ARTIST: DON MARTIN   **WRITER: CHARLIE KADAU**

ONE FINE DAY AT A TELEVISION STATION

It seems that Charles Berlitz, the renowned writer of language books and the founder of ma
language schools made a drastic oversight in his teaching methods! Mr. Berlitz failed to c

MAD'S HANDY FOR

For Various Types of A

FOR THE TRAVELING YUPPIE IN SPAIN

Excuse me, where can I get my portable cellular phone repaired?
¿Disculpame, donde peudo reparar mi tefé-fono portátil celular?

Don't bother with the tour bus, sir. We're renting today's excursion on videocassette.
No se preocupe por el autobús, señor. Vamos a alquilar la excursión de hoy en videocassette.

We need plane reservations to get back by Tuesday afternoon. We want to rest up a bit before we watch *thirtysomething.*
Necesitamos las reservaciones de avión para llegar para el martes. Queremos descansar antes de mirar thirtysomething.

No stamps please. I'll be faxing this postcard.
Mingunos sellos, por favor. Voy a fax esta tarjeta postal.

FOR THE TRAVELING CALIFORNIA AIRHEAD IN FRANCE

Frightful, dude! That ugly chick keeps glaring at me!
Fais gaffe, mec! Cette horrible gonzesse me regarde!

Hey, I speak a little French. Like BON Jovi, man!
Hé, je parle un peu Française, comme BON Jovi!

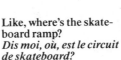

Like, where's the skateboard ramp?
Dis moi, où, est le circuit de skateboard?

Dude, what a rad soufflé!
Ma parole, quel soufflé extra!

You call yourself a fancy restaurant? I don't see anything by Bartles and Jaymes on this wine list!
Vous vous prétendez un restaurant chic? Je ne vois même pas de Bartles et Jaymes sur la liste des vins!

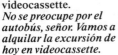

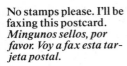

ARTIST: SERGIO ARAG

der that different people have different needs, especially when traveling abroad on vacation.
a valiant attempt to correct Chuck's oversights, we offer the following translation manual:

IGN PHRASE GUIDE

ricans in Various Lands

FOR THE SLIGHTLY OBESE TRAVELING IN GERMANY

s, it's impressive, but
es it have a snack bar?
ia, sehr eindrucksvoll!
er gibts hier auch
en McDonald's?

cuse me, are you
rough with those
ashed potatoes and
uerkraut?
tschuldigung, sind
e fertig mit den Brat-
rtoffeln und dem
uerkraut?

ase pardon my sweat.
mir leid, aber ich
witze immer so!

at is the plural of
twurst?
s is die Mehrzahl von
twurst?

, it's not nice to make
of the overweight,
little Nazi scum!
s ist aber gar nicht
t, dass du dich über
Dicken lustig
chst, du mieses
nes Nazischwein!

ER: AMY GILLETT

FOR THE TRAVELING SENIOR CITIZEN IN ITALY

What? What did you
say? You'll have to speak
up!
Si che cos' ha detto?
Deve parlare piu forte!

Excuse me, have you
seen my teeth anywhere?
Mi scusi, ma lei ha
visto da qualche parte
i miei denti?

Why did I ever come
here? My shoes are
pinching! My back is
aching! My arteries are
clogging!
Perchè sono venuto
qua? Le mie scarpe mi
stanno pizzicando! La
Mia schiena mi fa
malissimo! Le mie
arterie si stanno
bloccando!

Hey, Guido! Did you
know that American
women reach their
sexual prime at 75?
Eh, Guido! Sapevi che
le donne Americane
raggiungiono il loro
periodo di grande
passione sessuale
all'eta di 75 anni?

Do you sell plastic dis-
posable undergarments?
Si vende la mutandine
di plastica?

ONE BALMY NOVEMBER MORNING

ARTIST: DON MARTIN **WRITER: STANLEY SWIERSZ**

There's a growing phenomenon in America these days. Special interest groups are forcing their personal morality on everyone else! Self-appointed do-gooders like housewife Terry Rakolta and the Reverend Donald Wildmon are spearheading movements to pressure major companies into yanking their advertising from "offensive" TV programs like *Married with Children*. (And greedy, spineless companies are caving in!) That's bad enough, but we think it's going to get even worse. MAD envisions a day...

WHEN PRESSURE GROUPS *REALLY* TAKE OVER

ARTIST: BOB CLARKE   WRITER LOU SILVERSTONE

Dear General Mills,

On your Wheaties packages, you have been featuring Olympic Gold Medal winners such as swimmers, basketball players, gymnasts and runners. However, you have never once featured a medal winner in the Pistol and Rifle shoot.

We at the NRA think this is part of a Commie-inspired anti-gun movement. We have millions of members, all of whom eat breakfast cereal. If you expect us to eat the "Breakfast of Champions" you'd better rectify this un-American situation immediately.

Patriotically,
Stu Meats

General **⑤** Mills

Dear Mr. Meats,

General Mills owes all gun owners a heartfelt apology. We never intended to slight those magnificent athletes who compete in the Pistol and Rifle Shoot. We hold these marksmen in the highest esteem and believe them to be excellent role models for America's youth.

Your letter has convinced us to feature these unsung heroes prominently on all Wheaties boxes. Not only that, but we'll be giving away a loaded .22 caliber handgun in each box of Wheaties which will encourage children to start shooting.

Thanks for contacting us—and rest assured that at General Mills we believe firmly in the right of every American to bear arms, no matter how prone to violence they may be.

For God and Country,

Public Relations,
General Mills

To 7-Eleven Inc.,

As the wife of a compulsive gambler, I am outraged by the crass manner in which your store encourages and promotes excessive gambling.

The name "7-Eleven" is the battle cry of derelict, low-life crap shooters when they are rolling dice.

Whenever my poor husband sees one of your wretched stores he walks out on me and goes looking for a dice game or a seedy betting parlor.

I have organized a group of concerned housewives who firmly believe that their husbands' addiction to gambling is directly linked to 7-Eleven. We are planning nationwide demonstrations in front of all your stores and a high profile media campaign that will expose you for the unsavory characters we know you to be.

With deepest concern,
Mabel Duck

7-ELEVEN

Dear Mrs. Duck,

We beg your pardon. It never occurred to us that the name 7-Eleven could be an inducement for people to gamble. Thanks to your astute letter, we've taken action to remedy this situation and chosen a new number as our store name, a number that our research team assures us has nothing to do with gambling and will definitely not offend anyone. The number is 666.

It is our sincere hope this move meets with your approval.

Best regards,

Consumer Relations
7-Eleven

DEAR IZOD,

As a member of the Alligator Preservation Society, I feel it is my duty to call to your attention that the alligator is an endangered species on the verge of extinction. Your callous depiction of alligators on your sport shirts condones and encourages the senseless hunting and mutilation of these poor creatures.

On behalf of my organization, I demand you stop your ruthless exploitation of alligators and remove them from all your merchandise at once. Failure to comply with our wishes will result in our staging massive demonstrations in the parking lots of all stores that sell IZOD products.

Yours for alligators,
Henrik Spume

Dear Mr. Spume,

Let me assure you that it was never our intent to portray alligators in a negative way, nor do we mean to support the killing of these truly wonderful reptiles. Indeed, it troubles us to hear that they are an endangered species. In fact, we've decided to no longer use them as our trademark and replace them with creatures which we are certain are in much more plentiful supply —cockroaches and deer ticks. Thanks for calling this to our attention.

Best wishes,

Customer Service Dept.
IZOD

To: Kelloggs Cereal Co.

I resent your putting "Snap, Crackle and Pop" on the boxes of Rice Crispies. These characters are an obvious sacrilegeous mocking of the Father, Son and Holy Spirit. My Organization, The Alabama Mothers for Christian Cereal boxes, plan to boycott all Kelloggs products unless the demonic trilogy is eliminated

Yours in God,
Mr. Hans Brickface

K KELLOGG'S OF BATTLE CREEK

Dear Mr. Brickface,

Kelloggs is extremely grateful to you for pointing out the inherent blasphemous nature of Snap, Crackle and Pop. This terrible triumvirate will never appear on any of our products again.

It will please you to know that our Rice Krispies package has been completely redesigned and now features the prophets Moses, Ezekiel and Jeremiah. Now, when milk is added, our cereal no longer goes "Snap, Crackle, Pop," but instead chants the Twenty-First Psalm in Latin. We appreciate you setting us straight!

Best wishes,

Marketing Dept.
Kelloggs of Battle Creek

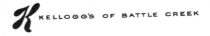

To Perdue Chicken Co.

Last night, while I was watching TV with my children, a commercial for your product was aired. I was absolutely taken aback by its sleazy content. Frank Perdue was talking like a dirty old man about "juicy thighs" and "tender young breasts" for the whole world to hear! Please be informed that I plan on spearheading a nationwide boycott of your company unless you do something to end this kind of blatent depravity in your advertising!

Respectfully,
Ted Tub

PERDUE

Dear Mr. Tub,

We are terribly sorry you found our commercial featuring Frank Perdue offensive. You will be happy to know that starting today all poultry appearing in our ads will be wearing clothing. Also, we have decided to put more energy into marketing the more acceptable, less disgusting parts of the chicken such as the neck, gizzard and head.

As for Mr. Perdue himself, we have replaced him with a claymation dwarf. Thanks for writing.

Sincerely,

Corporate Office
Perdue Farms

DEAR MIDAS MUFFLER INC.,

As PRESIDENT OF PEOPLE FOR PURITY IN PROGRAMMING, I AM WRITING TO EXPRESS MY OUTRAGE REGARDING YOUR OBSCENE TELEVISION COMMERCIALS. THESE ADS, FEATURING BIG SWEATY MECHANICS SPEWING FORTH THEIR FILTHY OBSESSIONS WITH LUBE JOBS AND TAIL PIPES, SHOULD BE BANNED! IT'S OBVIOUS TO US THAT MIDAS IS AN ACRONYM FOR MEN INVOLVED IN DERANGED AND AWFUL SEX AND THAT YOU ARE RESPONSIBLE FOR THE CORRUPTION OF OUR YOUTH AND THE DECAY OF OUR SOCIETY. WE WILL DO EVERYTHING IN OUR POWER TO ALERT THE PUBLIC OF YOUR SICK PERVERSIONS.

NEWT SNOUTFISH
PRESIDENT, P.P.P.

---

mIDAS

Dear Mr. Snoutfish,

We are always pleased to receive thoughtful letters such as yours. It will please you to know that just seconds after reading your letter our president was so upset that he jumped off the 96th floor of our building and killed himself. We have filed for bankruptcy and are going out of business forever. We deeply appreciate your concern.

Sincerely,

Media Relations Dept.
Midas Muffler, Inc.

Take a rubber-faced widower starting his life over, two grown daughters still seeking their dad's love, a lumbering dog, a great time slot—and what have you got? Unfortunately, you've got an ...

Hi, I'm **Richard Hooligan!** In this series I play **Harried Westin,** a recently-widowed pediatrician, the **most eligible bachelor** in all of Miami! What that means is: I don't have a **prostate problem** and I'm not a **Cuban Drug Czar!** Please meet my TV family!

I'm **Carrot Westin,** a depressed, angst-ridden, neurotic, hypochondriac divorcee! I'm all **doom and gloom!** The people from "Thirty-something" have told me to "lighten up"!

I'm **Boobra Westin,** the other daughter! I'm an under-cover cop! Unlike my sister, I'm **perky** and **bubbly! Why?** Because I spend most of my time **under the covers** with **cops!** Do I **look** like a police officer to you? The people who cast me in this role also cast **Pat Sajak** as the lead in *King Lear!*

Oooh, when I see a cop that looks as good as Boobra, I want to **take the law into my own hands!** I'm **Churley!** You may remember me from the **Joe Isuzu** ads! In this series I play a character like that, only without the **charm!** Here, I'm a **sleazy cruise ship officer.** How sleazy? On my last voyage, my best friend was a **porthole!**

YOU CAN CALL A DOCTOR A QUACK, BUT YOU CAN'T DUCK HIS BILL. ANON.

TRUTH METER

LIE

I'm **Luhverne!** A sassy hillbilly nurse! I'm an **R.N.—Real Nasty!** I bring a sarcastic, biting edge to this show! Let me put it this way: If **Minnie Pearl** and **Sam Kinison** had a child, **I'd** be it! I'd be **prettier,** but I'd be it!

MAX

KORN

VARIETY

I'm **Dreyfoos,** the **smartest dog** in TV! How smart? Smart enough to turn down the title role in that dog of a Tom Hanks film, *Turner and Hooch!* Before I **go** on *Variety,* I **read** it!

IIIQT DRUCKER

Empty Mess

ARTIST: MORT DRUCKER   WRITER: JOSH GORDON

123

ONE SPECIAL DAY IN THE DUNGEON

ARTIST: DON MARTIN

WRITER: ANTONIO PROHIAS

Dirty, rotten lies! Nobody likes lies! After all, our nation is founded on truth! But nowada

POLITICAL H

THE HALF-TRUTH IS:
"The depletion of the ozone layer is not an immediate threat…"

THE WHOLE TRUTH IS:
"…because the 'Greenhouse Effect' will kill us first!"

THE HALF-TRUTH IS:
"The homeless prefer to live on the street…"

THE HALF-TRUTH IS:
"The war on drugs is being won…"

THE WHOLE TRUTH IS:
"…by the South American Drug Lords!"

THE HALF-TRUTH IS:
"The government is ignoring our hostages…"

THE HALF-TRUTH IS:
"More nuclear power plants mean more jobs…"

THE WHOLE TRUTH IS:
"…for cancer specialists!"

THE HALF-TRUTH IS:
"The cure for cancer takes a long time to discover…"

EUREKA!

some truths are even bigger lies than lies! You'll see what we mean after checking out these...

HALF-TRUTHS

ARTIST: GEORGE WOODBRIDGE   WRITER: CHRIS HART

THE HALF-TRUTH IS:
"The plan to build a Star Wars defense system isn't a fantasy..."

THE WHOLE TRUTH IS:
"...but the hope that it will actually work is!"

THE WHOLE TRUTH IS:
"...which makes perfect sense if you've ever seen a public shelter!"

THE HALF-TRUTH IS:
"Capital punishment is a strong deterrent..."

THE WHOLE TRUTH IS:
"...the same way the hostages scared the government!"

THE WHOLE TRUTH IS:
"...but only to the guy who receives it!"

THE WHOLE TRUTH IS:
"...because once they find it, the searchers will be out of a job!"

THE HALF TRUTH IS:
"Some African nations don't have money for food and medicine..."

THE WHOLE TRUTH IS:
"...only for guns and tanks!"

Readers rejoice! It's time once again for MAD Switcheroos! And what, oh ye of faulty memory may ask, are MAD Switcheroos? Pay attention this time! What's the difference

MORE MAD SWIT

ARTIST: AL JAFFE

Q. What's the difference between a cheap eatery and Geraldo Rivera?

A. A cheap eatery serves up **HASH AND TRIPE;**

A. Geraldo Rivera serves up_____.

Q. What's the difference between a nervous collapse and an IRS audit?

A. A nervous collapse is a **BREAKDOWN THAT SHAKES YOU;**

A. An IRS audit is a_____
_____.

Q. What's the difference between a poultry lab and a sleazy lawyer?

A. A poultry lab takes in **CLUCKERS FOR SCIENCE;**

A. A sleazy lawyer takes in_____.

CHEROOS

WRITER: FRANK JACOBS

Q. What's the difference between a spanking and a tourist in Mexico?

A. A spanking
RATTLES THE BUNS;

A. A tourist in Mexico
_____.

Q. What's the difference between a horse-player and Jason?

A. A horse player
BACKS UP A HUNCH;

A. Jason_____
_____.

Q. What's the difference between a smoker and Kermit the Frog?

A. A smoker craves a
CIG IN THE PACK;

A. Kermit the frog
craves a_____.

DUCK EDWING ON THE LOOS

ARTIST AND WRITER: DUCK EDWING

AT THE ZOO

ONE INSANE AFTERNOON ON INTERSTATE 80

TV gets blasted for being a mind-numbing time-waster, programmed solely for air-headed couch potatoes. But isn't that criticism a bit harsh? MAD thinks TV can be very enlightening! In fact, every sitcom, soap opera and crime show gives us ideas we just don't get anywhere else. You'll see what we mean when we point out these...

IMPORTANT THINGS WE'D NEVER LEARN WITHOUT TV

In cases where large estates are willed to two or more beneficiaries, one of them is certain to murder the other before the money can be distributed.

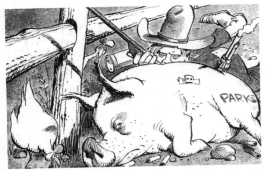

The financial crisis crippling American agriculture has come about because most farmers are demented hermits who spend all their time shooting at strangers.

ARTIST: MORT DRUCKER   **WRITER: TOM KOCH**

Under our present judicial system, many dangerous criminals now end up in a courtroom where so much horseplay is in progress that the judge forgets to sentence them.

The average parent is either a single mom with no social life or a divorced dad who can't cook. Couples seldom have kids, but may adopt ethnic, wise-cracking orphans.

All slum dwellers have three things in common: They never use good grammar, they never wash their kids' faces, and they never open their doors more than a crack.

If heavy drinking is done with buddies and confined to places of good fellowship, one can booze it up for years without becoming an alcoholic—or even getting tipsy.

All private eyes keep their own office in an impossible mess, but are skilled at finding every important paper in a strange office in 30 seconds—in the dark.

The average American ten-year-old no longer wants to be a fireman or an astronaut when he grows up. He wants to be Henny Youngman.

ONE FINE EVENING ON A STREET CORNER

THE PERILOUS PIONEER PREDICAMENT

ARTIST AND WRITER: DUCK EDWING

ONE DARK NIGHT ON THE EAST COAST

THE MACABRE MORTICIANS' MELODRAMA

ARTIST AND WRITER: DUCK EDWING

As a medical officer, I'd like to **know** what I'm **supposed to do** on this **sub!**

Stop always **asking** about **your role!**

I **can't!** The one time I **didn't ask** about my role, I **wound up** in the *Rocky Horror Picture Show* looking like **this...**

TIM CURRY IN "THE ROCKY HORROR SHOW"

We have **absolutely no defense** against the **new class** of **Russian submarines!**

It looks like the **United States** is in a "**no-win**" situation!

What do you mean, sir?

Right now the government is **unprepared** to face the **threat of war.** In a **few months,** it'll be **unprepared** to face the **threat** of **peace!**

Hmmm... I don't think the **crew** has been **impressed** with the **seriousness** of **our mission!**

What happened to the political officer?

I had to **get rid of him** so we could carry out **our plan!**

I **can't believe** that you **killed** him with your **bare hands!**

Why not? I used to do it **all the time** when I played **James Bond!**

WHAT A COUNTRY!

With our new **propulsion device** we make **no noise** that the enemy can **pick up.** We only **emit** very authentic **whale sounds!**

That means we can go **totally undetected!**

Not quite...

How about a n... **quiet dinner** o... **crustaceans,** a... then back to... **my place?**

DUCK EDWING

REALLY AXE UP!

ARTIST AND WRITER:

DUCK EDWING

EARLY ONE MORNING IN AN AFRICAN JUNGLE

ONE FINE AFTERNOON DOWNTOWN

THE PERILOUS PACIFIC PICKLE

ARTIST AND WRITER: DUCK EDWING

Long before Batman made it to the big screen, the Caped Crusader enjoyed success in a ridiculously overdone and campy 60's TV show. Each week the Dynamic Duo would chase an "arch criminal" portrayed by a has-been, washed up actor who couldn't get work anywhere else! This got us thinking (which is a rare thing indeed!): If Batman returned to television now, there'd be a whole new group of has-beens to choose from! So here, along with sample plotlines and some random scenes, are a few of our selections for...

Villains Awaiting Batman's Return to TV

ARTIST: RICK TULKA

WRITERS: JOE RAIOLA
AND CHARLIE KADAU

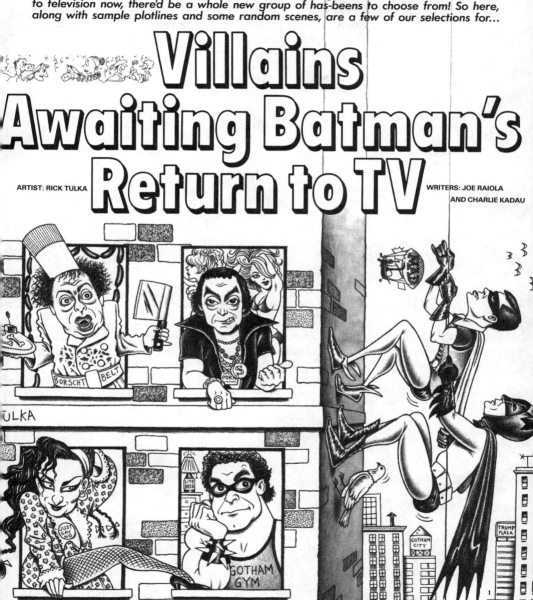

JACKIE MASON as THE CATERER

The criminally insane master chef supplies free gourmet food to the Gotham City Police so they do nothing but eat, gain weight and become too fat and lazy to stop his sinister crime spree!

BOY GEORGE as CROSS-DRESSER

Master criminal Cross-Dresser escapes from prison disguised as Commissioner Gordon's daughter. He blackmails Thomas Hovel, the curator of the Gotham City Museum, into giving him the priceless painting "Blue Boy" by threatening to release compromising photos of Hovel wearing a strapless evening gown with matching pumps!

BOB GUCCIONE as SLEAZEBAG

Sleazebag sponsors Tina Tramp as his own erotic entrant in the usually pure and moral Miss Gotham City Pageant! Tina is so much more aggressively sexy and seductive than the other contestants that she is sure to be named the winner by the aroused judges—leaving Sleazebag to steal the jeweled tiara given to the winner!

Well, **Miss Tramp**, *(drool)* when...I mean if, you're chosen **Miss Gotham City**, *(slobber)* how would you use your **body**, I mean **title**, to **improve society**?

Well, the **first thing** I'd do would be..

I'll answer that for her! She'll be a **forthright, bold** and **controversial** Miss Gotham City! She'll lobby to make **mud wrestling** an **inter-collegiate event!** She'll defend the **first amendment rights** of **pageant judges** to spend time in her **hot tub** whenever **they want!** Come on honey, **show 'em your tattoo!**

So, **Sleazebag** thinks he can detain us by locking us in this **cramped peepshow booth!** I can melt the lock in a second by using my **Bat-Anti-Peepshow-Lock-Laser!** Reach for it in my **utility belt, Robin!**

Holy hormones! **Forget** about the **lock,** Batman! I'm **running out** of **quarters!** Can you **break a twenty?**

JOE PISCOPO as THE IRRITANT

Upon his release from jail, Batman's old nemesis, The Irritant, desperately seeks revenge against the Dynamic Duo. The obnoxious super-crook takes them by surprise in the Batcave and mercilessly tortures them with his grating personality and moronic behavior!

Did'ya ever notice how **supermarket receipts** are so **blurry?** Why **is that?** That's my **Andy Rooney** impression! Pretty good, huh? And I'm just **getting started!** Now I'm going to do my **two-hour Bruce Springsteen** impersonation without looking or sounding like him at **all!** Ha ha!

Holy lack of **talent!** My mind is turning to **putty!** This is the **worst punishment** we've ever been **subjected to!**

I only hope we **escape** before he does his **Lite Beer** commercials! I really **hate** those **things!**

Batman! Are you **all right?** What **happened** to the **Irritant?**

I **shot him!** Let that be a **lesson** to you, **Robin!** Even the most **dedicated crime fighters** have their **breaking point!**

I want to be **buried** in **Jersey,** do **you** want to be **buried** in **Jersey?**

LATE ONE AFTERNOON OUTSIDE OF ORLANDO

THE FREE-STYLE FIRING-SQUAD FIASCO

ARTIST AND WRITER: DUCK EDWING

When TV shows visit the homes of famous people they show the pool, the sauna, the 50-foot kitchen. But you never see any books. Why not? Can't celebrities read? Sure they can! So what books are they hiding? We did a little MAD investigating, crashed a few private libraries, and turned up these..

CELEBRIT

ARTIST: SAM

WAIT A MINUTE—I'M ON TV!

WAIT ANOTHER MINUTE—I'M IN COMMERCIALS!

WAIT AN HOUR—I'M IN MAD!

WAIT A FEW YEARS—I'LL BE A HAS-BEEN!

DAN RATHER
"The Day Cronkite Retired
(and Other Memorable Dates in History)"
"Loni Anderson's E-Z Guide to Sex Appeal
in Slipover Sweaters"
"Libel Laws and Their Little-Known Loopholes"
"The Barbara Walters Book of Pubwik Speaking & Ewo
"Proclaiming Election Winners on the Basis of Two Vote

1,001 CLEVER WAYS TO END A NEWSCAST

JOHN MADDEN
"Winter Catalog of Size 58 Slacks"
"Coaching: Springboard to TV Commercials"
"Dull Sports Anecdotes for All Occasions"
"Cosell's Guide to Making Football Sound
Complicated"
"How to Appear Laid Back When You're
Completely Hysterical"

THE BIG PICTURE BOOK of COLORFUL INVECTIVE

FRANK SINATRA
"Who's Who in Sicily"
"Who's Who in Las Vegas"
"Who's Who in Hoboken"
"Who's Who at the Bottom of the
East River"
"Good Manners, and Why Celebrities
Don't Need Them"
"Profiles in Arrogance—Louis XIV
to Leonard Brenner"

I AM THE SECRET SQUARE by the Late Paul Lynde

JOAN RIVERS
"Good Taste, and How to Get Rich by Ignoring It"
"Use Nervous Mannerisms to Drive Your Friends Bonk
"Bette Midler's 101 Tips for Becoming a Classy Broad"
"The Sean Penn Guide to Total Politeness"
"How to Lose Old Friends and Use New Ones"

READING LISTS

WRITER: TOM KOCH

BROOKE SHIELDS
"Retaining Your Sex Appeal Beyond Puberty"
"Actor's Guide to Unskilled Movie Directors"
"Groucho Marx on Beauty for Bushy Eyebrows"
"Speaking Lines You Don't Understand:
    The Method Actor's Bible"
"How to Cut the Umbilical Cord by Age 50"

GEORGE STEINBRENNER
"Build Your Self-Esteem by Owning Athletes"
"Everything You Need to Know about Baseball,
    as Told by the Three Stooges"
"Biographies of Famous Unlikable People"
"Are Throwaway Managers Worth Recycling?"
"The Yankee Tradition—and 500 Ways to Destroy It"

AYATOLLAH KHOMEINI
"Burning the American Flag—and Other Party Games"
"Mecca on Five Drachmas a Day"
"The Beard Lice Breeder's Handbook"
"*The Pope Is Satan!* and Other Bedtime Stories for Children"

MICHAEL JACKSON
"The Ink Spots and Other
    Lifelong Boy Sopranos"
"Dare to Wear Epaulets"
"How to Profit from Your Strangeness"
"What the Well-Dressed Man
    Should Wear—on One Hand"

ONE FINE TUESDAY IN THE DUNGEON

THE REFRIGERATED ROCKY RUN-THROUGH

ARTIST AND WRITER: DUCK EDWING

THE EXCRUCIATING ESCAPE EXTRAVAGANZA

We're looking for people who are looking for a course on how to write children's books.

By Chic Glitz
Dean of Words

Home of the Home Study Institute for the Discovery of Hidden Talents in the Field of Writing Children's Books deep in the Connecticut woods. The Institute is located in a dilapidated shack behind this Victorian mansion.

RECENT GOVERNMENT FIGURES INDICATE there's now a better than 50/50 chance that everyone reading this ad was once a child. That means you've already done all the necessary research needed to create a child's book. Now all you have to do is write one!

Writing children's books is as easy as A, B, 3! Kids don't know from grammar, punctuation and style. To them, a book is just a string of words on pages. You don't have to use big words *or* know how to spell correctly!

Important details

Of course, there *are* fine points to be learned before writing children's books. Should you submit your story in crayon on white paper or type it on a brown paper bag? Who should you submit it to? General Motors or a book publisher? Should your book be illustrated, or maybe have drawn pictures?

That's where we come in. We're the Home Study Institute for the Discovery of Hidden Talents in the Field of Writing Children's Books. We're listed in the Guinness Book of World Records as the learning institution with the longest name! What better reference is there than that?

Lingering doubts?

You may still ask yourself: Am I qualified to be a writer? If you can write a check in the amount of $350—and the bank is so moved by your writing that they pay the amount of the check to us, then you're qualified!

After receiving Lesson One, "How to Sharpen a Pencil," you will be able to say to your friends, "Hey, I'm a writer"! Then, we will send you (at additional cost, of course) your own business card that says: WRITER. If you so desire, you can add other information like your name, address and phone number, also at an additional cost.

Learn writing "tricks"

Above all, we'll teach you to be original and avoid common clichés, which is easy as pie! We pledge the grass won't be greener on the other side of the fence any more for you! But, since even the longest journey starts with one step and today is the first day of the rest of your life, remember: He who hesitates is lost! Fill out and mail in the attached coupon now!

If you want to start on the fabulous road to becoming a famous author EVEN FASTER and earn big bucks to help pay off the charges we'll put on your credit card, then call 1-800-WRITER *this second* and give us your VISA, MASTERCARD or AMERICAN EXPRESS number. SPECIAL OFFER: Give us all three credit card numbers and learn three times faster!

Satisfied students

Here are some comments from our graduates:

"I could hardly believe it when I opened the publisher's envelope and a check fell out! My first sale after mailing out 6,735 submissions! I'll be taking a break from my writing now to decide how to spend my $5 check!!"
—N.M., Poor, NM

"I used to waste valuable time doing nothing. But now, thanks to the Institute, I now waste valuable time writing unpublished kid's books!"—J.W., Skank, OR

"The Home Study Institute for the discovery of Hidden Talents in the Field of Writing Children's Books is the best course in the entire world! I never, ever thought I'd be paid for my writing, but I just got my first check for writing this favorable quote for them to use in their ad!!!"—D.D., Boatbasin, NY

Don't think, do it!

Our course will get you started on the road to becoming an author of children's books, or children's stories, or maybe just a single children's word. We GUARANTEE you that after taking the course no more than five times, you will definitely be published, or at the very least, xeroxed!

The Home Study Institute for the Discovery of Hidden Talents in the Field of Writing Children's Books
11 Verb Place Noun, Alaska

Dear Mr. Glitz: Enclosed is my check for $350, which covers EVERYTHING you can think of for the moment. But being extremely creative, I know I can expect many future charges. I understand that once my check clears, I am under no obligation whatsoever to even open my study-at-home course.

Mr.   Mrs.   Ms.   Miss

_____
Please circle one and print name clearly

_____
Street

_____
City

_____
State   Zip

WRITER: DICK DEBARTOLO

Today, you can divide everyone under 35 in America into one of two categories: Yuppies and Aspiring Yuppies. All Yuppies care about is maintaining and improving their Yupster status. All Aspiring Yuppies care about is joining the ranks of these heralded achievers. Whether you're a Yuppie or a would-be Yuppie, we thought you'd like to know how you're doing. That's why we devised this simple test that will answer the toughest question you'll ever face:

HOW DO YOU RATE AS A YUPPIE?

ARTIST: PAUL COKER   **WRITER: TOM KOCH**

YUPPIE CAREER GOALS

AWARD YOURSELF A PERFECT SCORE OF TEN if you have dreamed since childhood of becoming a wine steward, a dealer in commodity futures or a great humanitarian who brings joyous news of tax shelters to the middle class.

DEDUCT TWO POINTS FROM THIS TOTAL if you'd settle for becoming a rich suburban dentist or a Senator from a thinly populated western state.

DEDUCT NINE POINTS for any hidden desire to be school teacher, a social worker or an honest cop.

YUPPIE EATING HABITS

AWARD YOURSELF THE FULL TEN PO[INTS] if you maintain that everything one [eats] should first be pulverized in a Cuisi[nart] —including steak, grape nuts and pe[ach] cobbler a la mode.

DEDUCT FIVE POINTS if you actually [use] your microwave oven and me[tric] kitchen scale, instead of eating [out] every night with other Yuppies who [all] have fully equipped kitchens at hom[e].

DEDUCT EIGHT POINTS if you serve [all] the "in" foods, but buy domestic bra[nds] instead of imported so you'll h[ave] enough money left to pay your rent.

YUPPIE FRIENDS

AWARD YOURSELF A FULL TEN POINTS if the only social contact whose name you bother to remember is the doorman who can get you into a popular disco.

DEDUCT THREE POINTS FROM THAT TOTAL if you spend *Christmas* with relatives instead of at Aspen making contacts among influential people.

DEDUCT FIVE POINTS if you don't know a single overseas airline pilot who can bring back new flavors of Swedish fibre bread before they're available here.

YUPPIE IDOLS

AWARD YOURSELF THE MAXIMUM [TEN] POINTS if your favorite celebritie[s are] Bill Cosby, Lee Iacocca and Mary [Lou] Retton's agent. (Make it a TEN PL[US] if you refer to them as "role models[" in]stead of "favorite celebrities.")

DEDUCT TWO FROM THAT TOTAL i[f you] still have admiration for such out[dated] people as Gary Hart, Alan Alda, P[hyllis] George and Abraham Lincoln.

DEDUCT SEVEN POINTS if your [role] models are any of the regulars [in] those Lite Beer commercials.

YUPPIE READING

[AW]ARD YOURSELF A PERFECT TEN if the **[Wa]ll Street Journal** would fulfill your **[eve]ry** need to keep abreast of the day's **[im]portant happenings**—if only it car**[rie]d "Doonesbury."**

[DED]UCT TWO POINTS FROM THAT TOTAL **[if y]ou** also sneak an occasional look at **[Peo]ple** and **Us,** but only to see what **[oth]er** featherbrained social climbers **[are]** yourself are doing.

[DED]UCT SEVEN POINTS if you still suffer **[fro]m** claustrophobia when the latest **[Yup]phobia** is a fear of having poor peo**[ple]** brush up against you in their infe**[rio]r polyester clothing.**

YUPPIE LOVE LIFE

AWARD YOURSELF THE FULL TEN POINTS if you refuse to date members of the opposite sex until you've inspected their apartments, thus following the sensible adage, "It's not who you are that counts; it's what you own."

DEDUCT SIX POINTS if you're already engaged, but still haven't selected a big name lawyer to handle your future divorce, in case the marriage goes kaput.

DEDUCT NINE POINTS if you've dated that girl next door since you were 14 and plan to marry her even though she's now a mere data processor with absolutely no management level ambitions.

YUPPIE PARENTHOOD

AWARD YOURSELF A MAXIMUM SCORE OF TEN if you've arranged for your kid to be born in a socially prominent hospital so he can get into the proper day nursery so he'll qualify for a snobbish private boarding school so he'll be accepted at Dartmouth or Stanford, even if he's a nitwit.

DEDUCT FIVE POINTS if you refer to raising kids as "raising kids" instead of "parenting."

DEDUCT NINE POINTS if you would lack the clout to keep your wayward children out of jail when all your Yuppie friends can get their kids released to undergo psychological counseling.

YUPPIE DISEASES

[AWA]RD YOURSELF THE TEN POINT MAXI-[MU]M if your only doctor is a psychia-**[tris]t** who diagnoses every earache and **[ing]own toenail** as an emotional prob-**[lem]** from the stress of overwork.

[DED]UCT ONE POINT FROM THAT TOTAL if **[you]** quit going to a psychiatrist—but **[only]** because he made you lie on a couch **[in h]is** office that wasn't covered with Corinthian leather.

[DED]UCT EIGHT POINTS if you sometimes **[read]** one of those check-out stand tab-**[loid]s,** even if you can prove that you only **[buy]** it to line the bottom of your pedi-**[gree]d** myna's bird cage.

YUPPIE DRESSING

AWARD YOURSELF THE MAXIMUM SCORE OF TEN if you now live in a nudist camp because the wise decision to buy top quality running shoes has left you too poor to buy any other clothing.

DEDUCT THREE POINTS FROM THAT TOTAL if you've ever been seen wearing a belt buckle with your own initials on it, rather than those of Yves St. Laurent.

DEDUCT NINE POINTS if you think Brooks Brothers was the all-star third baseman who played for the Baltimore Orioles a few years back.

SCORING

Either add up your score manually, or award yourself an extra five points by having your home computer add it for you. However you do it, this is what your total means:

140-TO-160 POINTS Nice going! Your life-long passion for overachievement has again put you at the top. You are such a dedicated Yuppie that you'll be running a major corporation before you're 40—if your colleagues let you live that long.

110-TO-140 POINTS Not bad, but there is still a spark of ordinary common sense within you somewhere. Work harder to get rid of it.

90-TO-110 POINTS Strictly so-so. Either you're not willing to live beyond your means, or you have some wimpish hesitation about riding roughshod over others. Whatever the problem, you'll never rise beyond the middle class unless you get off your duff and start playing for keeps.

70-TO-90 POINTS You're truly a sad case. Try having yourself committed to a Young Professionals' Club and see if they can do anything for you.

BELOW 70 POINTS Hopeless! In fact, no one ever scored as poorly on this test—except for Bishop Tutu, a couple of Peace Corps volunteers and a Hindu untouchable named Skippy.

THE ALARMING ALIEN ATROCITY

ARTIST AND WRITER: DUCK EDWING

Thinking about what career to get into? Wondering whether or not you'll fit in? Well, here's the sixth in a series of tests designed to help you choose your future line of work. Mainly, discover your true abilities by taking...

MAD'S APTITUDE TEST NUMBER SIX
WILL YOU MAKE A GOOD
PSYCHIATRIST?

1. As a Psychiatrist, you suggest to a patient that sessions be daily instead of twice a week. This usually means that:
   A. The credit check you ran on him came back positive.
   B. She's gorgeous and sexy, so why shouldn't you get turned on as often as possible.
   C. Your regular bridge partner has moved away, and you've suddenly got this free time to fill.
   D. Any of the above.

2. From the pencil in his hand, we can tell that this Psychiatrist is:
   A. Making progress in finishing the crossword puzzle he began during his first session this morning.
   B. Finding out that he can draw a picture of Bugs Bunny from memory.
   C. Calculating how much of a "cost-of-living" increase he can add to his hourly fee and still hold on to his patients.
   D. Any of the above.

3. A woman patient confides that she carries on conversations with her St. Bernard, spends week-ends hiding in a closet, and is terrified of walking on linoleum. As a Psychiatrist, what do you say when she pleads for your advice?
   A. "How do YOU feel about it?"
   B. "I think you KNOW the answer to that already!"
   C. "What is it you REALLY want to tell me?"
   D. Any of the above.

4. Complete the following sentence: Running a Group Therapy session is helpful because _____.
   A. Listening to patients arguing and screaming at each other provides wonderful entertainment.
   B. One of the patients may come up with an insight that you were incapable of seeing by yourself.
   C. Sitting back and playing God is a real kick.
   D. All of the above.

5. A patient catches you falling asleep while he is pouring out a sob-filled tale of how he was ignored as a child. What is the proper response to his accusation?
   A. "I was merely testing your reaction to MY ignoring you!"
   B. "My powers of perception increase when I close my eyes!"
   C. "Your hour is up!"
   D. Any of the above.

6. From time to time you will ask a patient to describe his dreams. Listening to dreams helps you by:
   A. Providing you with some swell stories that you can share with your fellow Shrinks at the next annual convention.
   B. Giving you a chance to use impressive Shrink gibberish such as "suppressed anger," "unconscious urges" and "deep-seated ego manifestations."
   C. Getting your patients off their real problems, which you can't figure out anyway.
   D. All of the above.

7. Some patients become so dependent on you that they call you night and day with trivial problems. This should tell you that:
   A. It's time to include a fee for "Telephone Consultation" in your bill.
   B. You've got the sucker so strung out that he's hooked for another two years of treatment, at least.
   C. You can really get your jollies by busting his chops and putting him on "hold."
   D. Any of the above.

8. While interviewing a prospective patient, you suddenly learn that he is unemployed and without funds. What should you tell him?
   A. "Learning to live with your problems is often preferable to going through the agonies of analysis!"
   B. "You, I am happy to say, are what we Psychiatrists classify as 'normal'!"
   C. "I think I should see you twice a week! With any luck, I may be able to work you into my schedule in a year or two!"
   D. Any of the above.

9. After twelve years of therapy, a patient announces that he is making no progress and is quitting. Which of these is your most effective response?
   A. "Impatience has always been one of your problems, hasn't it?"
   B. "Quit if you wish, but I cannot take responsibility for the consequences!"
   C. "I was waiting for you to get to this point! Now, we can really begin to work!"
   D. Any of the above.

10. Eventually, of course, there comes a time when therapy is concluded. This usually happens when:
    A. The patient's awareness of your incompetence overrides his need for your help.
    B. The patient dies.
    C. You die.
    D. Any of the above.

SCORING

If you answered "D" to all questions, you have the ability to make a good Psychiatrist.

Recently, we asked one of our idiot artists to do a drawing of a Rock Concert. Unfortunately, he didn't do a very good

HOW MANY MISTAKES CA

ARTIST: GEORGE WOODBRI

ob. In fact, he made a lot of mistakes ... 20 in all! And
ow, it's up to you to find them. Which is why we're asking:

OU FIND IN THIS PICTURE?

TER: CHRIS HART

ANSWERS

1. The audience is smoking cigarettes with tobacco in them.

2. The fan running up to the stage is not being beaten up by the Security Guards.

3. The man with the plaid suit, black shoes and white socks is not an undercover narcotics agent.

4. The musicians are playing their final number, and they're not destroying a single instrument on stage.

5. The man is eating his French fries, rather than throwing them.

6. The beer isn't flat.

7. The tough dudes are relinquishing seats that don't belong to them.

8. The person in the first row got his ticket legally, without paying triple to a scalper.

9. The usher understands the seating arrangement of the concert hall.

10. The drummer is reading the sheet music.

11. The lead singer's hair has been washed and combed.

12. There are no misspellings on the banner.

13. The girls are dancing in the aisle so they won't obstruct the view of the people behind them.

14. This is the "Coke" that the band ordered for after the show.

15. The roadies are not wearing T-shirts with beer advertisements on them.

16. The guy is leaving the concert early because he has to get up for school the next morning.

17. The promoters have generously provided free programs to each of the $15-per-ticket customers.

18. The guitarist tuned his guitar before appearing on stage.

19. The band is playing overtime because the concert started late.

20. The guards are actually throwing away the liquor they confiscated.

THE TORTUROUS TRAPEZE TRAVESTY

ARTIST AND WRITER: DUCK EDWING

THE SADISTIC SHARPSHOOTER'S STUNT

ARTIST AND WRITER: DUCK EDWING

HOW MANY MISTAKES CAN YOU FIND IN THIS PICTURE OF

A FAST FOOD RESTAURANT?

ANSWERS

1. The teenagers are all chewing their food with the mouths closed.

2. The cheese for the cheeseburgers is made from natural ingredients, including milk.

3. The fish filet sandwiches taste better than the styrofoam boxes they come in.

4. The iced drink has more drink in it than ice.

5. The young man is resisting the temptation to stomp on the packet of mustard that someone has dropped on the ground.

6. The boy with the magic marker is writing on the note pad, not on the table.

7. The teenage employees are earning more than the minimum wage.

8. The plastic lids actually fit the cups, and prevent spilling and scalding.

9. The employee leaving the washroom actually washed his hands after using it.

10. The person parked in the "Handicapped" section is really handicapped.

11. There are no swarms of bees or flies hovering around the garbage cans.

12. The "Quarter-Pounder" actually weighs a quarter of a pound after it is cooked.

13. Old, stale, cold, unsold food is being replaced with freshly-cooked new food.

14. The customer is being asked if he wants his burger rare, medium or well-done.

15. Someone has actually won the fast-food restaurant's "Sweepstakes."

16. There are no bird droppings splattered on the outdoor patio tables.

17. The teenager is not tampering with the salt shaker so the cap will fall off when the salt is poured.

18. The customer has not created a state of panic by requesting a glass of water.

19. The guy who handles the food has cleaned his nails before reporting for work.

20. The hamburgers look just as big in person as they do on the TV commercials.

ARTIST: JACK DAVIS   WRITER: CHRIS HART

ONE DAY IN THE SUBURBS

ARTIST AND WRITER: DON MARTIN

THE ZIPPY ZOO ZAPPER

ARTIST AND WRITER: DUCK EDWING

MAD ISSUES 301-400
"THE RUSH TO ANTIETAM"

Thou shalt not pierce together parts of the body that are not naturally connected.

I heard your br jumped off a b

This is our first attempt at marriage counseling, Dr. Forman!

Best assured, you'll fine a therapist with a mod approach and an awar that comes from year of personal experience

You played very well, Mad! Wasn't that set fun?

Sure was! But you know what's even more fun?

I ♥ N.Y.

FLUORESCENT Conditioning Formula

Leprechaun Green

Destroy Your Natural Looking Haircolor

From World Leader in Technical Fouls

JUST FOR RODMAN Shampoo-In Haircolor

Leprechaun Green

Jenkins begins a new weight training regimen by taking it slowly to avoid injury.

Melvin still pees blood from the time his friend bet him he couldn't lift the washing machine.

one...

SNAP!

VERLAS

FETAL FILTERS 25 Waterproof Cigarettes

Being Unborn Never sted So Smooth!

Look through the official rule book for any major sport and you'll find more penalties than you ever hear about as a casual fan! To supplement your sports knowledge (dare we say, to give you athletic support??), we've compiled this modest collection of...

LITTLE-KNOWN SPORTS

"Resumption of Play before the Network Returns from a Commercial"

"Failure to 'Grandstand' by Player with a Million-Dollar Sneaker Endorsement Deal"

"Unseemly Display of Good Taste in Clothing Worn by Professional Golfer"

ARTIST: JACK DAVIS   **WRITER: MIKE SNIDER**

[AND RARELY CALLED]
INFRACTIONS

"Break-up of Bench-Clearing Brawl before Enough Highlight Film Has Been Shot for *News at 11*"

"Incomplete Sponsor-Decal Coverage on Car in a Nationally Televised Race"

"Failure to Dive into Press Table for Ball During a College Game with Pro Scouts in Attendance"

"Failure to Throw a Tantrum after Flagrant Pass Interference Call"

"Failure by a Team with One Hit to Accuse Opposing Pitcher of Doctoring the Ball"

Every year around Christmas, magazines are filled with articles about how millions of people suffer from Christmas depression (brought on, no doubt, by those very same articles!). Unlike

WHY WE GET THE

ARTIST: GEORGE WOODBRIDGE

Valentine's Day

... is the time of the year when our loved ones show their affection towards us by giving us a 20 lb. box of chocolate that's been sitting in a warehouse all year long.

President's Day

... is the time of the year when greedy store owners honor a President who never told a lie by running deceptive ads, and a President who freed the slaves by keeping American consumers in continual debt.

Arbor Day

... is the time of the year when politicians who have passed legislation that's destroyed rivers and forests show their concern for ecology by planting a tree at a shopping mall.

Memorial Day

... is the time of the year when television announcers tell us to drive carefully so that we can watch race-car drivers kill themselves during the Indianapolis 500.

other magazines, though, MAD would <u>never</u> print depressing articles about Christmas. No, we'd rather run a depressing article about <u>every</u> holiday! So get ready as we give you a rundown of...

HOLIDAY BLAHS

WRITER: BARRY LIEBMAN

St. Patrick's Day

... is the time of the year when we show our respect for Irish-Americans by getting stinking drunk in their honor and throwing up our guts at their parade.

Mother's and Father's Day

... are the times of the year when every piece of junk that can't be unloaded on anybody at any other time is advertised as being "perfect for both Mom and Dad."

Labor Day

... is the time of the year when we celebrate our last remaining days of vacation by going out and enduring endless traffic jams, or staying in and enduring twenty hours of Jerry Lewis.

Columbus Day

... is the time of the year when we commemorate a man who lost two boats and ended up totally off-course by keeping the post office closed.

Halloween

... is the time of the year when stories of ghosts, goblins, and things that go bump in the night pale next to stories about psychos poisoning Trick or Treat candy.

Election Day

... is the time of the year when we officially give someone who has spent $20 million to get a $100,000 job the chance to manage our money.

Veteran's Day

... is the time of the year when we show our appreciation to all the old soldiers who hated marching in 10-mile hikes by allowing them to march in 10-mile parades.

Thanksgiving

... is the time of the year when we honor the notion of sharing by recounting how the Indians fed the same people who would eventually steal their land away from them.

Christmas

... is the time of the year when parents have to explain why the same Santa who's so worried about kids being naughty or nice is urging them to smoke and drink in cigarette and liquor ads.

New Year's Eve

... is the time of the year when all the restaurants and night clubs show their holiday spirit by handing out noise-makers and raising their prices 400%.

The most controversial new TV show this past year is a gritty, tough-talking series about New York City cops! Many parents object to its use of "realistic" language and we know why! Even though *parents* use "realistic" language when their kids aren't around, they don't want their *kids* using it! It's the old parental double standard! (The fact that their kids already know these words and use them regularly is besides the point!) But in this case, it may have some merit! After all, just because parents are vulgar, foul- mouthed low- lives doesn't mean their off- spring should be too! So, it's in deference to parents everywhere that we have refrained from using "realistic" language in our satire of this controversial hit series we call...

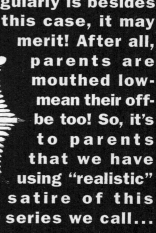

BOOBS

ARTIST: MORT DRUCKER   WRITER: STAN HART

WARNING: The following program may contain scenes with some violence. If you want scenes with *more* violence, stay tuned for your local news!

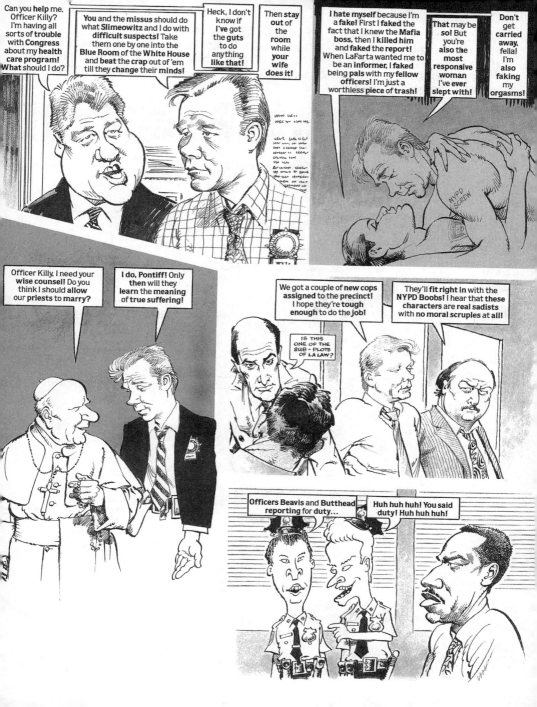

Most people have a silly belief that only athletes have use for sports equipment. Hogwash! Even a clod who has not lifted a Fungo bat or tossed a bocci ball in a decade has a real use for such stuff. Athletic inactivity should not deny anybody the inherent right to use sports paraphernalia. We will now demonstrate how your dinky, miserable, little existence can be immensely improved by just simply...

Using Sports Equipment
in Everyday Life

ARTIST AND WRITER: PAUL PETER PORGES

Lacrosse Stick/ Boiled Egg Scooper

Football Yard Marker/ Mud Scraper

Baseball Catcher's Mitt/Hot Bun Holder

Hockey Stick/ Slap Shoot Pooper Scooper

Baseball Cleats/ Kitchen Garden Seeder

Tennis Net/ Extended Family Hammock

Bike Helmet/ Appetizing Jello Mold Maker

In the old days when
dispute you had plenty
failed there was alw
kidnapping and even
we're much less civili
imagine how the past w

IF OTHER HIS
HAD BEEN AS "
AS OURS

ARTIST: GEORGE WOODBRID

...the discoverer of fire would have been swamped by "product liability" lawsuits!

...Mongolian invaders would have brought down the Gr
Wall of China in court by charging it was an "eyeso
that "obstructed the view" and "lowered property valu

...lawyers for a defeated Troy would have sued the Greeks, calling the Trojan horse "deceptive packaging"!

...Isaac Newton would have sued the apple-orchard ow
for head injuries, who then would have countersued h
seeking half of the credit for the Theory of Grav

wanted to settle a
ptions. When talking
dueling, blackmail,
ure. Now, of course,
We go to court! But
have been different...

RICAL ERAS
WSUIT HAPPY"
TODAY

RITER: MIKE SNIDER

...the Visigoths would have sued the
Ostrogoths for "trade name-infringement"!

...instead of fleeing to America, the Puritans would
have stayed in England and filed a "religious discrim-
ination" suit—which would still be "on appeal" today!

...Hannibal's army would have been stopped dead in its
tracks by a Restraining Order from the CSPCE (Carthage
Society for the Prevention of Cruelty to Elephants)!

...Josephine would have had a pre-nuptial
agreement giving her half of everything
Napoleon accumulated during their marriage!

ENGAGEMENTS

THE LIGHTE

MOVIES

R SIDE OF...

ARTIST & WRITER:
DAVE BERG

SELECTIVITY

My son is a **genius!** Look at this stuff—**computers, VCRs, camcorders, CDs, tape decks**—there's not **one piece** of **equipment made** that he **can't handle!**

Except, of course, a **lawn mower!**

AGREEMENTS

Ben, **before** we get **married,** we'd better get **one** very **important issue** settled **right now!** Do you like a **large family?**

Yes, I most certainly **do,** Karen!

That's **good!** Knowing **my family,** there's a **good chance** they're **all** going to **move in with us!**

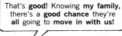

PREDICTIONS

Maybe **this** will **cheer** you up, **Mr. Gloom** and **Doom!** According to your **horoscope,** a lot of **money** is **coming your way!**

With **my luck** you know what **that** means, don't you?

VACATIONS

I just got back from **driving cross-country!**

In this **small car?** Who did you **go with?**

Five people I once **liked!**

SPORTS

STRATEGY

WARENESS

THE OFFICE

GIFTS

DOCTORS

Everyone wants to promote the importance of safe sex. There is, however, an even bigger issue than just the protection against the exchange of bodily fluids: it's what not to do with those pesky protectors when they're not in proper use. So, in MAD's always politically correct style and ribbed for your maximum pleasure we proudly present...

CONDOM ETIQUETTE

ARTIST AND WRITER: TOM CHENEY

"While condoms are available in a wide variety of styles, shapes and textures, it is considered thoughtful and mature to avoid extreme variations, especially with an inexperienced partner."

"Regardless of how casual a sexual encounter may be, it is tactless and crude to dispose of the condom in a manner which could only be construed as thoughtless or lazy."

"When it has been determined that a sexual encounter will NOT take place, it is not only immature, but rude, to employ the condom as a device for amusement."

"While it is appropriate to offer one's partner a choice of colors when selecting a condom, special care should be taken to insure that this option is not presented in an untimely fashion."

"Although most condoms are packaged with a complete set of instructions, it is considered rude and improper to read them immediately prior to use."

"While it is not inappropriate for one's partner to apply the condom, it is simply a matter of courtesy to insure that sufficient lighting is provided to prevent an embarrassing mishap."

"Special care should always be taken to insure that used condom wrappers are properly disposed of, particulary before beginning a relationship with a new partner."

"It can only be construed as a demonstration of tactlessness and vulgarity to attempt to obtain a refund for a condom which has failed to perform satisfactorily."

"Since all condoms have been electronically tested for structural integrity and safety at their factories, it is considered rude and untimely to make one's partner wait while conducting an additional field test."

"It is purely a matter of common sense to exercise great care when opening a condom wrapper with one's teeth, in order to avoid the accidental destruction of its contents."

filled

ARTIST: MORT DRUCKER   WRITER: STAN HART

To watch young adults concerned with **nothing** other than their **careers** and having **sex** is kinda **fun**, don't you think?

Not when you realize that these same **morons** vote in **elections**!

Which **stereotype** do you mean?

That **Jews** are **smarter** than **other** people!

...t at all! ...t helps ...ntradict ...he old ...reotype!

Okay guys, **what** do you **want** to do?

I know! Let's go to **Kramer's** pad! No one's ever actually **seen** it even though he lives **across** the **hall**!

Nah! Let's try to **top** some of the really **tasteless** adventures we've had, like the time we made **fun** of the **boy** in the **bubble**, or the **deaf-mute**, or the **paraplegic**, or those helpless **elderly** people! They were **riots**!

Can we **talk** about the **girl** I met the other day? We **might** be having a **relationship**!

A **meaningful** relationship?

I've **never** had a **meaningful** relationship!

Good! Since we've never had a **meaningful discussion** about **anything meaningful**, we can **talk** about it!

...o, I'm here to do a **CBS Reality Check** on this **show**! First, let's try to settle just where **reality** lies! Is **Jerry** supposed to be **Jerry Seinfeld**, the very successful comedian with his own **TV show**, best selling **book** and American Express **commercials**? Or is he just **playing** a character named **Jerry Seinfeld** who's only a **semi-successful comedian**? And isn't the **show**, which claims to be a **true** slice of New York life, **shot** in **Los Angeles**?

Hmmm, you **really** got your **work** cut out for yourself, fella!

You're so **seldom** at the **office!** Perhaps **book publishing** isn't your line of **work!**

What should **I** be **doing?**

Well, considering your **absentee record,** you might consider being in **congress!**

Hi, Elaine! What's **new?**

Nothing much!

Your Book, "Sein Language" was **dumped** as **Number One** on the **Best Seller List** and **replaced** by **Howard Stern's book** the minute it hit the bookstores!

Howard Stern aga[...] First he embarrasses me o[...] TV by asking abo[...] my **18 year old g**[...] friend! Now this[...]

THESE 5 PAGES ARE ABOUT ABSOLUTELY **NOTHING!**

?

Me again! If this were really the life of **Jerry Seinfeld,** Elaine, who works in the **publishing** world, would have told him **exactly** what was **new**...

Somebody's **knocking** at the **door!**

Who can it **be?** We're **all here!**

It **must** be our **cameo guest star!**

This **Seinfeld Show** is driving me **crazy!** Wherever I go, people want to know what **Kramer, George** and **Elaine** are **really** like! I'm at a loss to tell them because they **exist** only in your **sitcom** and not in **real life!**

I know what you mean, **Jerry!** People are always asking me about **Julia Louis-Dreyfus, Jason Alexander** and **Michael Richards!** But how should I know about **them** since they're **real people** with **real lives** and I'm only a **fringe stand-up comic** in this **sitcom!**

Hold it, fellas! Maybe **I** can **straighten** this out with a **CBS Reality Check!**

Yeah, **sure!** Like we'd **trust** a **CBS biggie** to help out an **NBC show** during **sweeps week!**

Which one said **that,** our **Jerry** or the **other Jerry?**

I'm getting a **migraine headache!** I've got to **lie down!**

At any given time, there are **millions** of people with **colds!** So **where** does all that **mucous** go? Maybe into our **streams** and **rivers** which feed into our **water supply!** And why isn't anyone **worrying** about that except **me?**

THE FASTEST ONE HALF HOUR ON TV.

We call this our **"Hall of Nations"**! Skinheads come from **all over the world**! The strong **bond** that keeps us **together** is love!

Love?

Right, the **love** of **hating**! The **English** skins **hate Pakistani** immigrants; the **French** skins **hate North African** immigrants; the **German** skins **hate Turkish** immigrants! We're just one **big angry family**!

We've **enjoyed** some of our **finest hours** recently in **Germany**! They're **terrorizing refugees** from **Third World Countries** to **stop** them from **taking** jobs from German workers!

But **they** do the **dirty**, **low paying jobs** German **workers won't do**! Like **cleaning** the **streets** and **picking up garbage**! If the **immigrants** **don't** do it, who **will**?

Hey, that's not **our** problem! We skinheads don't mind **living** like **pigs**! We're **tough**!

...must say that **flag** with a ...azi **swastika** is very ...off-putting! ...n't you guys ...ow what the Nazis did?

Don't believe it! It's **lying, revisionist** history! Just **like telling** us that **Columbus** was **Italian** or that **Einstein** was **smart** or that **George Washington Carver** knew from **peanuts**!

This is our **favorite** movie, **"The Third Reich"**!

But doesn't that show **Nazism** from its **rise** to **power** to its **ultimate downfall**?

Not when you only **play** the **first half over** and **over** again!

The next **speaker's great**! He's the **perfect spokesman** for our most **dearly held beliefs**! Maybe **you** heard of him—**Andrew Dice Clay**!

Yes I **have**! He's a **comedian**!

A comedian? Where'd **you** ever get a **dumb idea** like **that**?

...e **schedule** a lot of **activities**! ...his is one of our ...sports outings! ...hey're going for ...atting practice!

...here's the game?

What game? They're going to a gay bar!

This is our **Young Skinheads Group** of **pre-teenagers**! If we can **get** them while they're **young**, they're **ours** for **life**! We're just in time for their **cocktail hour**!

Aren't they **too young** to be **drinking cocktails**?

Those **cocktails** ain't **for drinking**! They're **for throwing**!

MAD CONTEMPLATES, INVESTIGATES, and FUMIGATES some...

AN ANTI-GRIDLOCK SH

SUPER-FAST FOOD

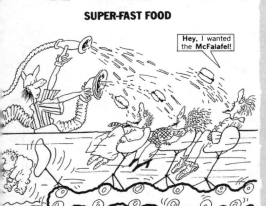

COUNTRY-WESTERN AEROBIC-STAIRMASTER SQUARE DANCING

AUDIENCE PARTICIPATION WRESTLEMANIA

THE GIANT MULTI-S

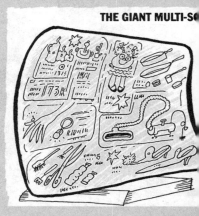

...BAD IDEAS Just Waiting to Happen!

MALL PEOPLE MOVER

A NEW EXPANSION TEAM FOR EVERY ZIP CODE

PORTABLE MICROWAVE SNACK OVEN

SHOPPERS CLUB

GENETICALLY ENGINEERED NO CHOLESTEROL FISH-FOWL

ARTIST AND WRITER: PAUL PETER PORGES

In the good ol' days, rock stars wanted to burn out before they faded away. Nowadays, Mick Jagger's got liver spots on

YOU'RE GETTING T

People get excited when they win something, but sometimes the things they win aren't worth getting excited about. You'll see what we're talking about when you scan these...

8 RUNNER-UP PRIZES THAT NOBODY CLAIMED

MACROBIOTIC LUNCH WITH SWAMI BA BA GANOUSH

SIX FREE LESSONS FROM A PRO SUMO WRESTLER

BACKSTAGE TOUR OF THE HIT FIRST GRADE PLAY "MR. VEGETABLE"

FRONT ROW SEATS TO AN ALPENHORN CONCERT

A WEEKEND AT A FULLY FURNISHED IGLOO

A PRIVATE CONSULTATION WITH A WORLD ECONOMIST

ARTIST AND WRITER: PAUL PETER PORGES

A COLLECTION OF THE TEN BEST HAIR REPLACEMENT COMMERCIAL TAPES FROM TV

GAMESMANSHIP HINTS FROM A CHAMPION SHUFFLEBOARD PLAYER

MAD'S INTERNATIONAL SIGNS FOR THE WORLD OF ROCK

THIS CONCERT PROTECTED BY RENT-A-COP SECURITY

ALL GOOD SEATS BELONG TO SCALPERS

PAPER-THIN T-SHIRTS ON SALE

SEATS DANGEROUSLY CLOSE TO SPEAKERS

BAND'S ARRIVAL TIME HIGHLY FLEXIBLE

ROTTEN OPENING ACT ON BOARD

DANGER

OVERZEALOUS BODYGUARDS

CAUTION!

LAZY SINGER LEADING AUDIENCE SINGALONGS

WILDING ZONE

ARTIST: SAM VIVIANO   WRITER: DESMOND DEVLIN

TEN CONCRETE LAWS OF HOME REPAIR!

HI THERE, DO-IT-YOURSELFERS! I'M HAP THE HANDYMAN HERE WITH SOME ADVICE FOR ALL YOU HOME CRAFTSMEN. BEFORE YOU TACKLE ANY PROJECT AROUND YOUR HOUSE, PUT DOWN YOUR BALL-PEEN HAMMER AND MEMORIZE THESE...

The most **important** part of your thermostat **will** be small enough to fit through the grill of the nearest heating vent.

If only **one shingle** on your house needs replacing, it **will** be located next to the biggest hornet's nest in the world.

The **only time** you will **ever** drop a screwdriver in the toilet will be when someone has forgotten to flush it.

ARTIST AND WRITER: TOM CHENEY

Products labeled, "Use only in well ventilated areas," will be needed **only** in rooms that don't have windows.

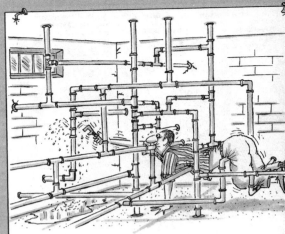

The pipe that **always** leaks will be the only one that can't be reached without removing ten other pipes that **never** leak.

The **only** extension cord you have that's long enough to reach the job site will be **the one** you accidentally cut through.

No matter **where** you choose to drill a hole in the wall, it **will** be where pipes are hidden behind the plaster.

When people hear the word gross, they normally think of open sewers, bleeding sores or rancid luncheon meats. But when you're a MAD reader your first thought is probably Al Jaffee! So, it's with that thought in mind that we proudly present...

Al Jaffee GETS GROSS

ARTIST AND WRITER: AL JAFFEE

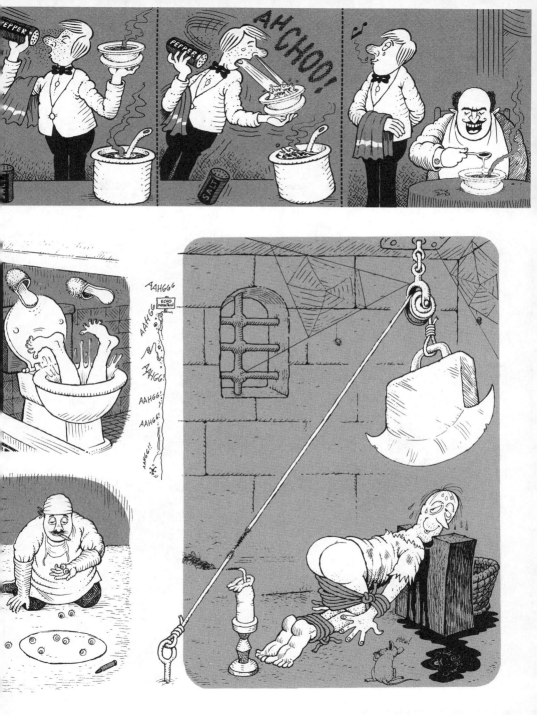

Not too long ago, the Surgeon General of the United States, Dr. Joycelyn Elders, suggested that it might be helpful to teach "do-it-yourself" sex in the classroom. Since the president is an advocate of having sex with at least one other person (not necessarily his wife), he fired her the next day! But it led us to wonder what would really happen...

IF "DO-IT-YOURSELF" SEX Were Taught in Public Schools

ARTIST: PAUL COKER   WRITER: STAN HART

This new Megadeth video sucks!

That's my heart monitor, dickweed!

They say that time is the great equalizer. They also say that with age comes wisdom. While we're not quite sure who "they" are, "they" obviously haven't watched MTV lately, because if "they" had, "they" would realize that the increasing years will be meaningless...

Senility bites!

What did you say, Stimpy?

WHEN BEAVIS & BUTT-HEAD GROW OLD!

Hi, I'm Tabitha Soren with *MTV News*. Today, Courtney Love Cobain Dando Reznor Bon Jovi announced her engagement to 4-year-old Elvis Jackson! It will be the first marriage for the son of retired superstar Michael Jackson and Lisa Marie Presley, who recently celebrated their 50th anniversary together!

MTV NEWS

Who the hell is Michael Jackson?

You should remember him — he's your hero! He wore one white glove when he played with his monkey!

Shut up, suckwad!

ARTIST: SAM VIVIANO   WRITER: DESMOND DEVLIN

The reclusive Michael Jackson hasn't been seen in public since 2018, when his face exploded on stage at Woodstock III!

Whoa! That was cool!

Hi, I'm Tabitha Soren with TV

However, Tito Jackson, whose 28 multi-platinum albums have made him the most successful of the Jackson family, said that Michael would be online at the ceremony itself!

Huh-huh-huh! You know that Elvis Jackson guy who's getting married? Huh-huh-huh! Afterwards, on his honeymoon night, I bet he gets some!

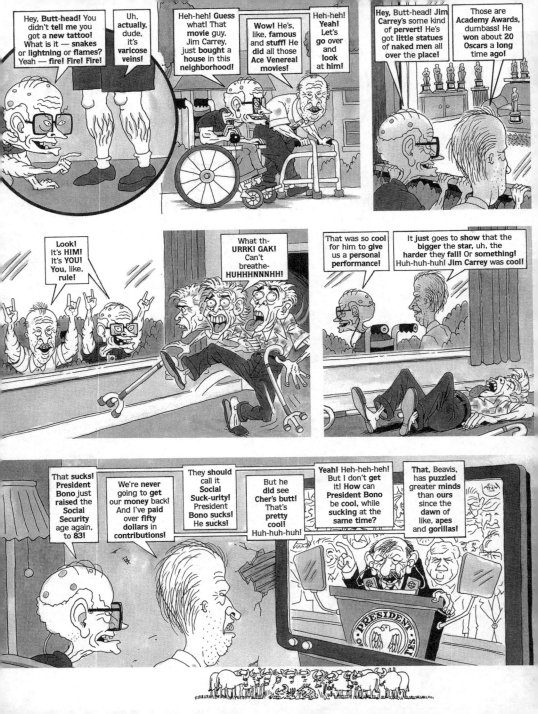

It's summertime! Time to get out and enjoy the great outdoors! But let's face it, just the very fact that you read MAD intros means you're a troubled individual, with a few, shall we say quirks...idiosyncrasies...personal peccadilloes! Yes, you have special needs, needs that an ordinary, run of the mill, normal camp could never satisfy! No, you definitely need one of these

SUMMER CAMPS

FOR KIDS WITH

UNIQUE PROBLEMS

ARTIST AND WRITER: PAUL PETER PORGES

CAMP DAMP—For Chronic Bedwetters

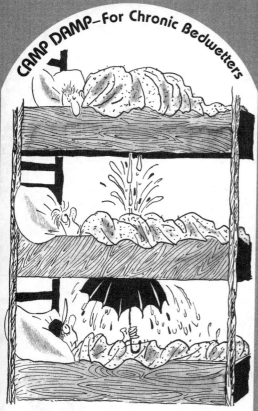

CAMP LIABILITY—For Accident-Prone Children

Serenely settled on the banks of the majestic Whiz River in Pete, New Jersey, **CAMP DAMP** encourages boys and girls of all ages to get in touch with themselves and confront their problem amidst babbling brooks, flowing rivers and trickling streams.
(Enroll early, as camp fills up quickly.)

Just a stone's throw away from New Jersey's finest trauma center, **CAMP LIABILITY** is a hotbed for those youngsters who seem destined to break a leg, maim a pet, disfigure a playmate or be somehow responsible for the death of an entire camp's population. New this year: Hayrides In An Ambulance!

CAMP LOTTA-LOTTA OOZE—For Boys & Girls With Sensitive Skin

Perched high in the tree-lined hills of Wawawa, New Jersey, CAMP LOTTA-LOTTA-OOZE caters to the special needs of youngsters afflicted with zits, assorted blackheads, white heads and unsightly facial boils, sores, hives and fissures. A courteous staff administers midnight hot, cold and warm compresses.

CAMP MONO-MONO—For Tired Children Of All Ages

Set beautifully in the idyllic countryside of Idyllic Countryside, New Jersey, CAMP MONO-MONO is the perfect spot for lethargic teenagers with low-grade fevers and swollen glands. With over 30 fun activities to not take part in, it's the choice place to sleep the summer away!

CAMP DORK—For Supernerds

Sleepily situated in reclaimed swamp-lands, just minutes from the charming old factory section of Bayonne, New Jersey, CAMP DORK is a favorite gathering spot of the socially challenged. Activities include: *Crafts That No One Needs, Sporting Events Currently Out Of Favor With The General Population* and strict observance of the 6PM lights-out curfew.

CAMP HOSTILITY—For Mean-Spirited Teens

Located in the pastoral grasslands of Wammelsdorf, New Jersey, CAMP HOSTILITY, owned and operated by recently paroled felons, boasts world class facilities in the teaching of revenge, senseless and brutal physical retaliation, sore losing and unsportsmanlike conduct. A midsummer visit by Charles Barkley has been scheduled!

CAMP BENADRYL—For Kids With Severe Allergies

Nestled in the bucolic fields and woodlands of Prozac Pines, New Jersey, CAMP BENADRYL offers a varied selection of fun activities for boys and girls allergic to pollen, ragweed, grass, mosquitoes, bees, deer flies or just being outdoors. The camp's mess tent is located in a hermetically sealed bubble.

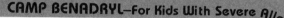

CAMP HOW-STERN—For Gross & Vulgar Youths

Tucked neatly in the rolling plains of Road Kill, New Jersey, CAMP HOW-STERN provides a supervisor-free atmosphere, ideal for tasteless practical jokes, obsessing over sex, and shameless displays of exhibitionism. July 4th is Lesbian Parent Weekend. (Visitation may also be arranged on a pay-per-view basis.)

Long ago a young entrepreneur invented the garden shears. Since then the wonderful world of botany has never been the same. Some say it was the most important discovery in the field since photosynthesis. As coincidence would have it, many schools that teach the concept of photosynthesis also happen to have athletic programs, which brings us to...

SPORTS ODDITIES

ARTIST AND WRITER: JOHN CALDWELL

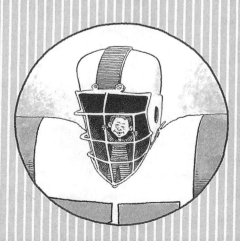

Sure, parents are suposed to provide their pathetic offspring with food and shelter— but for how long? 18 years? 21 years? 25 years? What, you've moved out and now moved back in? Why you lazy, ignorant, good for nothing deadbeat of an ungrateful, insignificant, absolutely useless waste of DNA! Can't you take a hint? Haven't you noticed any of these...

not-so-subtle signs YOUR PARENTS t

It's Time YOU Moved Out Of THEIR H

DEAD-BEAT CLUB

CLASS

8

When you ask your dad to lend you $50 he gives it to you in travelers' checks!

All over the house you keep finding pamphlets entitled "Religious Cults—They're Free, They're Fun, They're For You!"

Your bed is donated to the Salvation Army—while you're sleeping in it!

Your mom does a needlepoint wall-hanging which reads "Life Begins At The Moment Your Last Blood-Sucking, Unemployed Loser Of A Kid Moves Out!"

Although it's not Thanksgiving and you're over 21, you still have to eat your meals at the "little table"!

The Club is installed on the refrigerator door!

You wake up one morning to find in your bed the head oif your old hobbyhorse!

When your friends call, your dad puts them on hold and then leaves for work!

Every time your mom serves alphabet soup the words "go away" are floating in your bowl!

DON'T COME BACK

ARTIST: GREG THEAKSTON   WRITER: DENNIS SNEE

NT IS A DANGER

ARTIST: ANGELO TORRES   WRITER: DICK DEBARTOLO

I'm **Admiral Rear!** I'm a very **sick man!** But I'm thankful it's only **physical!** Not like all these **mental sickos** around me!

I'm **Fearless Cortex**, freelance spy! I'm **dishonest, despicable**, and I'd **sell** my **best friend** down the river for a **price!** What am I doing **here** in the **Oval** office? I always drop by because I feel **at home** with so **many** of these **government officials!**

IF YOU FILL IT IT WILL FLOW

JUST SAY YES

I'm **Ernest Escargot**, drug kingpin! One of my **drug-smuggling partners** crossed me, so I had my **men** board his **yacht** and **wipe out** him and his entire **family!** But I'm not a man without a **heart** — I belong to the **"Help Feed the Sharks" Foundation!**

That **slain man** was a **friend** of mine! Do the Colombians think we're **powerless?** Do they think they can **get away** with this **sort of thing?** What's the **real story**, Jock?

Basically, **Mr. President**, we are **powerless** and they can **get away** with this **sort of thing!**

There are some things I **don't** want to **hear!** Like the **truth!** Now go **fix it!** And the **next time** you **tell** me the **truth**, it had better be **good!** Even if you **have** to **lie!**

Do the **doctors** know **where** your **cancer** is **located?**

In the **diplomatic pouch!** They're going to **operate**, even though they tell me it **won't help** a bit!

Then **why** do it?

Figure it out, Jock! As a **government bureaucrat**, I have a great **medical plan!** And the **doctors** feel it would be a **damn shame** to waste it!

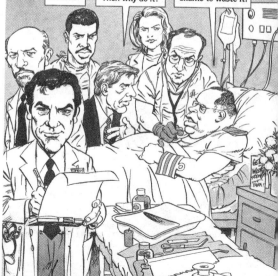

EACH YEAR, TOY MANUFACTURERS COME UP WITH THOUSANDS OF IDEAS FOR NEW BOARD GAMES. A SELECT FEW ARE PRODUCED AND GO ON TO BECOME KIDS' FAVORITES (E.G. MONOPOLY). OTHERS ARE PRODUCED AND GO ON TO BE MASSIVE FAILURES (E.G. THE MAD MAGAZINE GAME)! BUT, FOR ONE REASON OR ANOTHER, MOST NEVER EVEN MAKE IT PAST THE DESIGN STAGE, LIKE THESE . . .

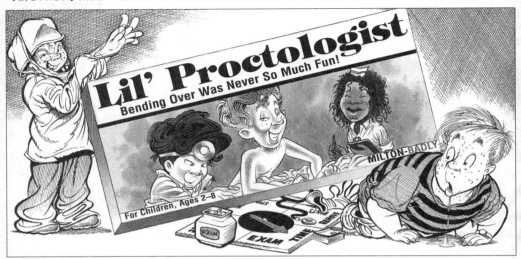

REASON FOR REJECTION: Small children may choke on enclosed rubber gloves.

REASON FOR REJECTION: Consumers likely to be interested in a professional wrestling game probably unable to read the instructions.

BOARD GAME REJECTS

ARTIST: STEVE SMALLWOOD   WRITER: MICHAEL GOODWIN

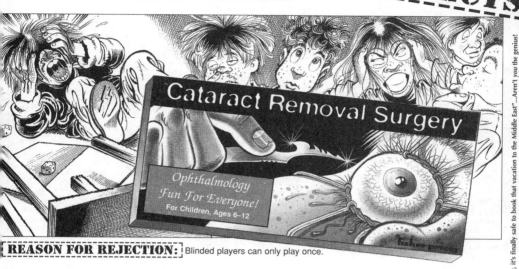

REASON FOR REJECTION: Blinded players can only play once.

REASON FOR REJECTION: Company attorneys felt selling handguns to minors was "probably illegal."

When the PLO and Israel signed their milestone Peace Accord, you said to your wife, "Honey, it's finally safe to book that vacation to the Middle East"...Aren't you the genius!

THE *MAD WORLD*

A *MAD* LOOK AT DENTISTS

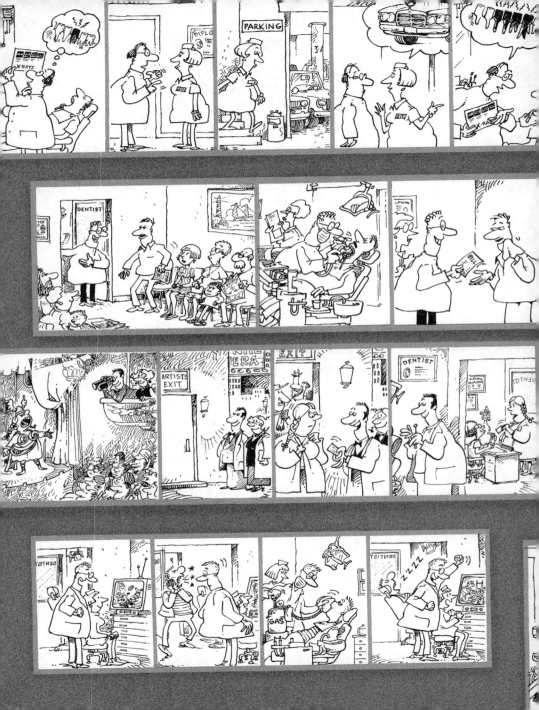

No matter what you do, one day you will start behaving just like the people you once vowed to be completely different from: your mother and father! It's a humiliating and terrifying life transition. The only thing you can do is to be aware of the symptoms and desperately try to fight it off! So stand up straight and pay attention as MAD reveals...

Your first thought upon seeing the new Playboy centerfold is, "Geez, I wonder what her parents must think."

You refuse to go all the way with your dinner date unless he eats all his broccoli.

SURE SIGNS THAT YOU'RE TURNING INTO YOUR

When a friend shows you his new Air Jordans, you press the toe to see if he has enough room.

You automatically assume that someone who hasn't arrived home on time is lying dead in a gutter.

You don't join the rest of the audience in shouting "You suck!" to the opening band at a concert because you don't want to hurt its members' feelings.

Your first reaction upon being handed a joint at a party is to wipe off the tip, shake your head and mutter to yourself, "Germs, germs."

You only go to the mall to buy something...and only if it's practical...and only if it's in a store than doesn't play that loud rap music.

You know which one is Ebert, but you're not sure which one is Beavis.

You're a recent college grad ready to make your mark in the world! You've got an apartment, you've got a job and you've even got an active social life! You've got it all, baby—except a future! Don't believe us? Then take a look at...

A DAY IN THE LIFE OF A SINGLE CAREER GIRL IN THE BIG CITY

ARTIST: CAROL LAY　WRITER: PEGGY DOODY

Hurriedly dress without saying a word to him, ditch him at the deli and hide at the opposite end of the subway platform.

Get to work late. The entire office is in a closed door meeting in the boss' office.

Your boss introduces you to the Harvard grad son of her best friend and tells you to walk him through everything he needs to know to do your job.

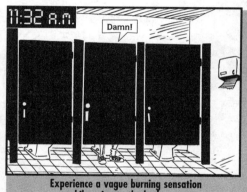

Experience a vague burning sensation while going to the bathroom.

Come back from smoking to find a large crowd gathered around your desk marveling at the smutty bouquet last night's date sent you.

Try in vain to make a personal call without anyone hearing you.

A DAY IN THE LIFE OF A SINGLE CAREER GIRL IN THE BIG CITY

8:15 p.m.

Finally get home. Eat entire bag of cheese puffs for dinner and lapse into MSG stupor.

12:25 a.m.

Get a mysterious phone call from unidentified weirdo.

1:15 a.m.

Can't fall asleep because you're wired from all the coffee you drank during the day and you're parched from the cheese puffs you ate for dinner.

2:35 a.m.

That's **it!** I'm becoming a lesbian!

After stumbling into a fitful sleep, awaken to the return of the burning sensation. Finally nod off at 5:45.

7:30 a.m.

Time to get up and start another great day!

No. 409
une 038

Our Price
4,560 Yen
Cheap!
5,560 Yen
Canada

MAD

:cording to scientists, there are two traits that separate man from beast. The first is humans' inability to lick their wn privates (but that's another article)! The second is their borderline obsession with their future. And since we :re at MAD are only human (despite reports to the contrary), we called the Psychic Friends Network to ask them hat MAD would be like decades from now. Aside from telling us that it would still suck, they sent us...

MAD IN THE YEAR 2038

ARTISTS: AL JAFFEE, MORT DRUCKER, DAVE MANAK, GERRY GERSTEN, DUCK EDWING, DAVE BERG, SERGIO ARAGONES

WRITER: DESMOND DEVLIN

SNAPPY ANSWERS TO STUPID QUESTIONS

THE MAD NASTY FILE, VOL. 53

WOOD-YI ALLEN

CO-PRESIDENTS ASHLEY AND MARY-KATE OLSEN

...Have worked out a schedule where Mary-Kate runs the country Mondays, Wednesdays and Fridays, and Ashley handles things Tuesdays, Thursdays and Saturdays (Sunday is Malibu Barbie Play Day).

...Have combined to be twice as incompetent and corrupt as President Baio was all by himself.

...Spoke for a grateful nation during their inaugural address when they called the ethnic cleansing by Serb death squads "totally gross."

...Wishes his father had named him something less stupid — like Satchel, or Zelig.

...Can't afford to sit in his dad's old Knicks seats anymore, because Mia's kids split Woody's inheritance 53 ways.

...Is neurotically jealous of Ingmar Bergman's kid.

You May Have Been a TEST TUBE BABY If...

...your parents' talk with you about the birds and the bees includes the phrase "the cyclotronic sperm spinner."

...every Thanksgiving the sight of the turkey baster fills you with a sudden rush of tangled emotions.

...you're deathly afraid of getting into one of those enclosed-glass hotel elevators.

A MAD LOOK AT ALZHEIMER'S
JUST MARRIED
HOTEL
PL-276
WHAT?
— ARROZ
— CAMARONES
— TOMATES
— PAY MARK E.
— ARROZ
TOP OF PAGE

A MAD PEEK BEHIND THE SCENES AT MICHAEL JORDAN'S FUNERAL

PREPAREDNESS

I knew this **bomb shelter** would come in handy! While they **incinerate** the **Earth** up there, we've got **canned meat, canned vegetables, canned soup** and **canned drinks!** I remembered **everything** we need to **survive** the **apocalypse!**

Yeah, **everything** except the **can opener!**

THE LIGHTER SIDE OF...

CONVENIENCES

Boy, did my folks **lay down the law!** They told me that unless I **passed** all **my classes** and did all **my chores,** I couldn't **go out with Marcie** on the weekends!

Wow, **that's rough!** So **what did you do?**

I **bought** one of those **home cyborgs!** He did all my **homework,** and I got **straight A's!** Then he **cleaned** the **house** so well, Dad gave me a **bonus** in **my allowance!** He does **everything better** than I **ever could!**

Cool! He sounds absolutely **fantastic!** Let me **see him!**

You can't! He's out with **Marcie!**

DOCTORS

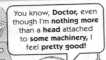

You know, **Doctor,** even though I'm **nothing more** than a **head** attached to **some machinery,** I feel **pretty good!**

It's true, **Kaputnik-XF7,** you're in **excellent shape!** However, there is **bad news** to **report...**

...you have **head lice!**

Oh no!

david Berg

Always make every effort to keep hands, hair, clothing and jewelry clear of the garbage disposal unit while vomiting in your host's kitchen sink!

When it becomes apparent that you are about to pass out, serious trampling injuries can be avoided by quietly directing yourself to a low-traffic area prior to losing consciousness!

Embarrassing and potentially serious injury can be avoided by asking your host or hostess for assistance in locating the bathroom light switch. What feels like a toilet in a darkened room may instead be a life-threatening appliance when used improperly!

BEHIND THE INEBRIATE BALL DEPT.

Some people were born to party, and to party hard! C'mon, you know who you are out there! But like any other hazardous situation, you have to be quite careful when you wanna get down and boogie! So before you go and ruin another good shirt with your own vomit here's MAD's

SAFETY PARTY

The safety-conscious party animal knows that it's important NEVER to stand on the "hinge" side of a bathroom door!

When the time comes to dance on the bar while performing a striptease, it is important to avoid injury by first removing any bottles, spills or beer nuts, which could cause a sudden loss of balance!

Depending on your level of intoxication, a common cushion or pillow may bear a striking resemblance to a full bag of potato chips. Select your snacks with care at all times to avoid the irreversible effects of Dacron Polyester poisoning!

To avoid the risk of accidental poisoning, never consume the contents of a bottle or container when you are too intoxicated to read or understand what's on the label!

TIPS FOR THE ANIMAL

ARTIST & WRITER: TOM CHENEY

When operating motor vehicles indoors, insure that adequate ventilation is provided to avoid exposing yourself and others to dangerous levels of carbon monoxide from engine exhaust!

Always walk, never run, during the mandatory "wearing of the lampshade," as there may be hazards of which you are visually unaware!

When it comes time to trash your host's home or apartment, it is important to avoid the risk of electric shock by first unplugging any appliances you intend to destroy!

For years, nothing has baffled the scientific community more than trying to figure out what is causing all that angst and malaise among America's young adults! Finally, they realized there was only one duo who could solve this unsolved mystery, to answer this unanswerable question, to crack this uncrackable code, to—ah, you get the point! Anyway, they called in the country's premier investigative duo, Mulder and Scully, to crack the secrets of...

EPISODE 6: CLOSE ENCOUNTERS OF THE CAFFEINATED KIND

Assistant Director Skinner is forced to take Mulder's theory about extraterrestrials posing as coffee vendors seriously when their "Shoppes" begin replicating themselves on street-corners all over America.

Hmmm, you're right! This is the **THIRD** one in the **last five blocks!**

And look: **"Starbucks"?** **STAR-bucks?!** What more do you need, a **name tag** that says, "Hello. I'm **E.T.**"!?

I'm sending this off to the **lab.** No telling what could **happen** if it got out into the **general population!**

THE GENERATION

ARTIST: TIMOTHY SHAMEY
WRITER: MIKE SNIDER

EPISODE 11: CHILDREN OF THE LOST COMBS

It's a puzzle wrapped in an enigma that Mulder and Scully must try and solve: How can a generation that spends so much time obsessing over their hair always look like they just got out of bed?! (Episode also features the first appearance of the mysterious Zima-Slurping Man.)

It's... it's **almost** as if they... **DON'T KNOW** how they **look!**

My **guess** is they've all been **infected** with a **parasite** that attacks the **brain center** controlling the **ability** to say "No" to **goofy hairstyles!**

Mmm!

X FILES

EPISODE 17: DAWN OF THE NIGHT OF THE CALVIN KLEIN ZOMBIES

With the assistance of a subservient national media, a megalomaniacal fashion designer unleashes his army of anorexic, heroin-addicted walking dead upon unsuspecting consumers. His dastardly goal: To put his own name on the jeans of everyone born since 1965!

EPISODE 23: PIERCED NATION

Mulder suspects an intergalactic conspiracy when unexplainable holes suddenly begin appearing all over the bodies of America's youth — only to be filled by equally inexplicable "Jewelry-Like Implants" (JLIs).

EPISODE 28: THE VANISHING JOBS

With the assistance of Deep Dockers, a secret informant from another generation, Mulder and Scully investigate the strange disappearance of millions of jobs that pay more than minimum wage and don't require the wearing of silly paper hats!

EPISODE 43: SCHOOLHOUSE ROCK AROUND THE CLOCK

A series of cheesy-but-hummable educational TV spots from the '70s come back to haunt the generation that grew up on them, when it's discovered that they contain subliminal messages that turn viewers back into giddy, drooling children whenever they hear the songs again as adults!

EPISODE 31: JANEANE GARAFALO, WHO THE HELL ARE YOU?!?

When a second-rate stand-up comedienne with just a few TV and film roles to her credit becomes a generational icon, Mulder is covinced there's only one explanation: Mass hypnosis!

EPISODE 34: HOME SWEET, LIKE, Y'KNOW, HOME

Some mysterious force is magnetically keeping people in their 20s and 30s — even those with good jobs — from moving out on their own! Mulder and Scully must find a way to counteract it to prevent the bankruptcy of a generation of parents and the U.S. apartment-rental market!

The services suffer frequent interruptions as a "technician" checks the formaldehyde level every 300 mourners

The open casket presentation leaves a lot to be desired

Well, Gramps has finally kicked the bucket, and gone are the good old days when you could just dig a hole in the backyard and plant him! Now you have to take the time out of your busy schedule to find a place that will give the old geezer a decent send-off without blowing all of your inheritance! So before you rush down to the local crematorium that's offering 10% off coupons in the Pennysaver, be sure you read...

CLUES YOU'VE CHOSEN A REALLY BAD FUNERAL PARLOR

**ARTIST AND WRITER:
JOHN CALDWELL**

In place of the usual collage of snapshots chronicling the life of the deceased: grisly autopsy photos

CLUES YOU'VE CHOSEN A REALLY BAD FUNERAL PARLOR

Enroute to the cemetery, the funeral director leads the procession through his cousin's car wash

At the memorial service, you're not thoroughly convinced your Aunt Thelma would have wanted a magician

The crematory urn suspiciously resembles a 7-11 Big Gulp beverage container

Instead of respectfully greeting mourners at the door, the funeral director hustles tickets for a 50/50 raffle

The customary moment of silence is conducted by a mime

What is described in the brochure as a "non-sectarian cleric" turns out to be more accurately labeled as a "Toothless, snake-handling, wack job"

Due to a questionable co-op advertising deal, a guy in a peanut suit spends the evening mingling among the dearly beloved handing out samples

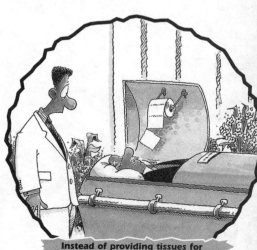

Instead of providing tissues for mourners, there's a roll of Charmin tacked over the deceased

July 10, 1998

Astronomers announce they have observed a huge asteroid headed this way, and calculate it will collide with Earth in 30 years.

Ever since it was determined that dinosaurs became extinct because an asteroid collided with Earth 65 million years ago, people have been asking, "Can it happen again? And if it does, will I still have to pay my property tax?" Movies like *Deep Impact* and *Armageddon* have tried to show us what it would be like if we discovered a comet or asteroid headed right for us — stories of bold plans to divert the threat, reassuring leaders, a responsible news media and everyday people performing heroic deeds. But that's the movies! If you want to find out what it would really be like, then read MAD'S...

COUNTDOWN to ARMAGEDDON

ARTIST: TOM BUNK   WRITER: MIKE MIKULA

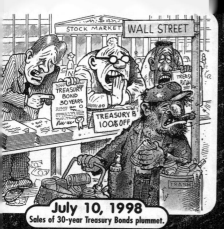

July 10, 1998
Sales of 30-year Treasury Bonds plummet.

July 12, 1998
Red-faced astronomers announce they forgot to carry the five, and now calculate the asteroid will miss Earth by several million miles.

Turns out what they **thought** was going to **destroy humanity** wasn't a **massive asteroid** at all...it was just **the shadow** from **Rosie O'Donnell's head!**

July 12, 1998
Every late night talk show host makes the identical joke.

OCTOBER 3, 2008
Astronomers realize they were right about the asteroid the first time, only now Earth has a mere twenty years left.

NOVEMBER 4, 2011
Vegas oddsmakers begin posting odds for the survival of various species.

SEPTEMBER 6, 2016
Last health food store in the world closes.

NOVEMBER 5, 2022
James Cameron is signed to produce a $1 billion movie based on the impending disaster — if he survives the collision.

JANUARY 29, 2023
Astronomers announce that previously unavailable technology has enabled them to make a more accurate calculation of when the asteroid will hit...and it's in three weeks.

FEBRUARY 2, 2023
IRS revenues dry up as a record percentage of taxpayers file extensions.

FEBRUARY 4, 2023
Increased attendance at churches, temples and mosques causes many houses of worship to structurally collapse, killing thousands

COUNTDOWN to ARMAGEDDON

FEBRUARY 14, 2023
The asteroid passes Earth, missing it by a million miles. Everyone goes back to their normal lives, embarrassed by their behavior over the past few weeks, but with a renewed passion for life and a sense of brotherhood and civility never before seen. It is truly the dawning of a golden age.

JANUARY 30, 2023
Nike sales skyrocket as millions of various cult members decide to jump the gun and kill themselves.

FEBRUARY 9, 2023
Nobody gives a #&@%! where they park anymore.

MARCH 3, 2023

It used to be a universal fact that school was a relatively safe place for kids. The occasional bully threatening someone for their lunch money or picking fights at recess were the most dangerous things going on. These days, however, there are guns, knives and horny custodians to worry about! How safe is your school? Unsure? Well, if the daily locker searches and metal detectors aren't enough of a clue, here's MAD's...

TIPOFFS THAT YOU GO TO A REALLY TOUGH SCHOOL

ARTIST: TIMOTHY SHAMEY   **WRITER: BARRY LIEBMANN**

The guidance counselors have all been replaced by hostage negotiators.

The most popular project in shop class is making shivs.

The debating team's idea of an effective rebuttal is to just give the finger.

Most students get out of writing "What I Did on my Summer Vacation" essays by pleading the Fifth Amendment.

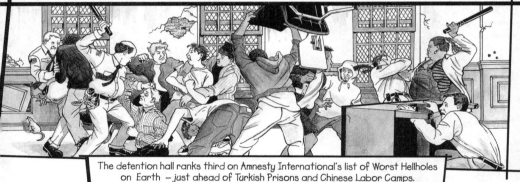

The detention hall ranks third on Amnesty International's list of Worst Hellholes on Earth — just ahead of Turkish Prisons and Chinese Labor Camps.

The senior play is always eagerly attended by scouts from the porno industry.

97% of all kids participating in Show and Tell first ask for immunity from prosecution.

English Composition class this year focuses on the proper punctuation of ransom notes.

How many **times** do I have to tell you! It's "Put **$10,000** in fives, COMMA, tens, COMMA and twenties, COMMA or I blow your #$%^& kid's head off, **EXCLAMATION POINT!**

There hasn't been a class reunion in 20 years because the whereabouts of most former students are protected by the government's Witness Relocation Program.

The introduction of the graduation commencement speaker always includes the phrase, "Indicted, but never convicted."

If Tom lays $15 on the six and $10 on the hard eight and craps out, how much money did he lose?

Math is taught through the use of a floating craps game.

Your school's alumni population decreases every time another state brings back the death penalty.

COMMUNICATION

PREDICTIONS

CRIME

THERAPY

PRIORITIES

CONSIDERATION

THE OFFICE

APPRECIATION

DOCTORS

Do you have a filthy %$^#*@& mouth?

Do you regularly use the **%$#&^#@** F-word? Has George Carlin ever threatened to wash your **%$#@&*!** mouth out with soap? Did Mike Tyson ever ask you to watch your **#$@&^*%** language? If you answered "**^%$%&*** yeah!" to one or more of these questions, you have a serious social problem. So unless your immediate supervisor is named Gotti or you're dating Courtney Love, it's likely your propensity for garbage gab is holding you back! But not to worry! As a public service we've devised an easy, cuss-cutting program that's guaranteed to improve your **%#$&** lexicon. Simply read on as we lead you through...

The MAD Guide to Cleaning Up Your

*!% &

VOCABULARY

Rather than setting the bar impossibly high by trying to go "cold turkey," set aside one day a week to vent your vulgarities.

Learn to say it with flowers instead.

Whenever possible, resort to a rebus.

ARTIST AND WRITER: JOHN CALDWELL

FUDGE!!!

Every morning, before leaving home, bang your thumb with a hammer. Repeat until every conceivable vulgarity is out of your system.

HEY! I GOT A ✿#¡✲ SPLENDID IDEA! LET'S GRAB A COUPLE OF ✲BEYAPH✲ REFRESHING BREWS AND CATCH A ✲FUVAVABEF✲ SPIRITED BALL GAME!

Spend more time around people who are less likely to cuss.

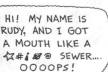

HI!. MY NAME IS RUDY, AND I GOT A MOUTH LIKE A ✿#¡✲@ SEWER.... OOOOPS!

Form a local chapter of Obscenity Anonymous.

Get the seven basic bad words off your chest in a civil manner, while, at the same time, enjoying the aerobic benefits of semaphore.

AAAAAW!!! ASTERISK! EXCLAMATION POINT! COLON! SATURN! STAR! AMPERSAND!

SMASH!

Get in the habit of verbalizing the comic strip versions of what you're trying to say.

Try picturing your mother in place of the target of your wrath.

What are most Americans hooked on? Sex? Yeah. Booze? Right again! Phonics? Sure! But for the purpose of this article, let's all agree that Americans are hooked mainly on pills, potions and ointments — legal or otherwise! Which leads us at MAD, the perverse pushers of poetry, to present...

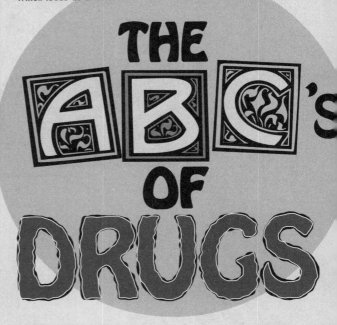

THE ABC's OF DRUGS

ARTIST: RICK TULKA

WRITER: FRANK JACOBS

A is for Aspirin
The first drug you'll swallow;
It won't be your last—
Loads of others will follow.

is for Birth Control Pills
Which are worth ev'ry buck;
Forget to take one —
Baby, you're outta luck!

is for Cocaine
Not addictive, you say?
You just use it to "cope"
Twenty times ev'ry day.

is for Date Rape Drugs
She'll pass out without fail;
Save a few for yourself
When you're gang-raped in jail.

is for Ecstasy
Gets you hot beyond measure;
If you can't find a date,
Hey, there's always self-pleasure!

THE ABC's OF DRUGS

F is for Fertility Drugs
Mom's doing just fine;
She hoped for a girl —
Big surprise — she got nine!

G is for Ginkgo
An herbal success,
Though what value it has
Is most anyone's guess.

H is for Heroin
Did it leave her half dead?
Or is it a pose
For a Calvin Klein spread?

I is for Ibuprofen
Which trendy pills now contain;
Got no money? No problem,
Then live with your pain.

J is for Joint
Should some Narc give you grief,
Say you've never inhaled,
Then sing "Hail to the Chief."

K is for Kaopectate
When the runs make you ill,
After downing some school
Cafeteria swill.

L is for LSD
Take a tab — soon you'll see,
That your lamp's talking Freud
With a moose in a tree.

 is for Minoxidil
A hair-raising drug;
Takes a year to grow fuzz —
Give it up! Buy a rug!

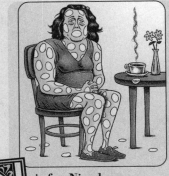

 is for Nicoderm
There's only one catch:
Though you no longer smoke,
You're now hooked on the patch.

 is for Oxy 10
Got a zit? This may stop 'em;
But why bother when
It's more fun just to pop 'em!

is for Prozac
Which ends the depression
You get from the cost
Of an analyst's session.

is for Quinterra
What's it for? We've no clue;
We're just thankful we've foun[d]
A drug starting with "Q."

 is for Ritalin
When a kid's not attentive;
Though a kick in the butt
Seems a stronger incentive.

is for Steroids
Guy, you're built like a truck;
But despite abs of steel,
Girls still know you're a schmuck.

THE ABC's OF DRUGS

T is for Tinactin
Which battles foot fungus,
Or soothing your crotch
When that itch is humungous.

U is for Uppers
When term papers you sweat;
But why stay up all night?
Swipe 'em straight off the 'Net!

V is for Viagra
When your problem's acute;
Don't despair—gulp one down,
Then stand up and salute!

W is for Weed
In a rolled cigarette;
What's that? We did "Joint"?
When you're stoned you forget.

X is for Xantax
Side effects? Yessiree!
Impotence? No problem—
Just go back to "V."

Ah, those years long
ago, we look back
on them still,

When folks seldom
got hooked on some
new-fangled pill;

Who'd have thought
in that era of horses
and buggies

We'd wind up today
— just a nation
of druggies.

Y is for Youth Cream
Hides each wrinkle and line;
What a shame it can't hide
That you weigh 3-0-9.

Z is for Zyban and Zantac and Zerit
Each year more appear till we barely can bear it;
There's Zyrtec and Zestril and so many more,
Like Zoloft and Zomig — God knows what's in store?

TULKA

MAD MINI MOVIES

Featuring The Fickle Finger of Fate

ARTIST AND WRITER: AL JAFFEE

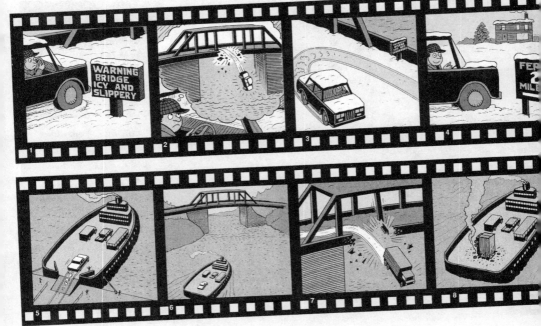

WHY DO WE BELIEVE

The math teacher who insists that algebraic skills will help you later in life...

...when all it got him was a lifetime job teaching algebra?

WHY DO WE BELIEVE

The rapper who kicks it stupid hard about pop-pop-popping tha police in Compton.

...when the only time he even sees a cop is when his infra red security-cam picks up a disturbance in Sector G of his Bel-Air estate?

You gotta believe! Believe in Tinkerbell—believe in magic—believe in all those endearing young charms—believe in the Easter Bunny

WHY DO W

WHY DO WE BELIEVE

The morning radio traffic reports that promise to get you out of that highway gridlock, and zip you to work on time...

...when every other exhaust-sucking schmuck on the road is hearing the exact same report, and swerving to the same exact "all-clear alternate route" that you are heading to?

WHY DO WE BELIEVE

The White House insider whose subpoena testimony in the courtroom consists only the words "I," "cannot," and "remember

...when the instant the trial's over and their immunity k in, they've cut a 5 million dollar deal to spill everything scorching behind-the-scenes autobiography?

The boyfriend who whispers that you're the most beautiful vision imaginable...

...when he's looking at you through candlelight, at night, with a bottle of wine sloshing around in his stomach?

A national rifle association that says it promotes gun safety and personal security...

...when the main freebie that comes with membership is a $20,000 insurance policy for accidental death or dismemberment?

ve in peanut butter—believe that God plays dice with the world—believe for every drop of rain that falls, a flower grows—but why, oh

: BELIEVE...

ARTIST: GEORGE WOODBRIDGE   WRITER: DESMOND DEVLIN

That Bill Clinton's universal health care package is the answer to all of our medical crises...

The former security guards of indicted celebrities, when they announce that they can no longer remain silent about their ex-bosses' sexual perversions...

...when they had no problem shutting up during the whole five years they were on the celeb's payroll?

WHY DO WE BELIEVE

Our dog when he acts like we're absolutely the greatest thing on Earth...

...when he thinks the second and third things are drinking
from the toilet and sniffing other dogs' day-old urine?

WHY DO WE BELIEVE

Doctors who insist that their job
requires all-access license plates and
parking privileges...

...when the last doctor to make an actual house call is the
one who was called when President McKinley was shot?

WHY DO WE BELIEVE

The faded rock legend who announces
this may be his last concert tour, in
order to pump up lousy ticket sales...

...when if it really works, and sales do go up, he'll
announce a tour next year, due to "overwhelming
demand by his fans"?

WHY DO WE BELIEVE

Television programmers who refuse t
run ads for condoms or public service
announcements for safe sex because
their audience wouldn't stand for it...

...when the other 23 hours and 59 minutes of their sched
ule is filled with drooling lustbags doing every smutty
thing possible (except watching condom ads)?

There are two kinds of lawyers, those who are bloodsucking, ambulance-chasing, slimy, bottom-feeding slugs, and those who are *incompetent* bloodsucking, ambulance-chasing, slimy bottom-feeding slugs! How to tell the difference is not always easy, as all of the following plaintiffs found out in our own little legal dissertation which we call...

SUREFIRE, NON-LITIGABLE SIGNS YOU'VE HIRED THE WRONG LAWYER

Before making an objection in court, he leans toward you and asks, "Which is the good one again, 'sustained' or 'overruled?'"

He keeps a tip jar on his desk!

He introduces you to his imaginary paralegal, Claudette!

ARTIST & WRITER: JOHN CALDWELL

SUREFIRE, NON-LITIGABLE SIGNS YOU'VE HIRED THE

WRONG LAWYER

His waiting room is always inexplicably filled with injured rodeo clowns!

In his closing statement he makes you moon the jury as he screams, "Is this the ass of a guilty man?!"

He represents you in an unnecessary surgery malpractice suit and winds up settling out of court for custody of your appendix!

Instead of a place in the Federal Witness Relocation Program, he gets you a free fashion makeover on the *Ricki Lake Show*!

He does his entire summation in mime!

While representing you in a paternity suit, his entire defense centers on the "Getting You to Try on the Condom" tactic!

During court proceedings, the only legal precedent he ever brings up is "Ali vs. Frazier, 1971!"

He shows up at your real estate closing dressed as Vasco da Gama and hops onto the table screaming, "I claim this territory for Phil and Donna Bucholtz!"

HEALTH

THE LIGHTER SIDE OF...

ARTIST AND WRITER: DAVE BERG

GAMBLING

PETS

OBJECTIVITY

The big baseball strike meant that fans never got to see the exciting first round of planned semi-playoffs... *So What's the Problem?*

POOR JUDGEMENT

Well, Andrew! You've **beaten me** in **straight sets!** What have you got to **say** for **yourself?**

Sorry, Boss!

MESSAGES

If you wish to **check** your **balances,** pres "**1**" **now!** If you wish to learn current **intere rates,** press "**2**" **now!** If you wish a list of available **investment** programs, press "**3**" ne If you wish to send a **FAX,** press "**4**" **now**

MATURITY

I can't believe that **today** is our son's **21st** birthday!

I know! It seems like only **yesterday** we were telling him to **stand up straight** and **close** his **mouth** when he **chews** his food!

THERAPY

Although this is our **first session** with you, **Dr. Forman,** both my husband and I have had **individual therapy** before coming to you!

Good! May I ask who your **therapists** were?

CRITICAL: CRIME

CRIME

If you desperately **long** for the **good old days** when you could **talk** to a **human being** on the phone, press "5" now!

It **was** yesterday!

I had my **hairdresser** and he had his **bartender!**

This is a **stick-up!**

Are you **aware** this is a **library?**

Don't give me that "we have **no money** routine!" I **know** you have **cash** collected from **overdue books!**

I'm referring to our **noise restrictions!** Is there a **silencer** on that **gun?**

THE OFFICE

NOW

Without intervention by big-city police, rival gangs are likely to wipe each other out in vicious flurries of violence...*So What's the Problem?*

DOCTORS

THE JOCULAR JURASSIC JOLT

ARTIST AND WRITER: DUCK EDWING

MAD ISSUES 401–500
"BEGINNINGS"

I'M INBRED AND I VOAT!

WHAT, ME WORRY?

NATIONAL SECURITY RISKS

It's so frustrating. Getting Brendan to tell you anything is impossible!

He went to the movies with Alison and then they snuck into the basement and made out.

How'd you get him to tell you all that?

I read it on his blog!

WRITERS AND ARTISTS: 3/DESIGN STUDIO · RAY ALMA · SERGIO ARAGONES · PETER BAGGE · ANTHONY BARBIERI · SCOTT
DICK DEBARTOLO · DESMOND DEVLIN · MORT DRUCKER · BRIAN & SEAN FARRELLY · MARK FREDRICKSON · DREW FRIEDMAN · MARC HEM
HERMANN MEJIA · ROBERTO PARADA · JOE RAIOLA · TOM RICHMOND · IRVING SCHILD · TIM SHAMEY · STAN SINBERG · SAM SISCO · MI

GOOD NAME FOR... | BAD NAME FOR...

Frozen vegetables | A suppository

Green Giant

STANKEE CANDLE

FLATULENT PONY

What's black and white and red all over? A penguin addicted to salsa!

GULF WARS
EPISODE II
CLONE · OF · THE · ATTACK

THE BUSH ADMINISTRATION

I brought some puzzles for you to try and finish before you die!

THE 50 WORST THINGS ABOUT

GARBAGE PAIL KISS

DUMBO BRITNEY & MENOPAUSAL MADONNA

M BUNK   TERESA BURNS PARKHURST   KENNY BYERLY   JOHN CALDWELL   PAUL COKER   RUSS COOPER   DAVE CROATTO
FFEE   CHARLIE KADAU   ARIE KAPLAN   ARNIE KOGEN   JEFF KRUSE   PETER KUPER   SCOTT MAIKO   JOSH MALINOW
OTT SONNEBORN   JACK SYRACUSE   ANGELO TORRES   RICK TULKA   P.C. VEY   RICHARD WILLIAMS   BILL WRAY

Here's the hot HBO series about four man-hungry Manhattan babes on the prowl. It's a comedy show and a suspense show. We don't know what's going to unravel first — the plot or their underwear! These women look like models but talk like hockey players! They call themselves sophisticated power chicks, but let's face it, they're basically nothing but...

SLUTS

I'm **Catty Broadshow!** I'm a **sex columnist** for a **New York** newspaper! I write about the **dating scene** in **Manhattan!** A statistic: There are **400,000 sex acts** a day in New York! About **100,000** of them **involve myself** and my **three friends!**

I'm **Slamantha Johns!** I'm the most **sex-crazed** of the **group!** I'm **HBO** without the **B** in it! You do the **math!** I will **@#%^&*** a **chair leg!** I make **Madonna** look like the **cast** of **7th Heaven!** My mantra: **been there, done him!**

I'm **Marimba Hopps!** I'm an **uptight lawyer!** I'm about as much **fun** as a **yeast infection!** You, the **MAD** reader, will **never know** what I'm **like** in bed! But let me **put** it this way, right now I'm **"faking"** this intro!

I'm **Shallow Yorkie!** I'm an art dealer! I'm the most **prim** of the **group!** When use the **"F"** word it's things like **"Flemis painter"** and **"Frame"!** Our show has become a **cult hit!** I wouldn't be surpris to **see** us in the **TV exhibit hall** at the **Smithsonian** with **Fonzie's jacket, Minn** Pearl's hat and **Slamantha's diaphragm**

Hello! We're **Mr. Biggie, Strive** and **Tripe!** We're **in** and **out** of the **show** *and* the **women** in the **show!** On this **series** the **traditional roles** are reversed! *We're* the **sex objects!**

Me again! I **forgot** to **mention** that around here size *does* matter! The **size** of the **TV audience!** We'll do **anything** to get **ratings!** We'll get **naked** at the **drop of a hat!** In fact, that's **episode 16!** But I'm **getting ahead** of myself! I'll be doing the **running narration** — starting now!

ARTIST: MORT DRUCKER

WRITER: JOSH GORDON

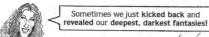

Sometimes we just **kicked back** and **revealed** our **deepest, darkest fantasies!**

Okay, girls, **what's** your greatest **sexual turn-on?** Mine is being **stark naked** on a **lobster boat** with George Clooney!

In a **church tower!** With a **priest,** a **bikini-clad coed** and a **deformed bell ringer!**

It involves **pancake syrup,** a **dwarf** and the **cast** of *The West Wing!*

A **romantic walk** on the beach with a **charming** guy who proposes **marriage,** we end up with **two kids** and a **home** in the **country!**

Yucch! You're **grossing me out!** What a **freak!** Get a life!

The New York **singles scene** wasn't **easy!** We each **experienced** a period of **dating disasters!**

Catty, I am **leaving!** I just realized **something** about **you!**

What is it?

Your **sex** is as **mechanical** as your **acting!**

We have **selected** you! You are the **"chosen one"!** We are **here** to perform an **anal probe!**

Oh! You're **aliens** from **another planet?**

We're **three guys** from **the Bronx!**

He **left** me for this **hot Asian chick!**

It **happens!** But he said he **loved** me for my **personality!**

If you **believe** that, I've **got** a **dot-com stock** I'd like to **sell you!**

I know **you're** a **corporate billionaire,** but I'm **dumping** you for that **gardener!**

For heavens sake, **why** would you **do that?**

Duh! For the **ratings!** I'll be able to say **"weed whacker"** 22 times a show!

Move over Homer Simpson, there's a new dysfunctional TV patriarch in town!
And by the look of the ratings, he's biting the heads off the competition!
Unlike Springfield's favorite D'oh! boy, this guy is real. Maybe too real!
So if you've spent any time at all watching *The Osbournes* on MTV,
it must have occurred to you to ask the heavy metal musical question...

How **Cool** Would it be to be a Member of *Ozzy Osbourne's* Family?

How **Cool** Would it be to be a Member of ~~Ozzy Osbourne's~~ Family?

When you misbehave, you'd always be admonished with the same threat.

You'd experience the father/son bonding that only comes from tossing a big screen TV off a high-rise hotel balcony.

Bringing Pops to school would always add up to extra credit, be it Career Day, Show and Tell, or a D.A.R.E. lecture.

The reaction to Daddy having helped you with your %$#*ing homework would be %$#*ing priceless.

Lousy report cards could easily be slipped by during trips to the mall.

You'd marvel at Mom's ability to juggle her domestic chores with helping out in the family business.

As long as you're with the old man, your money would be no good on carnival rides.

Picking your parents out in the audience at your dance recitals would be a snap.

You'd have unique childhood memories, like checking to see if the Tooth Demon came.

Immediately following the terrorist attacks of September 11, 2001, news pundits and politicians told us two things: 1) We'll never be the same again, and 2) Let's get back to normal. Let's get back to normal? Are they kidding? We were never normal to begin with. And besides, how are we supposed to get back to normal when "we'll never be the same again"? This kind of idiotic advice from so-called experts and leaders might be the only thing that hasn't changed since that fateful day. Otherwise, here are examples of...

HOW EVERYTHING CHANGED AFTER THE ATTACKS

Osama bin Laden solidifies his standing as the most hated man in Afghanistan — at least until Geraldo arrives, and then it becomes a toss-up.

Pictures of Osama bin Laden replace Saddam Hussein and George W. Bush on gag toilet paper.

For the first time ever, sales of American flags surpass those of porn in the U.S.

The nation's airlines become 50% more secure, but only because there are 70% less passengers.

Americans sigh a breath of relief every time an airplane or train crash is blamed on the usual mechanical failure or worker incompetence.

ARTIST: PETER KUPER   WRITER: BARRY LIEBMANN